*Catalog of Aids for the Disabled*

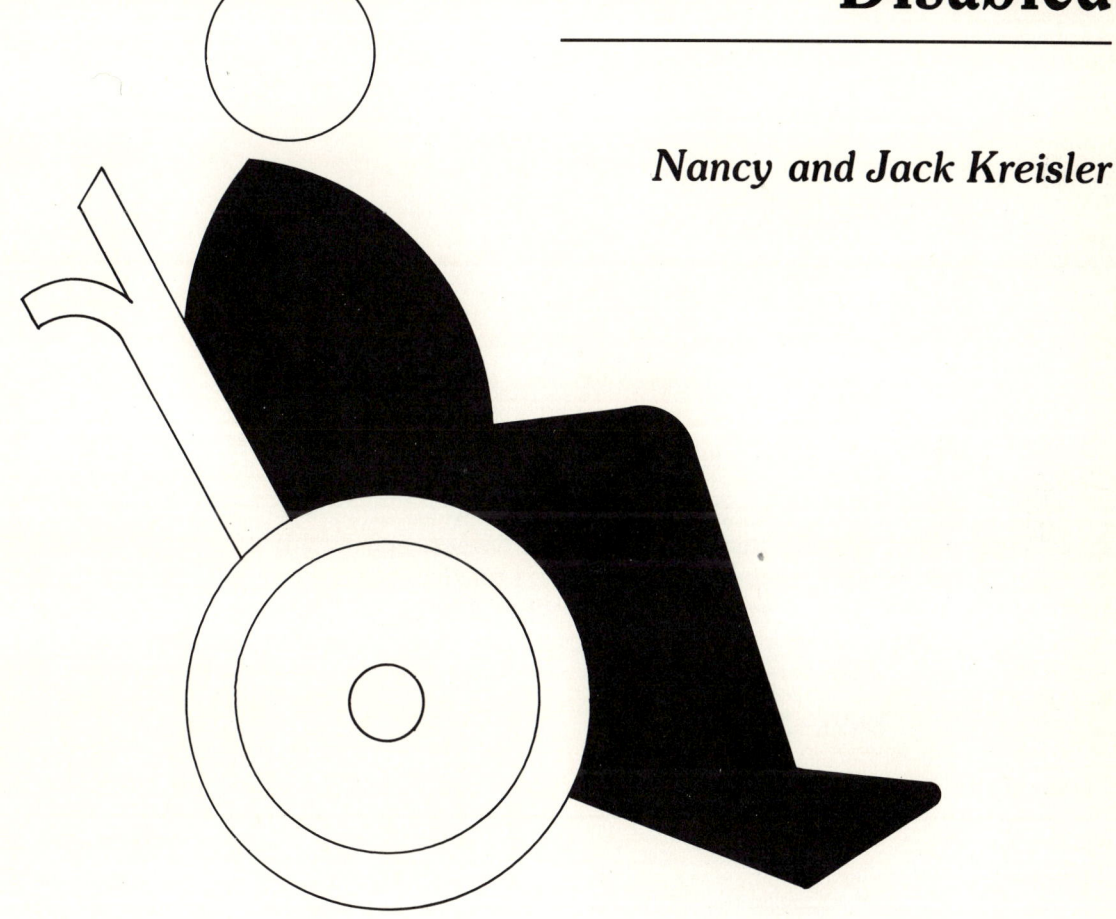

# Catalog of Aids for the Disabled

*Nancy and Jack Kreisler*

McGRAW-HILL BOOK COMPANY
New York  St. Louis  San Francisco
Toronto  Mexico  Hamburg  London
Montreal  Paris  Tokyo

We wish to express our thanks to several people: Our children Gary, Dawn Kristi, and Jack for their support; Pia Lindstrom for giving us the motivation and confidence to do this book; the TV viewers, both disabled and able-bodied, for their helpful suggestions; our editor, Lou Ashworth, who first approached us about this book and realized the great need for it. We appreciate her patience and expertise.

Copyright © 1982 by Nancy and Jack Kreisler.
All rights reserved.
Printed in the United States of America. Except as permitted under the Copyright Act of 1976, no part of this publication may be reproduced or distributed in any form or by any means, or stored in a data base or retrieval system, without the prior written permission of the publisher.

1 2 3 4 5 6 7 8 9 MUMU 8 7 6 5 4 3 2

ISBN 0-07-035475-8

LIBRARY OF CONGRESS CATALOGING IN PUBLICATION DATA

Kreisler, Nancy.
Catalog of aids for the disabled.
1. Self-help devices for the disabled—Catalogs.
2. Self-help devices for the disabled—United States
—Catalogs.  I. Kreisler, Jack.  II. Title.
RD755.K73          617          81-20929
ISBN 0-07-035475-8              AACR2

Book design by Judy Allan

# Preface

No one knows exactly how many people in the United States are physically disabled. Government figures vary from 35 to 50 million. Now, approximately one out of every two households in the United States is affected or involved to some degree with a disabled person. Nancy Kreisler is one of these disabled.

A former John Robert Powers model, she uses a wheelchair to get around as a result of polio. Although disabled, she brought up three children, took care of a house, traveled over 100,000 miles in a motor home, lectured, and appeared on television talk shows in the United States and Canada. As a result of over 330 television appearances, including a series on NBC-TV in New York and a current weekly hostess spot on NBC-TV in the Orlando–Daytona Beach area of Florida, she has accumulated personally, and also received from viewers, a great deal of information on useful aids and gadgets. The thousands of letters from her TV audience requesting advice about them also indicate a growing desire for a source of this information. Thus, Nancy realized there is a proven need for a guide describing useful equipment and aids to enable more independent functioning and to help make life easier for the millions of disabled, elderly, temporarily disabled, and the able-bodied persons who assist them.

It is surprising how little is known about what aids are available and where they can be obtained. There are aids for almost every kind of problem, if people only knew where to find them. We hope this book will help.

*Nancy and Jack Kreisler*

# *Foreword*

Some years ago I interviewed Nancy Kreisler for NBC-TV in New York. She was so filled with enthusiasm and information that she became a regular on our news broadcast. She talked about helpful ideas for the handicapped and, being in a wheelchair herself, she was able to testify to their usefulness.

Nancy had information that could be used not only for the handicapped but for the elderly and the injured. She always had so much more information than we had time for that I suggested she write a book to get it all in. I am so pleased she has actually done it.

Nancy Kreisler is a special person, and with her astonishingly positive and happy outlook she is an inspiration to me. As Nancy said, "All of us are handicapped in some way, but with some it just shows more." I believe that is true.

Pia Lindstrom

## *How to Use This Book*

There are 13 sections listing aids and equipment.
Each item has:
1. A photograph (when necessary);
2. A description;
3. A price category—
    A  (less than $17)
    B  ($17 to $58)
    C  ($58 to $115)
    D  ($115 to $460)
    E  ($460 to $1150)
    F  (Over $1150)
4. The name of a supplier or other sources where the aid can be obtained.

The Appendix lists:
    1. Organizations, agencies, and other sources of useful information.
    2. Periodicals that may be helpful.

In using this book, please remember that some aids may no longer be manufactured exactly as specified, some companies may have gone out of business suddenly, or prices may have changed. Where available, we have listed a variety of similar items to make alternate selection possible.

Many of these aids can be found in local stores: department, hardware, locksmith, hospital supply, etc. If they cannot be found, the companies mentioned in this book for a particular aid can either supply or direct you to a supplier of the item.

If you are under a physician's care for your disability, check with your doctor before purchasing *any* major equipment for health care.

# Contents

| | |
|---|---|
| *Preface* | v |
| *Foreword* | vi |
| *How to Use This Book* | vii |

1. *In and Out of Bed* — 1
   Alarms / Beds / Bed Aids / Blanket Aids / Lifts / Mattresses and Aids / Pillows and Backrests / Pockets / Trays and Tables / Miscellaneous

2. *Personal Care* — 15
   BATHING: Brushes / In Bed / Bars / Seats / Lifts / Tubs and Showers
   EXERCISE: Hands / Legs / Whirlpool / Miscellaneous
   GROOMING: Teeth / Hair / Mirrors / Nails / Scissors / Miscellaneous
   HEALTH CARE: Blood Pressure / Heat Pads / Medical Emergency / Massage / "Talking" Aids / Miscellaneous
   PERSONAL HYGIENE: Toilets / Seats / Rails / Miscellaneous

3. *Dressing* — 55
   Clothing Aids / Shoes and Aids / Stocking Aids / Miscellaneous

4. *Meal Preparation* — 67
   Small Appliances / Cutting Boards / Cookbooks / Holders / Mix and Chop / Openers / Pans and Aids / Peelers / Racks / Knives and Slicing Tools / Stoves and Ovens / Tongs and Turners / Miscellaneous

5. *Eating* — 87
   Dishes / Drinking Vessels / Nonslip Aids / Utensils / Miscellaneous

6. *Getting Around* — 99
   SITTING: Cushions / Lift Chairs / Leg Extenders / Miscellaneous
   WALKING: Bags / Canes / Ice Grippers / Walkers / Electronic Guide / Rails
   WHEELCHAIRS: Handpower / Electric / Portable / Reclining / Stair-Climbing / Stand-Up / Travel / Miscellaneous
   WHEELCHAIR ACCESSORIES: Ash Trays / Bags / Brake / Crutch Holders / Cups / Leg Supports / Lapboards / Stabilizers / Miscellaneous
   TRANSFER: Portable Lifts / Wheelchair Lifts / Stair Lifts / Ramps / Transfer Boards
   SYMBOLS OF ACCESS

CONTENTS ix

7. *Household Activities* 143
   Cleaning / Kitchen / Laundry / Storage / Tools and Miscellaneous

8. *Access at Home and Elsewhere* 157
   Doors / Elevators / Lights / Locks / Reachers / Stools

9. *Communication* 165
   READING: Bookholders / Talking Books / Enlargers and Magnifiers / Eyeglasses / Page Turners / Large-Print Publications / Reading Machines / Variable Speech Controllers
   REMOTE CONTROLS: Environment / TV / Switch
   SPEAKING: Artificial Larynx / Silent Communicator / Voice Communicators
   TELEPHONE: Bells and Signals / Cordless / Automatic Dialers / Hearing Aids / Hearing-Impaired / Holders / Large Numbers / Silencer / Toll-Free Digest
   WRITING: Braille Electronic Writer / "Talking" Calculator / Typing and Writing / Miscellaneous
   MISCELLANEOUS: Intercom / Time / TV-Telecaption

10. *Recreation* 191
    Bicycles, Three-Wheelers, and Carts / Bowling / Cards and Aids / Computer and Electronic Games / Fishing / Games / Needlework and Sewing / Radios / Miscellaneous

11. *Travel* 205
    Baggage / Driving Controls and Aids / Lifts and Loaders / Vehicles / For Trips—Miscellaneous

12. *Accident Prevention at Home* 215
    Emergency Aids / Doors and Drawers / Miscellaneous

13. *Safety from Crime* 217
    Alarms / Locks / Timers / Miscellaneous

*Appendix* 225

*Useful Names and Addresses* 225
   Organizations, Agencies and other sources of help / Periodicals

*Photo Credits* 239

*Index* 241

# In and Out of Bed

**1**

## 1.1 WAKE-UP ALARM FOR HEARING-IMPAIRED

Edison Digitimer®. Has receptacle in back of clock for lamps or vibrators. When alarm goes off, lamps will flash on and off or bed will vibrate to awaken sleeper.

**PRICE B** From Vibralite Products, Inc.

## 1.2 CHILDREN'S BED-WETTING ALARM

Wee-Alert Buzzer. Helps condition sleeper to stop bed-wetting. Battery powered. Units are safe. When sheet becomes wet, alarm sounds. Does not interfere with sound sleep.

**PRICE B** From Sears

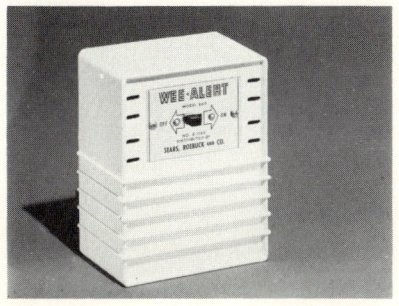

## 1.3 CHILDREN'S BED-WETTING ALARM

Lite-Alert Buzzer. Helps condition sleeper to stop bed-wetting. Buzzer plus light awaken sleeper when bed is wet. Operates on batteries (6-volt). Units are safe.

**PRICE B** From Sears

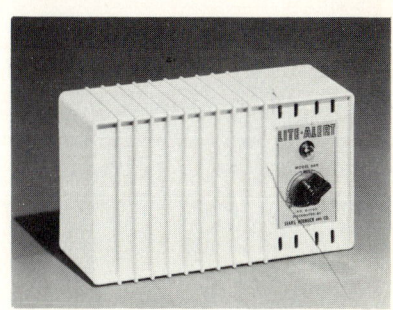

## 1.4 BED-WETTING ALARM

Dri-nite unit. Safely controls bed-wetting. Very sensitive, transistorized circuit. Loud sound system goes off when bed is wet.

**PRICE B** From Wal-Jan Surgical Products

## 1.5 WAKE-UP VIBRATOR FOR HEARING-IMPAIRED

The vibrator is used with Edison Digitimer® or the Vibralite® to provide vigorous vibration for waking the heavy sleeper.

**PRICE B** From Vibralite Products, Inc.

## 1.6 WAKE-UP BUZZER FOR HEARING-IMPAIRED

The buzzer is used with Edison Digitimer® or the Vibralite® to provide moderate vibration, under a pillow, to awaken the sleeper.

**PRICE B** From Vibralite Products, Inc.

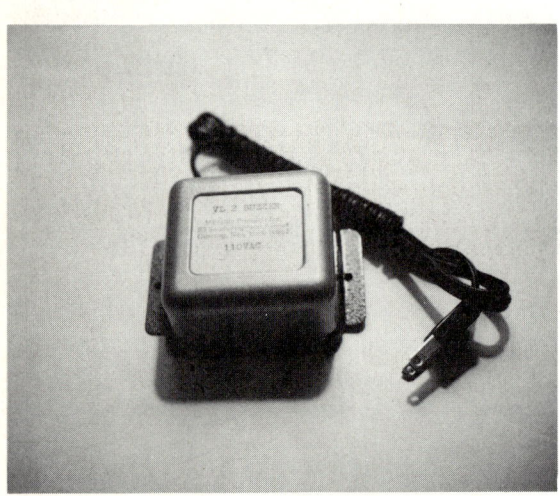

## 1.7 OVERHEAD TRAPEZE BAR

Aid for sitting up in bed. Can be used with almost any style of bed. Plastic-covered clamps protect finish of bed. Made of chrome-plated square steel tubing. Adjustable for height. User can pull self up by holding bar.

**PRICE D** From Preston

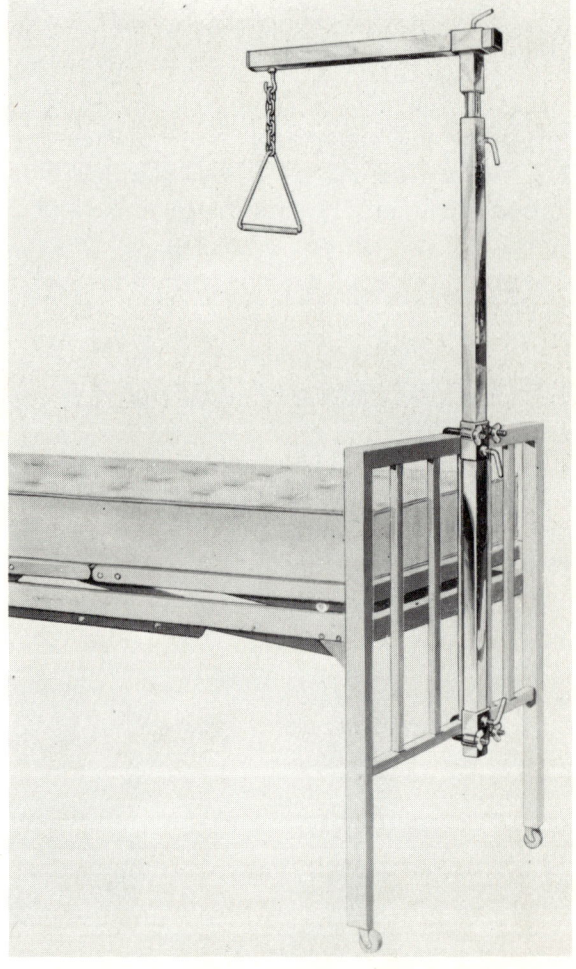

## 1.8 PORTABLE FOLDING BED BOARD
When placed under mattress, protects against sagging mattresses and gives firm comfort. Four folds, 5′ long, 1/2″ thick, made of 7-ply aircel board. 24″, 30″, 48″, and 60″ widths.

**PRICE A** (two smaller sizes) **B** (two larger sizes) From Better Sleep (24″ & 30″) (48″ & 60″)

## 1.9 BED BLOCK
Used to lift lower or upper half of bed. Lightweight aluminum cones are available 6″ and 8″ high. Fit under legs of bed.

**PRICE A** From Camp International

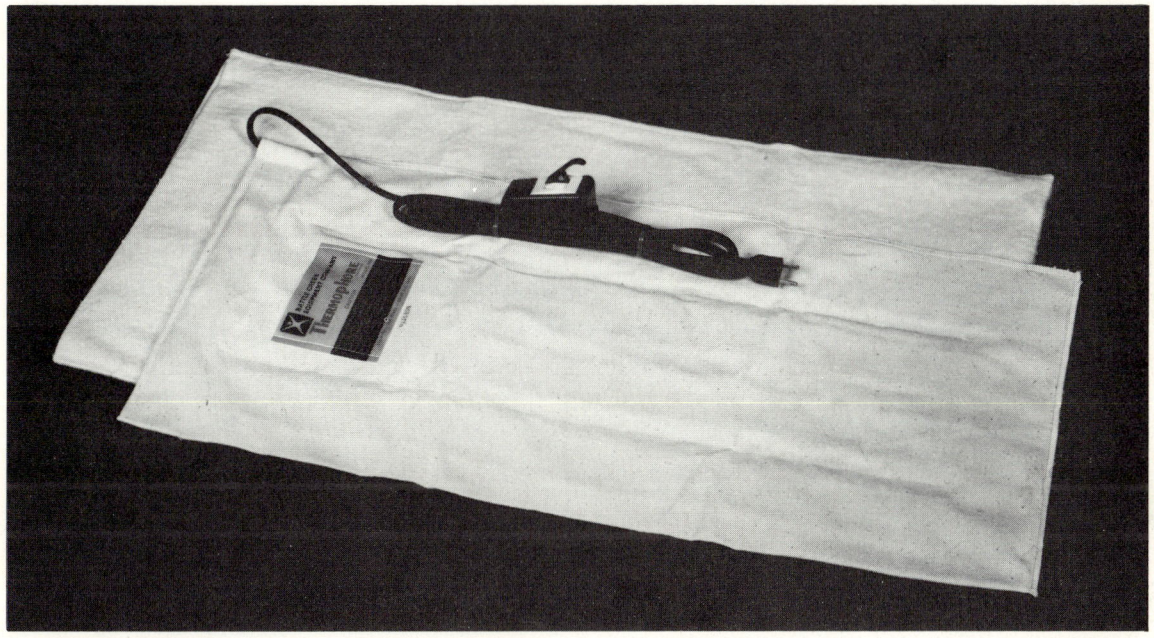

## 1.10a BED WARMER
Slips under lower bedsheet out of sight to provide warmth for feet and legs. Size: 36″ long, 17″ wide.

**PRICE B** From Battle Creek Equipment Co.

## 1.10b BED WARMER
Maintains steady warmth to feet and legs all night long. Goes under bottom sheet and mattress cover. Size: 18″ by 36″.

**PRICE A** From Battle Creek Equipment Co.

## 1.11 DELUXE BLANKET SUPPORT

Lifts regular, contoured or electric blankets, for foot freedom in bed. Fits all beds. Arms cross and fold invisibly flat when bed is made. Extended, stabilized base and wings create shelf for bedspread and blanket.

**PRICE A** From Better Sleep

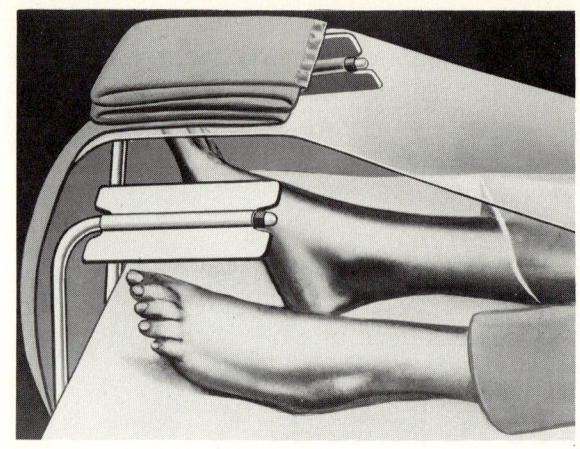

## 1.12 SUPER BLANKET SUPPORT

Use where cover contact must be avoided. It will "tent" cover almost to your hips. Lifts covers 13" high for an area 24" by 14". Disassembles for flat storage.

**PRICE B** From Better Sleep (similar from Aparco)

## 1.13 FOLDING BED BLANKET CRADLE

A desirable support to keep sheets and blankets from touching a person. Use two on either side to form tent for any part of body.

**PRICE B** From Camp International

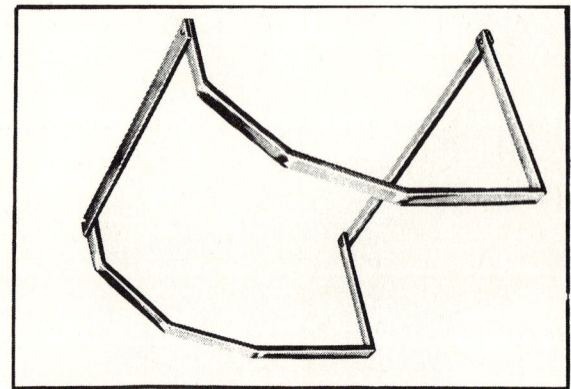

## 1.14 BED READER

Enables a person to read in bed while lying flat on the back. Holds large or small books or magazines. Permits easy turning of pages. Has adjustable frame. Book rests on, and is read through, clear plastic surface. Doesn't restrict head or arm movement. Folds automatically to flat 29" by 23". Height adjusts from 15" to 24".

**PRICE B** From Maddak

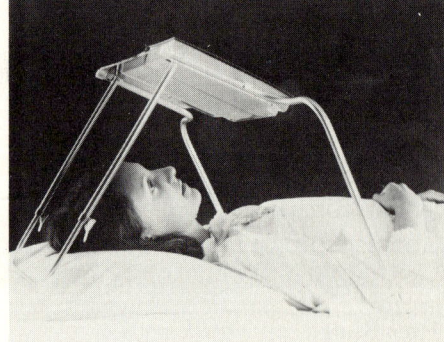

## 1.15 ELECTRIC ADJUSTABLE BED
Elevates head, feet, or both. Looks the same as conventional bed and is same height. Just plug into any outlet. Various sizes and widths.

**PRICE D** From Electropedic Products

## 1.16 SEMI-ELECTRIC BED
Bed adjusts from 18″ to 27″ from floor by crank at foot of bed. Two motors operate by remote control to lift head or foot of bed. Size 36″ by 87″.

**PRICE E** From Sears

## 1.17 ELECTRIC EASE-O-MATIC SPRINGS
Entire spring unit replaces box spring. Fits any bed frame. Powerful motor responds when button is pushed for back up or down, foot up or down. Mattress extra.

**PRICE D** From Sears

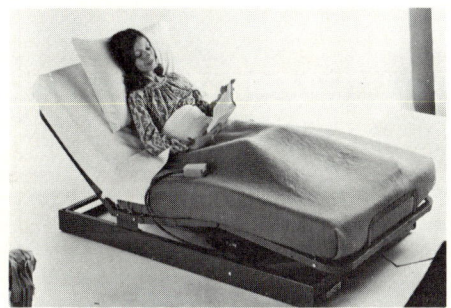

## 1.18 ELECTRIC EASE-O-MATIC BED
Two powerful motors operate by remote control. Back up or down, foot up or down. Frame fits conventional, twin or full-size headboard. Has electric outlet at foot of bed for lamp or appliance. Switch-on remote control can turn off appliance or lamp. Comes complete with innerspring mattress. Frame 80″ by 30″ by 17″ high.

**PRICE E** From Sears

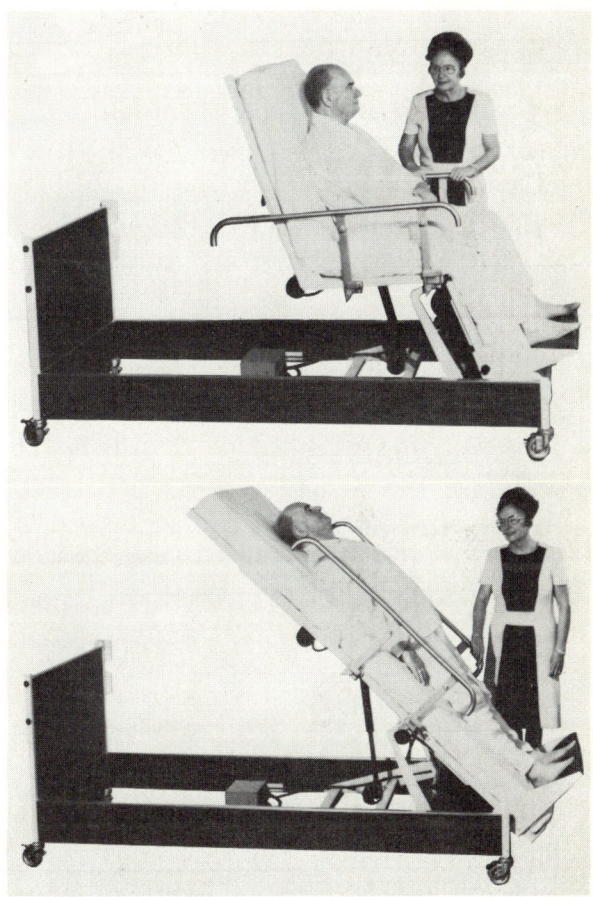

## 1.19 LONG-TERM-CARE BED
Electric powered. Height, 19¼″. Tilt position up to 45°. Vertical chair position. Special mattress system greatly reduces pressure on skin.

**PRICE F** From Burke

## 1.20 ADJUSTABLE BED BACKREST
Washable cover slips off when desired. Adjust by lifting guide rod and sliding lock plate into position. For bed, lawn, or beach.

**PRICE A** From Camp International

## 1.21 DELUXE FOLDING BACKREST
Five adjustable positions. Elastics hold pillow. Nonskid base. Backrest 16″ wide by 24″ high. Supports head and back. Weighs less than 4 lb. Folds thin for storage. For use in bed.

**PRICE A** From Better Sleep

## 1.22 MATTRESS RAISER
Easily adjustable to four heights. For under mattress at foot or head of bed. Anodized aluminum. Height 3½″ to 19″, width 31½″, depth 23″.

**PRICE B** From EDCO/Pasco

## 1.23 BED RAILS
Telescopic rails assure complete protection. Attach to any hospital bed spring fabric of widths from 34″ to 36½″. Use ¾ or full length. Length 48″ to 74″. Keeps user from falling out of bed.

**PRICE C** From Professional Convalescent Products

## 1.24 MANUALLY ADJUSTABLE BED
Bed height adjusts from 18″ to 27″ from floor. Three cranks at foot of bed: one for raising head; one for raising foot; one for adjusting spring height from floor. Size 36″ by 87″.

**PRICE D** From Sears

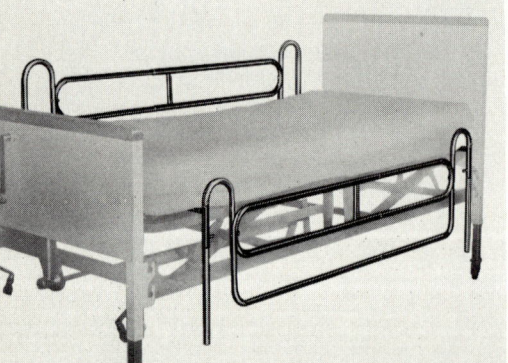
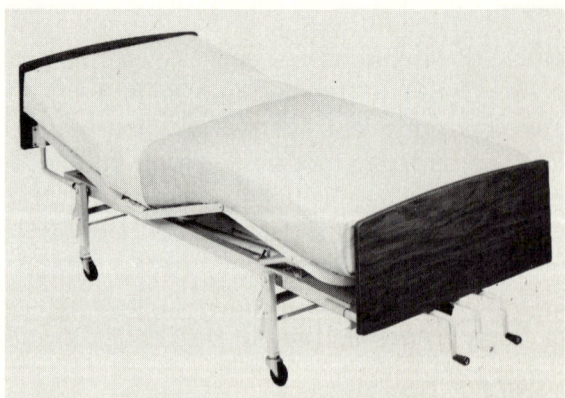

## 1.25 MANUALLY ADJUSTABLE BED
Has three adjustment cranks. One for mattress height from floor 17" to 27", two cranks for spring adjustment, head and foot up and down. Walnut-finish head and foot board. Length, 84".

**PRICE D** From Professional Convalescent Products

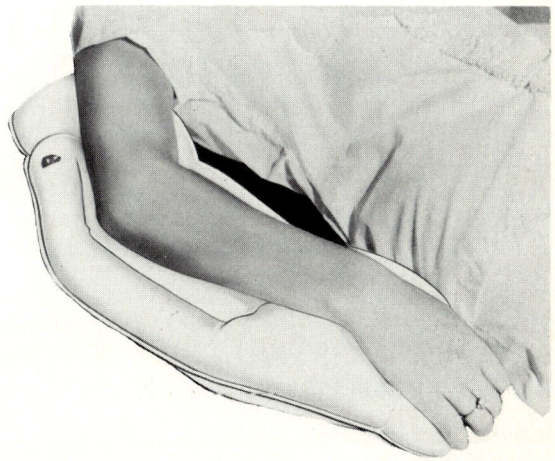

## 1.26 ARM CUSHION
Cushions shoulders, elbow and wrist joints, and fingers. Cradles arms. Helps relieve aches and soreness.

**PRICE A** From Better Sleep / FashionAble

## 1.27 FOAM WEDGE CUSHION
Foam slant is a light foam wedge for use on top of mattress to support back and torso on gradual slope, for all-night comfort. Can also be used as backrest. One-piece urethane foam. 27" long by 24" wide. Comes in various thicknesses (at top of wedge): 4", $7^{1}/_{2}$", 10", $12^{1}/_{2}$".

**PRICE B** From Better Sleep

## 1.28 FOAM WEDGE LEG REST
NuFoam® leg rest used to flex knees on while in bed. Also provides nonskid pocket to prevent sliding down bed while sleeping elevated. Made of foam 24" wide by 9" long by $3^{1}/_{2}$" high.

**PRICE A** From Better Sleep

## 1.29 BED POCKET
Fits between spring and mattress on bed. Holds magazines, books, etc. for convenient temporary storage. Also fits over arm and under cushion of most chairs and sofas. Pocket is 12" wide by 8" deep, is lined and made in either vinyl or fabric.

**PRICE B** From Ventura (Fireside)

### 1.30 BED POCKET
Attaches to side bar of bed rail. Holds magazines, eyeglasses, toilet articles, etc. Single Velcro tab equalizes pocket with raising and lowering of side bar. 9¼" by 9½".

**PRICE A** From Handee For You

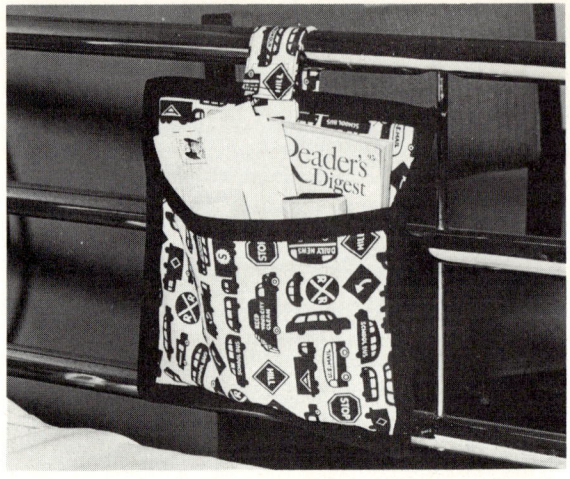

### 1.31 EYEGLASS HOLDER
Spec-Caddy™ holds eyeglasses. It is a large, cushioned, lined pouch with Velcro strap which secures it to bed rails, walkers, wheelchairs, garden chairs, etc. Fits structural supports up to 1½" diameter round or 1¼" square.

**PRICE A** From Maddak

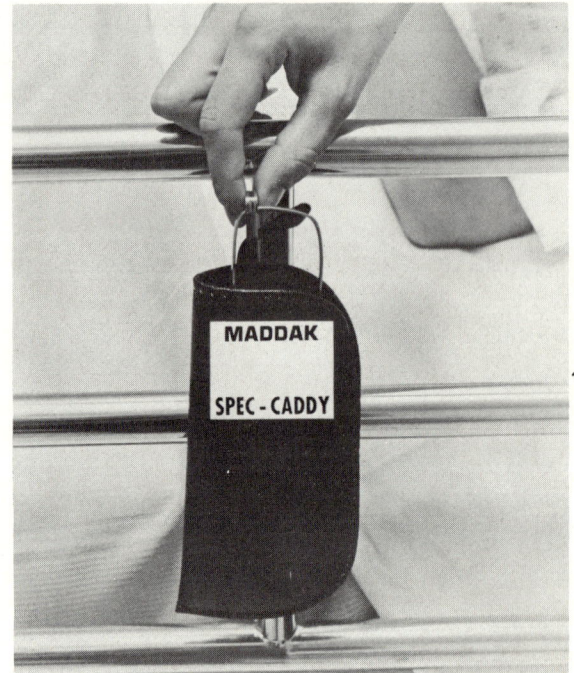

### 1.32 TIME-ON-CEILING
Regular clock projects time quietly in digital numbers on ceiling. Invisible beam has no glare to disturb sleep. Has snooze alarm and AM/FM radio. Other models without radio.

**PRICE**—with radio, **C**. Without radio, **B**. From Hammacher Schlemmer

## 1.33 TV VIEWER

Tele-Vue reclining viewer fits over glasses. 5½" long mirror permits wide viewing area. Lets user watch TV from flat position.

**PRICE A** From Bernell

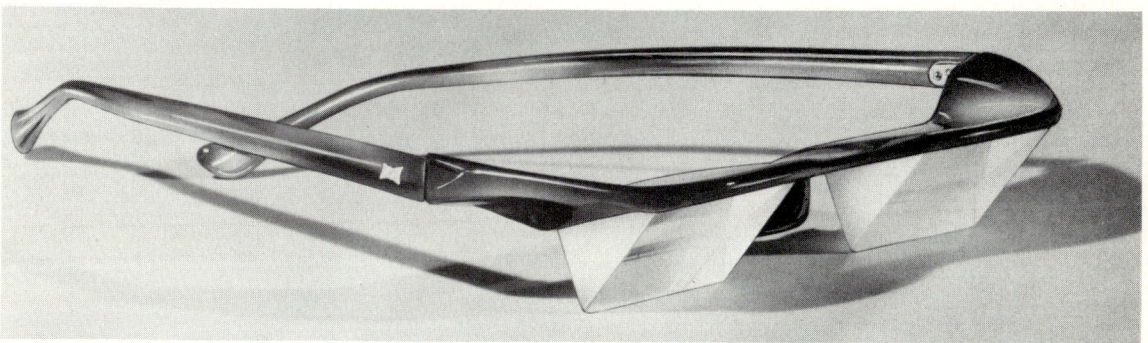

## 1.34 BEDSPECS

Prism glasses permit user to watch TV or read while lying down flat. Can be worn over glasses. Glasses allow user to see straight ahead (at right angle) while looking at ceiling.

**PRICE B** From Preston / Cleo / Bernell

## 1.35 BEDLIFT–HOIST

A self-lift transporter permits disabled to get into and out of bed unassisted. Motorized both vertically and horizontally. Free-standing or ceiling-mounted. Lifts up to 500 lb. Powered by house current.

**PRICE E** From Holo Industries (Self-Lift)™

### 1.36 BEDLIFT–HOIST
Self-operating bedlift is designed so disabled can get in and out of bed unassisted. Lifts person out of wheelchair and rotates him into bed. Lift is adjustable to various lengths and heights. Powered by 12-volt D.C. battery.

**PRICE F** From Wilch Manufacturing Inc.

### 1.37 MATTRESS TOPPER
Urethane foam 3/4" thick for top of mattress. Cool in summer, warm in winter. Protects, conceals mattress lumps, nonallergic, mildew-resistant. Can also be used for playpens, boats, exercise mats. Cut to any size or shape with scissors. Sizes 36" by 70" and 50" by 70".

**PRICE A** From Better Sleep

### 1.38 MATTRESS EXTENDER
Adds 6" to bed length. Adjustable for mattresses from 3 1/2" to 9" thick. Is foam padded with inner spring. If bed has foot board, side rail extenders are needed. Good for very tall person.

**PRICE B** From Better Sleep (available for twin or full mattresses)

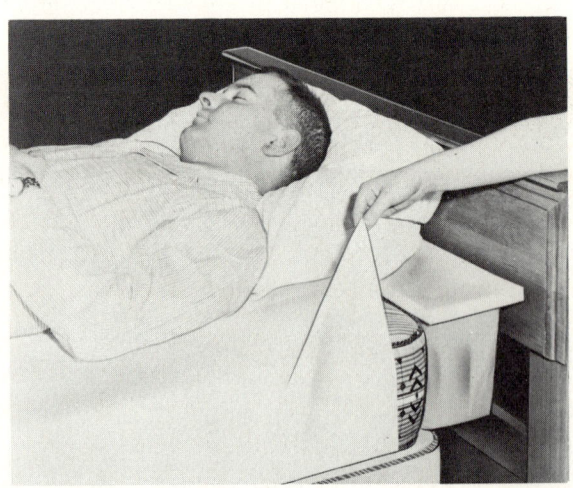

### 1.39 SIDE RAIL EXTENDER
To be used with mattress extender if bed has foot board. It gives 6" of extra length between foot board and headboard of bed. Fits 85% of beds now made. If length is incorrect for your bed, check with supplier for other available extenders.

**PRICE B** From Better Sleep

### 1.40 WATER FLOTATION MATTRESS
Inexpensive water flotation mattress, covered with unique formulation of vinyl and nylon. Reduces and distributes pressure over user's bony prominences while supporting body evenly. Helps curtail perspiration. Can be used over regular mattress. Helps prevent and treat irritation of skin caused by long confinement to bed.

**PRICE B** From Jefferson Industries Inc.

## 1.41 DRY FLOTATION MATTRESS
The Roho Dry Flotation mattress uses four lightweight air-inflated sections each 20″ by 34″, joined by Velcro strips. Its purpose is to minimize interference with existing blood circulation, prevent pressure sores, and aid in their cure.

**PRICE D** From Roho Research & Development


## 1.42 FLOTATION MATTRESS
Lightweight flotation mattress effective in helping prevent bed sores. Aqua-Pedic® mattress is a low-cost method of flotation. Has solid foam pillow area. Holds less than 20 gallons of tap water. Thick foam insulates user from water temperature. Can be elevated to all bed positions.

**PRICE D** From Aquatherm


## 1.43 MATTRESS RAISER
Nu-Slant® mattress raiser can be placed between mattress and spring at either head or foot of bed. Adjusts from 5″ to 14″ high. Folds flat when not in use. Folds in half for travel. Weighs 8 lb. Made of mahogany plywood. 27″ long and fits either 36″ to 39″ or 48″ to 54″ bed widths. Special sizes are available on request.

**PRICE B** From Better Sleep

### 1.44  MATTRESS RAISER
Aluminum frame can be used under mattress at foot or head of bed. Several height adjustments. Lifts user's head or feet.

**PRICE B**  From Camp International

### 1.45  HEAD PILLOW
Ther-A-Pedic® pillow designed to support and cradle the head, reduce spinal distortion and induce better sleep through relaxation. Solid urethane foam, nonallergic, nontoxic, odorless and dust-free.

**PRICE A**  From Better Sleep

### 1.46  ANTI-WRINKLE AIR PILLOW
Protects face from impressed wrinkles of pillow. Preserves hair style. Comfortable for arthritics. Size 17" by 9", has soft foam casing. Covers available.

**PRICE A**  From Better Sleep

### 1.48  RELAXING AIR PILLOW
For relaxing anywhere. Crescent-shaped air pillow cradles neck and supports head. Folds to fit purse or pocket. Comes with choice of zipper cover.

**PRICE A**  From Better Sleep

### 1.47  AIR HEAD PILLOW
Relax-A-Pedic® air pillow is adjustable to give perfect fit in any sleeping position. Helps relieve arthritic-like pain, neck kinks, and restless sleep.

**PRICE A**  From Better Sleep

### 1.49  SLEEP SOUND
Induces sleep and relaxation by lulling user in a vacuum of scientifically blended, non-noisy, rhythmic tones. Screens out disturbing noise. Has soft "white sound." Weight 3 lb.

**PRICE B**  From Hammacher Schlemmer / FashionAble

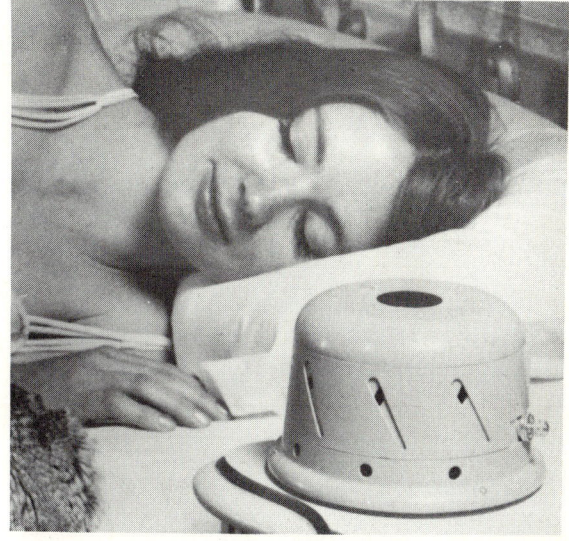

### 1.50  BED TRAY
Adjusts from flat to completely upright. For reading, writing, eating, in bed or chair. Adjustable center section. Has side pockets for books, magazines. Size 15" by 28" by 8½" high.

**PRICE B**  From Sears

### 1.51  BED TRAY
Formica tray with book clips and bottom rim. Tray tilts, and folds for storage. Size 13" by 20" for reading, writing, in bed.

**PRICE B**  From Wal-Jan

### 1.52  BED TRAY
Large tray enables person to eat, write, and work comfortably in bed. Aluminum frame, Fiberglass tray. 8" tray height gives good clearance for blankets. Food tray fits easily on bed tray. Folds flat. Size 18" by 24" by 3" folded. Weight 4½ lb.

**PRICE B**  From Aparco

### 1.53 MULTI-POSITION TABLE
Top resists heat, stains, alcohol. Raised edge keeps objects from falling off. Top 24" by 16". Tilts in any direction. Adjusts to seven positions. Adjustable height 25" to 38". Folds to 4". Easy roll three-ball caster. 15 lb. For reading, writing, eating, games.

**PRICE C** From Hammacher Schlemmer

### 1.54 MULTI-POSITION TABLE
For convenient dining, reading, writing, in bed. Chrome-plated stand adjusts for height. Top tilts and locks in five positions. Stain resistant, mar-proof. Nonglare finish. Has four wheels.

**PRICE D** From Everest & Jennings

# Personal Care ②

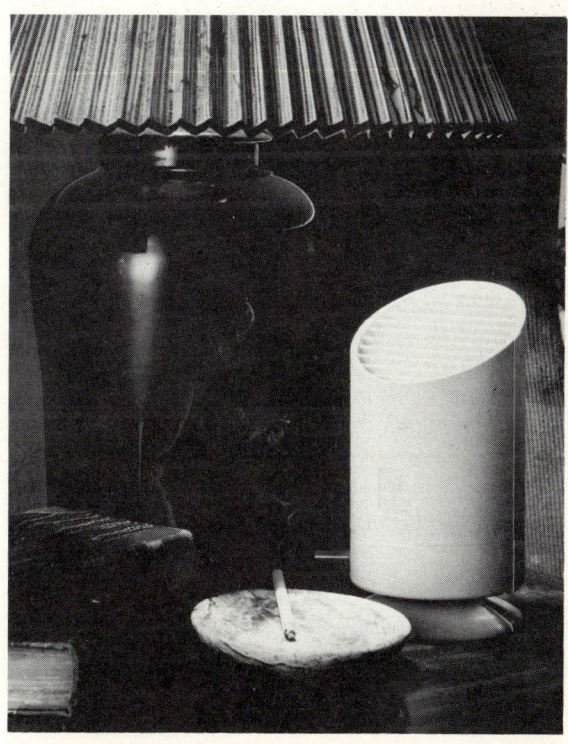

**2.1 AIR PURIFIER**
The Good-Air Ecologizer removes odors, tobacco smoke, pollen, and dust from indoor air. It cleans and deodorizes it by constant air re-circulation and natural filtration. Unit contains a filter filled with CA/90-saturated, absorbent particles. With normal use filter should be changed every three months. Unit comes with one filter; extra filters must be purchased separately. 4 lb. weight.

**PRICE B** From Rush Hampton Ind. / Hammacher Schlemmer

### 2.2 WHEELCHAIR BATHROOM
Featured are one-piece Fiberglass stall shower that wheelchair can move into; 18"-high toilet that permits easy movement to and from wheelchair; and a sink that allows wheelchair to slide beneath it.

  **PRICE F** From Universal-Rundle (See Index for wheelchair shower, wheelchair sink, wheelchair toilet)

### 2.3 SUCTION DENTURE BRUSH
A new way to get complete access to both sides of denture brush. Strong suction cups hold base firmly. Brush is positioned for easy, one-hand cleaning of dentures.

  **PRICE A** From Cleo

### 2.4 LARGE HANDLE TOOTHBRUSH
Toothbrush has large plastic handle for people with poor grasp. Lightweight and durable.

  **PRICE A** From Cleo

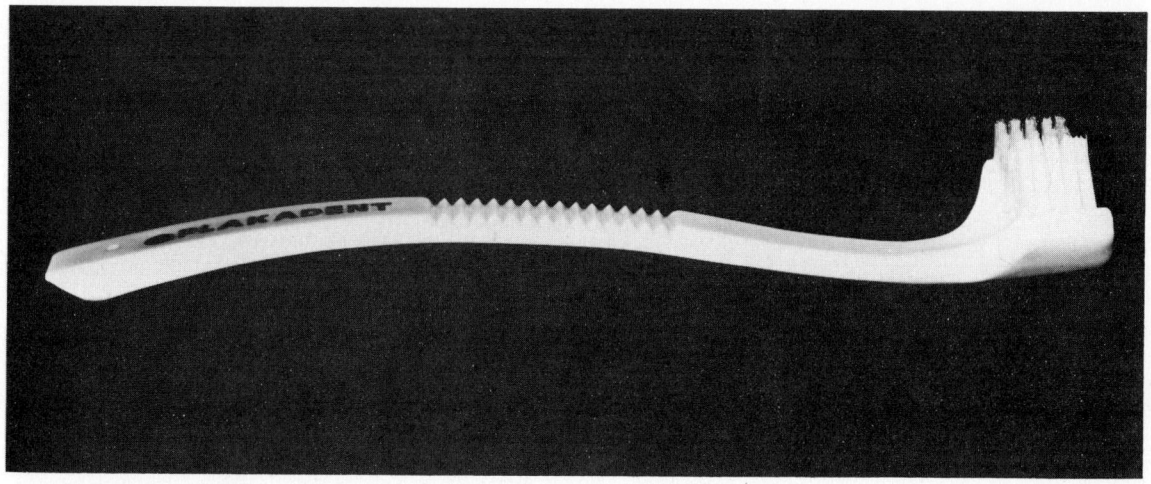

## 2.5 ANGLE TOOTHBRUSH
Twin brushes at 45° angle brush both teeth and gums with straight strokes. Has contoured, grooved handle and soft nylon bristles.

**PRICE A** From Plakadent International (Plakadent Double Header)

## 2.6 LONG HANDLE BACKBRUSH
Has adjustable angle. Lets user with limited motion scrub back and legs. Angle is locked with wing nut. Aluminum handle with rubber cover.

**PRICE A** From Cleo

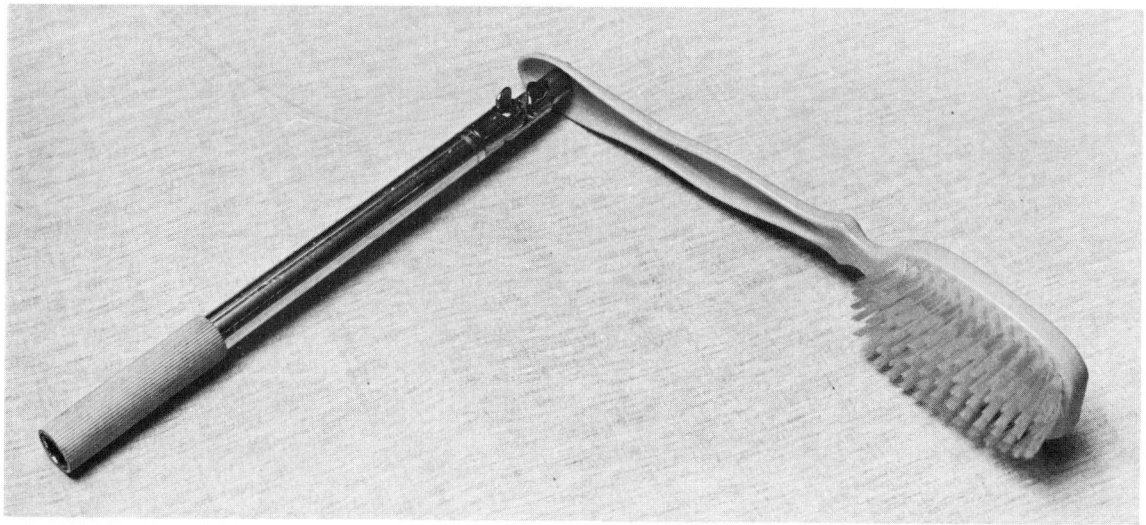

### 2.7 VELCRO HANDLE HAIRBRUSH
Has soft plastic teeth for men's and women's hair. Has easy-to-fasten handle for individuals with limited grasp. Locks firmly to your hand. Durable black plastic. Washable.

**PRICE A** From Cleo

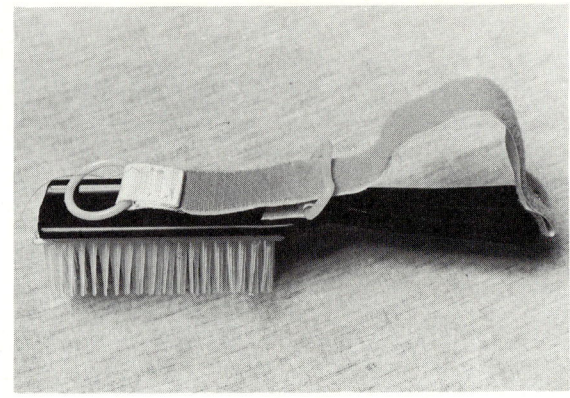

### 2.8 BACKBRUSH WITH SOAP
Good for one-hand use or limited range of motion. Soap is in the sponge. No reaching for soap. Slip sponge off plastic handle, insert soap in pocket in sponge, replace handle. Length of brush and handle: 16$\frac{1}{2}$".

**PRICE A** From Cleo

### 2.9 SUCTION BRUSH
Hand and nail brush with rubber suction cups to attach to sink or tub. Has plastic back and nylon bristles. Good for those who have use of only one hand.

**PRICE A** From Cleo

### 2.10 BATHING SCRUB CLOTH
Terri Cloth Super Soaper enables individual with limited motion to bathe all areas of the body. Has thumb holes on each end. A pocket in middle closes with Velcro and holds soap.

**PRICE A** From MED

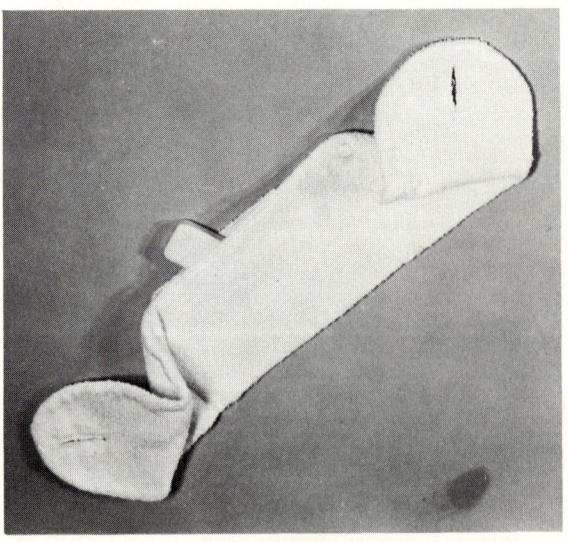

PERSONAL CARE 19

### 2.11a  BATHTUB READER
Bather can read comfortably in bathtub or whirlpool. Good for hydro-therapy and relaxation therapy. Fits all style and size bathtubs. Fits metal whirlpool tanks. Uses only one tub wall. Bathtub Reader can be lifted on or off tubs directly. Book fits on plexiglass tray.

   **PRICE B**  From Aparco Inc.

### 2.11b  BATH PILLOW
Wet-proof, held in place by two suction cups. Adjustable height and softness. Inflate by mouth to degree of firmness desired. 9" by 18". Relax in bathtub with this tranquilizing pillow.

   **PRICE A**  From Better Sleep

### 2.12  BATH IN BED
An easy way to have a tub bath or hydrotherapy in bed. May be stored in small space. Easy to assemble. Size 12" by 28" by 74". No motors, pumps, or electricity.

   **PRICE D**  From Hoffman Manufacturing Co.

### 2.13  BATH IN BED
Makes it possible to bathe in bed. Person is rolled on tub which is then inflated around him. Good for traveling if bathtubs are unaccessible. Inflated size (inside) 60" by 21" by 8½". Weight 6 lb.

**PRICE D**  From Bathing Aids to Handicapped

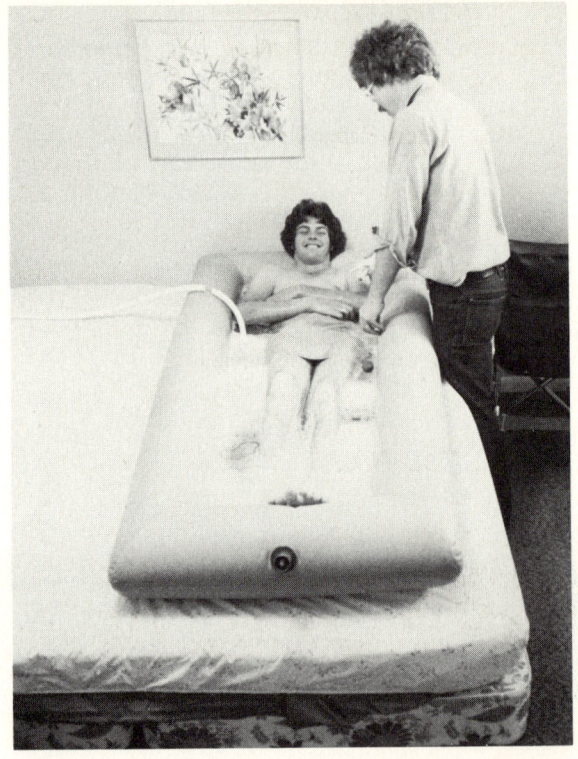

### 2.14  BATHTUB LIFT SEAT
Helps one in and out of the bathtub. Buoyant, soft, complete with back, sides and safety strap. Suction cups adhere to tub and hold user in place. Release cups and one is lifted with a minimum of effort.

**PRICE B**  From Better Sleep

PERSONAL CARE 21

## 2.15 BATH OVERFLOW CAP
Soakers Delite is a suction rubber cap to cover and control tub overflow valve. Allows tub water level to raise 1" to 3" higher by rotating the cap.

**PRICE A** From Better Sleep

## 2.16 GRAB BAR
One-inch diameter nylon coated steel tubing 16" long. Extends 4" from wall. For safety in and out of tub or shower.

**PRICE B** From Everest & Jennings

## 2.17 GRAB BAR
16" by 32" left angle grab bar. Also comes in right angle. Aids in getting in and out of shower or tub and steadies user when standing.

**PRICE B** From Lumex

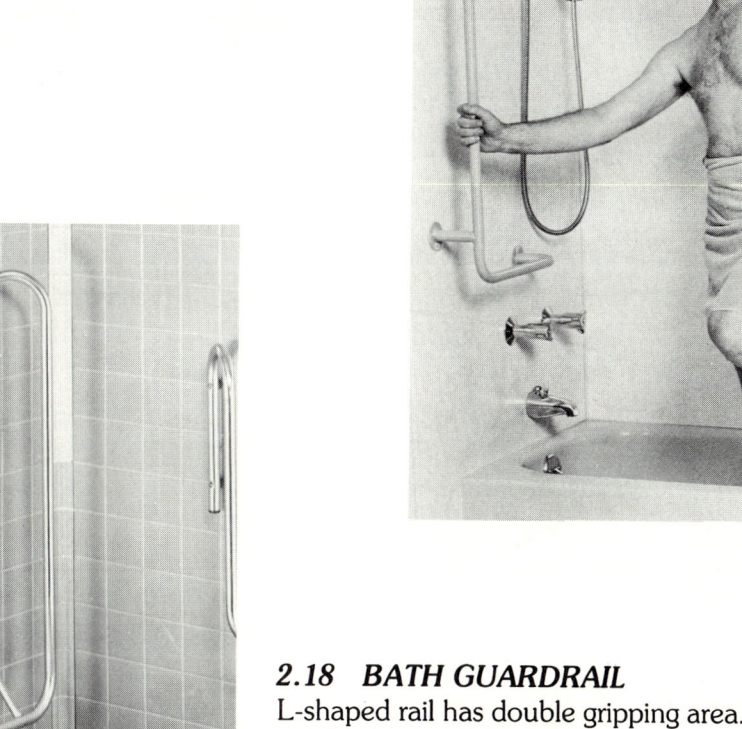

## 2.18 BATH GUARDRAIL
L-shaped rail has double gripping area. 18" by 38" long. Aids getting into or out of tub or shower. Aids in standing.

**PRICE B** From Sears

### 2.19 TUB BENCH
Low enough to let tub water cover lower part of body. 5" high. Vinyl-coated steel resists rust and chipping. Self-leveling plastic feet.

**PRICE B** From Everest & Jennings
(similar, Hausman)

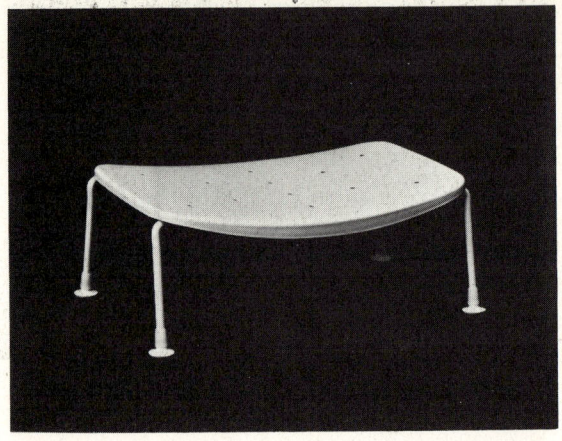

### 2.20 BATH BENCH
Adjustable bath bench. Seat height 14" to 20". Width 20". Seat depth 12". Anodized aluminum frame. Plastic seat with assist handles and drain holes for water. Four legs angle out to resist tipping. Suction tips on legs.

**PRICE B** From EDCO/Pasco

### 2.21 BATH BENCH
Protective white plastic-coated. Rubber-tipped feet. 11" high, 16" wide, 11" deep.

**PRICE B** From Frohock Stewart, Inc. (similar bench available from Everest & Jennings)

### 2.22 BATH BENCH WITH BACK
Chair back and side rests provide support for bathers with balance problems. Self-leveling plastic feet. Seat width 16". White vinyl-coated steel resists rust and chipping. $18^{1/2}$" seat height. Back support, 10".

**PRICE C** From Everest & Jennings

### 2.23 BATH BENCH WITH BACK-ADJUSTABLE
Seat height 14" to 20". Width 20". Seat depth 12". Plastic back and seat have water drain holes and assist handles. Suction legs tilt out to resist tipping. Anodized aluminum frame.

**PRICE B** From EDCO/Pasco (similar, Cleo; Frohock Stewart)

## 2.24 CUSHIONED BATH BENCH
Adjustable height padded bath seat. Thick polyurethane cushions heat sealed in vinyl. Back has adjustable padded cushions. Seat height $16\frac{1}{2}''$ to $20\frac{1}{2}''$. Highly rust-resistant.

**PRICE C** From Lumex, Inc.

## 2.25 BATH BENCH—ADJUSTABLE
Made of cast and tubular aluminum with rubber feet to prevent sliding. Seat has wrinkled baked enamel finish. Seat 9" by $16\frac{1}{2}''$. Height adjusts from 9" to 14". Sturdy. Backrest firmly attached.

**PRICE B** From Bollen (Bath Seat with Back)

## 2.26 TUB SEAT
Side panels have friction grip pads that pivot to wedge into angle of tub. Seat adjusts from 21" to $24\frac{1}{2}''$ in width to fit most tubs at desired height inside tub. All metal parts finished in white baked enamel. Holds 300 lb.

**PRICE B** From Invacare

## 2.27 TUB SEAT
Adjustable cushioned frame smooth plastic seat. Frame hangs on bathtub edge. Adjustable to tub widths $21\frac{1}{2}''$ to $23\frac{1}{2}''$. Won't scratch tub. Seat 10" by 15".

**PRICE B** From Maddak

## 2.28 PADDED TRANSFER TUB SEAT
Aids in getting into tub. Allows shower curtain to close and water to drip into tub. Adjustable seat height 18" to 22". Legs inside tub have suction cups with release tabs. Polyurethane cushions heat sealed in vinyl. Back has adjustable cushions. Armrest 7" above seat. Highly rust-resistant.

**PRICE C** From Lumex Inc.

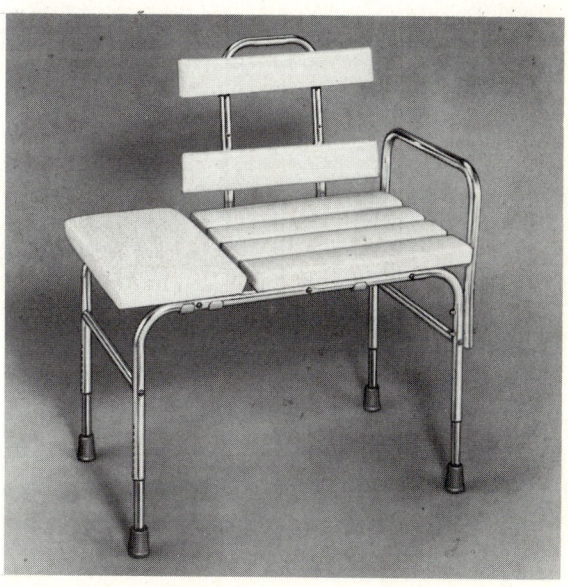

## 2.29 TRANSFER TUB SEAT

All-purpose bath seat adjusts to width of tub. Backrest may be mounted on either side of seat. Unit folds for storage. User sits on seat with legs outside tub. Lifts legs into tub one at a time.

**PRICE C** From Hausman
(similar, Lumex; E. F. Brewer)

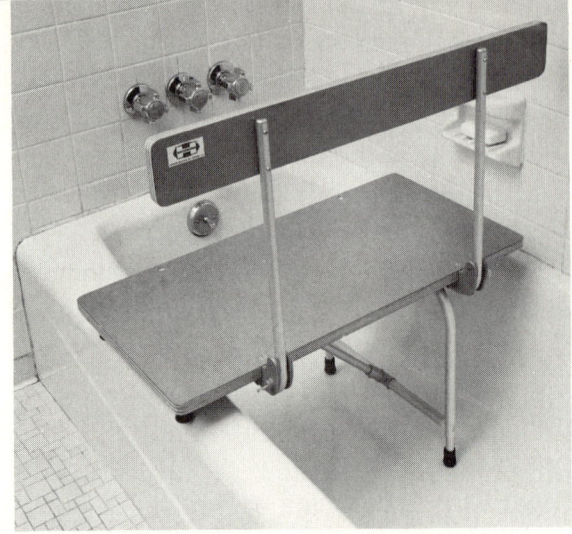

## 2.30 WATER-POWERED BATH LIFT

Aqualift™ provides safe, sure means to get into and out of bathtub. Can use with whirlpool. Does not interfere with normal tub use. Completely portable and nonelectrical. Weight 23 lb. Seat lowered height 3". Seat raised height 18".

**PRICE E** From Triaxon Inc.

## 2.31 WATER-POWERED BATH LIFT

Self-operated, no electricity. Fits all tubs, portable. Easy way to get into and out of bathtub. Weight 19 lb. Lifts over 300 lb. Lowers to 2" from tub bottom. Arms aid sitting. Options available.

**PRICE E** From J. E. Nolan & Company, Inc.

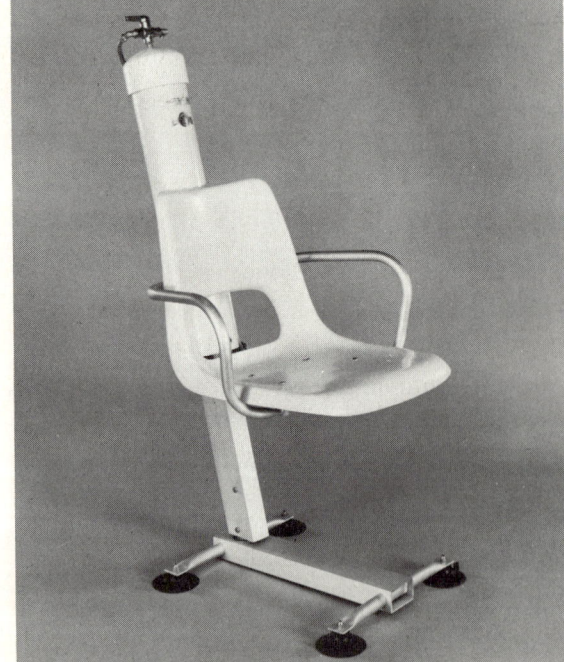

## 2.32 WATER-POWERED BATH LIFT

Easy way to get into and out of tub. Nonelectric. Uses water from replacement tub spout. All components resist water corrosion. Can be stopped in any position. Seat turns at all levels. Lifts 200 to 400 lb. depending on water pressure at lift. 22" of total lift. Seat rotates 360°.

**PRICE E** From Grant Water Corp.

## 2.33 WATER-POWERED BATH LIFT

Easy, independent, safe way to get into and out of bathtub. Portable, weight 26 lb. Nonelectric. Doesn't interfere with normal tub use. Size: $16^{1}/_{2}''$ long, 15" wide. 20 lb. water pressure lifts 150 lb.

**PRICE E** From CHEC Medical Products

## 2.34 BATH LIFT, WATER-PRESSURE

User adjusts lever to lower or raise out of tub. Chair swivels. Operates on normal water pressure. No electrical parts. Won't interfere with normal tub use.

**PRICE D** From Sears

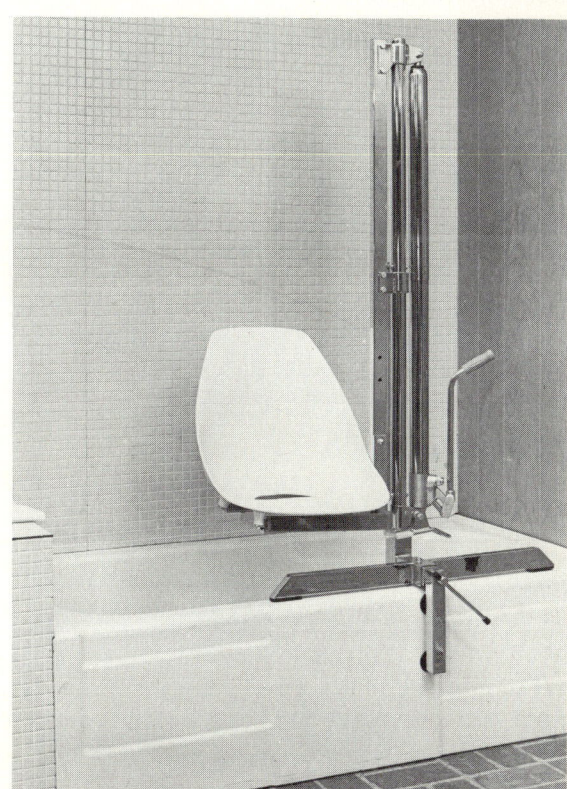

## 2.35 BATH LIFT, HYDRAULIC

Hoyer Hydraulic Lift is for persons who have some ability to help themselves and who wish to bathe in private. Can be operated by bather or helper. Seat raises, lowers, swings, locks in place. Cannot be used on rolled rimmed tub or Fiberglass tub.

**PRICE E** From Hoyer Bath Lift Mfg., Everest & Jennings

## 2.36 BATH LIFT, HYDRAULIC

Lowers or raises user in or out of tub. Chair rotates around and over tub and lowers into tub until it rests on bottom. Easily installed on any tub.

**PRICE E** From Invacare

## 2.37 BATH LIFT, MANUAL

Eaton E-Z Bath is a manual bath lift. Allows bather to slide from wheelchair onto unit. Fits into most tubs. Weighs 22 lb. and is portable. Seat is lowered by turning of crank.

**PRICE D** From Eaton E-Z Bath™ Company (E-Z Bath)

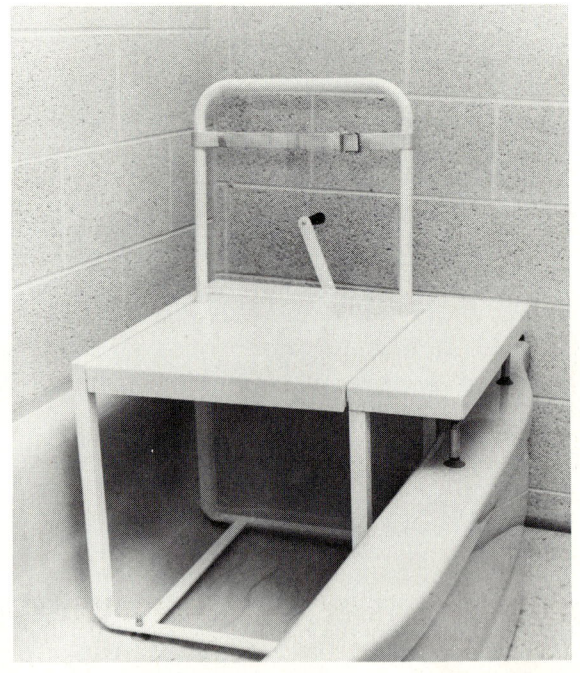

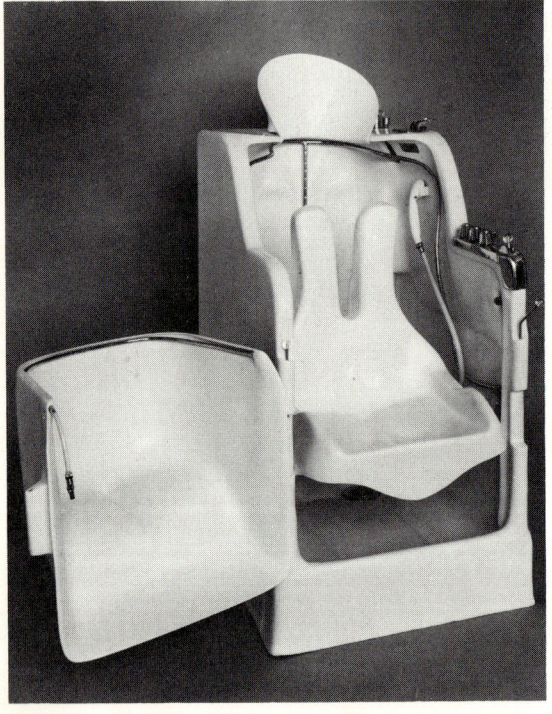

## 2.38 SIT-DOWN SHOWER

Hygienically bathes people safely and efficiently. Can be used for sitz bath, shampoo, foot and body shower, people with lower-body casts. Hydro-powered seat, thermostatic temperature control. Liquid soap injection system. Height, 47"; width, 27". Required floor space, 60" width by 66" depth.

**PRICE F** From Easy Bath™

## 2.39 WALK-IN BATHTUB
Bath-Aid is a walk-in, sit-down bathtub. It eliminates need in some cases for hoists and lifts. It can be used as shower, bathtub and with whirlpool. Made of Fiberglass. Is 43" wide by 31" deep by 36" high.

**PRICE F** From Amsco

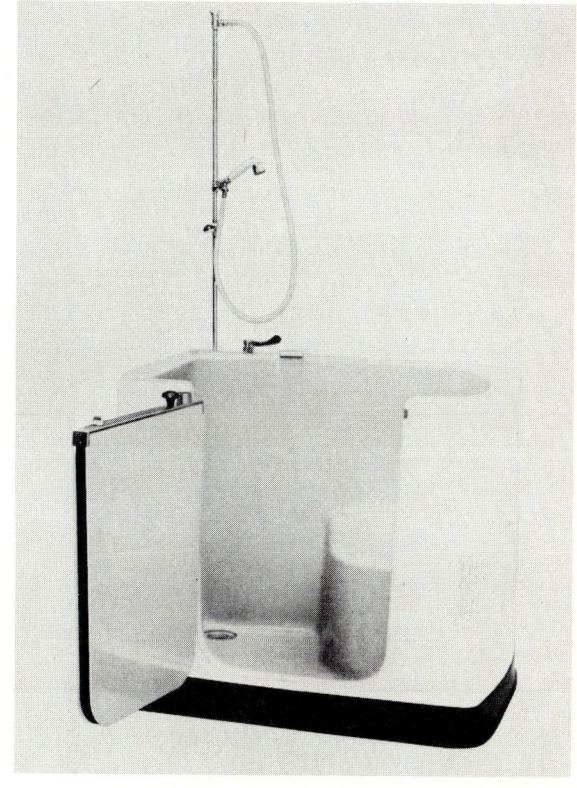

## 2.40 BLOOD PRESSURE KIT
Inexpensive kit. Cuff for inflating. Has touch-and-hold closure for proper fit. Vinyl zip case.

**PRICE B** From Sears (similar, Cleo)

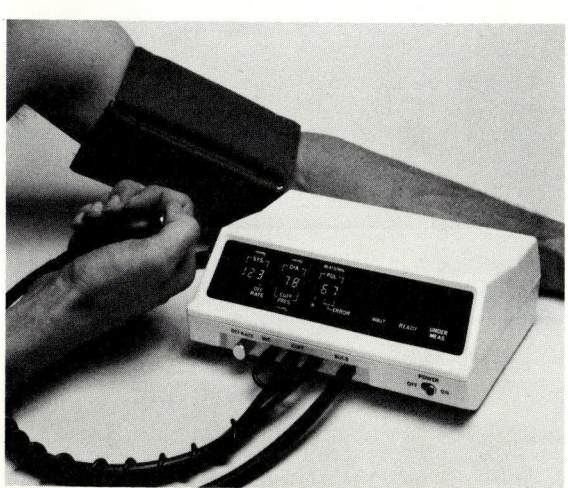

## 2.41 ELECTRIC BLOOD PRESSURE KIT
Designed for easy self-use. No stethoscope needed. Digital read-out.

**PRICE C** From Sears

## 2.42 LARGE HANDLE AFRO-COMB AND NAIL FILE

Comb and nail file are cemented into filled bicycle-type handles with finger grip knobs. Handles made of resilient vinyl. For either hand. Good for persons with weak hand grip.

**PRICE A (each)** From Maddak / Comfort-Able-Aids

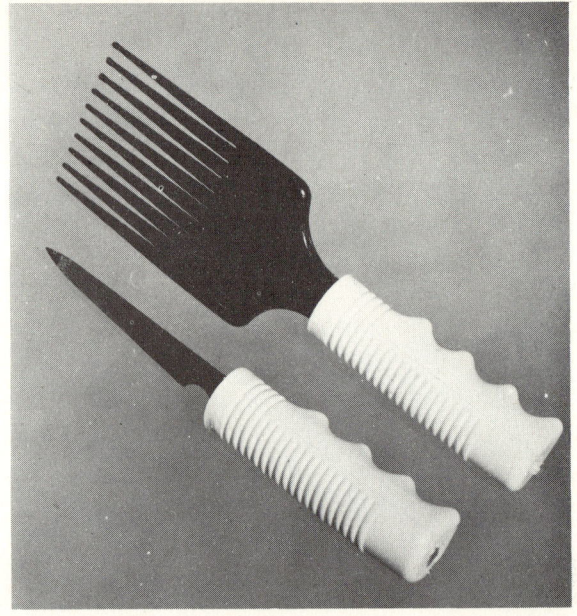

## 2.43 LARGE HANDLE COMB AND BRUSH

Comb and brush are joined to specially shaped oversized handles of durable plastic. Convenient for either hand for users with grasping difficulties.

**PRICE A (each)** From Comfort-Able-Aids

## 2.44 COMB ON HANDLE

20" double T-bar handle with adjustable swivel angle. All plastic. Also with choice of afro comb. For people with limited arm motion.

**PRICE A** From Maddak

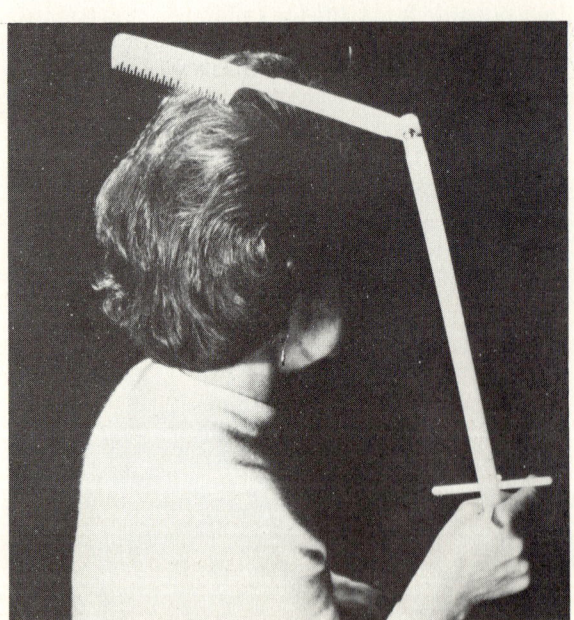

## 2.45 EXTENSION COMB
Long-handled comb has positive lock setting at joint. Aluminum comb won't break or bend. Aluminum shaft can be bent to give best combing pattern. Expandable handle can also be bent to fit the hand. Length 20″. Good for those with reaching difficulties.

**PRICE A** From Cleo

## 2.46 ALL-PURPOSE DISPENSER
Pumps just the right amount of lotion, conditioner, shampoo, hand cleaner, etc. Comes individually or in sets. 16 oz. capacity in each. Attaches to wall or tile with epoxy adhesive. Useful for those who have difficulty bending, reaching, or holding.

**PRICE A** From Camping World

## 2.47 HAND AND ARM EXERCISER
Improves gripping power, flexibility and muscle strength. Works against gyroscope rotor inside plastic sphere.

**PRICE A** From Zeus Manufacturing (Dyna Bee™)

## 2.48 EXERCISER—LEGS
Ideal for individual who must exercise but cannot sit safely on a bicycle. Portable, lightweight. Attaches to any straight-back chair or tubular bed. Pedals have toe and heel to hold feet in place. Adjustable resistance mechanism. Fits all leg lengths for any age. Stores in small space.

**PRICE D** From Preston / Dakon Corp.

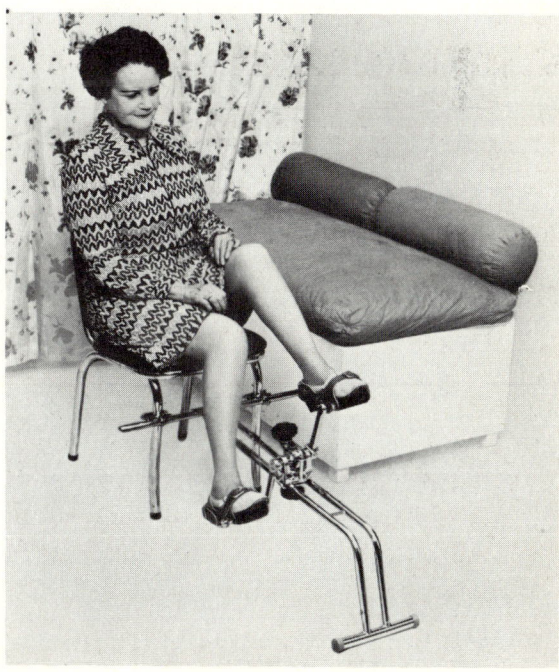

### 2.49 HAND EXERCISER

Hand Gym® for proper exercise of hands affected by injury or disease. Can be adjusted for various size hands. Measures 5½" by 6½" by 7½". Weighs 12 oz. Comes with 30-page illustrated instruction book.

**PRICE B** From Maddak / S. E. Kewer

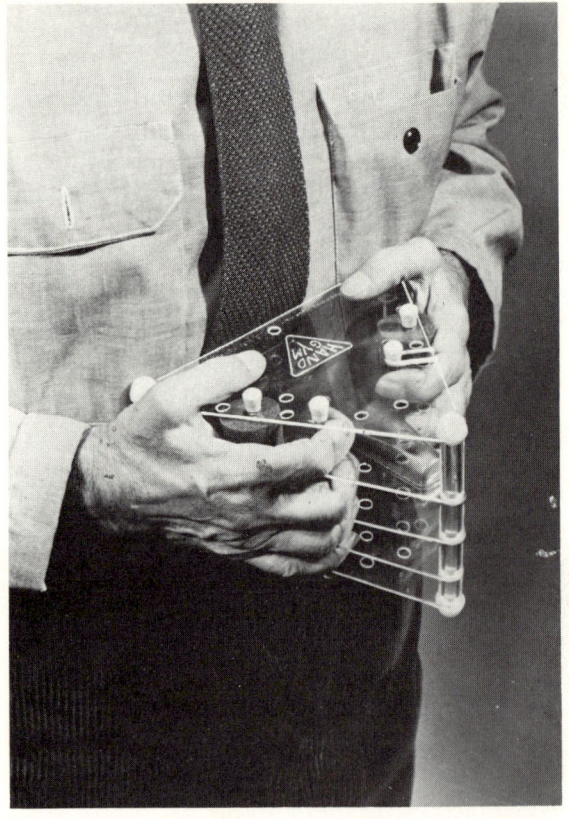

### 2.50 HAND EXERCISER

Thera-Plast® is a therapeutic aid to strengthen fingers, hands, wrists, forearm. Can be pulled, bounced, manipulated or worked in the mass. Available in 2-oz. or 1-lb. size.

**PRICE A** From Thera Plast Company (A surgical supply company may carry this item.)

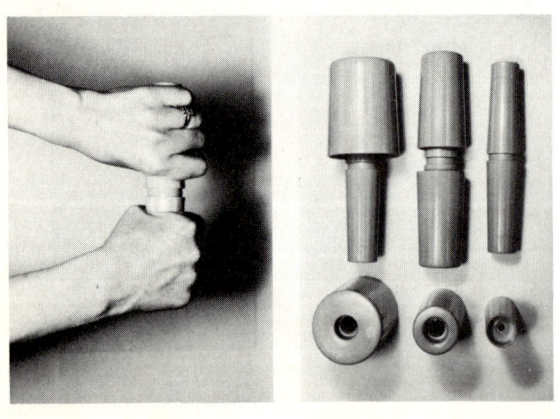

### 2.51 EXERCISER—HANDS, ARMS, SHOULDERS

Exer-Twist® exercises grip, wrist, arms, chest and shoulders. Resistance is adjustable. Additional snap-on grips 2" or 3" wider are available.

**PRICE A** From Maddak

PERSONAL CARE  31

## 2.52 JOGGING EXERCISER
Provides a good heart-strengthening exercise that requires little coordination. Provides exercise equivalent of anything from walk to run. Jarless exercise is very gentle on the joints. Smoother than walking. Adjustable for height and leg resistance. Has various accessories.

**PRICE D** From PSI

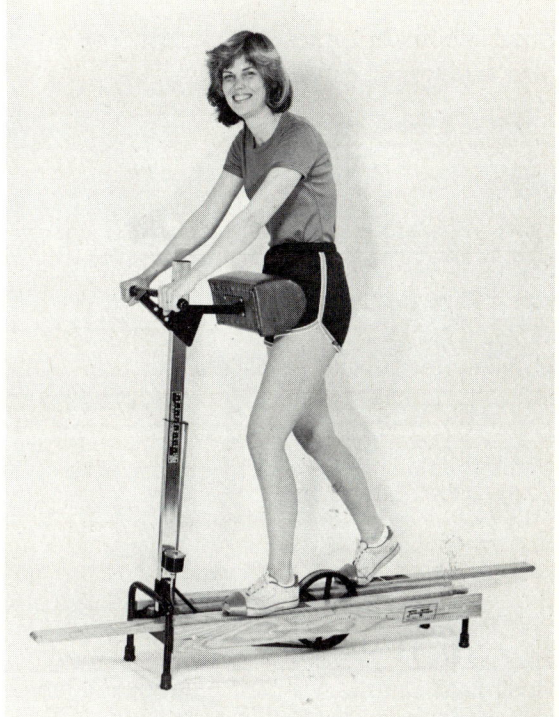

## 2.53 HAND EXERCISER
Rubber hand grip contoured to give all fingers equal exercise.

**PRICE A** From Cleo

## 2.54 DENTAL FLOSS HOLDER
Floss 'Em® is an easy way to clean between the teeth. Holds spool of floss conveniently; uses a small amount; guides floss between teeth with prongs to eliminate "sawing" back and forth; keeps even tension of floss; releases instantly if floss gets wedged between teeth. 28-yard spool of unwaxed dental floss in handle.

**PRICE A** From American Coil

## 2.55 HEATING PAD
Knee, elbow, or shoulder heat pad. Size adjustable with Velcro closure. Washable cover. Three heat settings. 7′ cord.

**PRICE B**  From FashionAble

## 2.56 HEATING MUFF
Arthro-Muff™ for hands, elbows, knees, and feet. Helps relieve pain of aching muscles and joints. Can be used with moist or dry heat. Stretch cuffs. Velcro adjustable closure. Three settings—low, medium, high. Washable.

**PRICE B**  From Sears

## 2.57 HEAT MASK
Moist heat sinus facial mask. Choose either dry heat or moist heat. Three heat settings. 100% wetproof.

**PRICE B**  From Oster Corp.

## 2.58 HEAT PADS
To fit neck, leg, or wrist. Electric moist heat pads. Generates moisture without use of water. Three heat settings. Size 13″ by 14″, 4″ by 14″.

**PRICE A (each)**  From Cleo

## 2.59 MOIST HEAT PAD, LARGE
Generates moisture without use of water. Three heat settings. Size 13″ by 27″.

**PRICE B**  From Cleo; (similar, Battle Creek—Sm-M-Lg; Everest & Jennings)

## 2.60 PORTABLE HAIR STYLER-DRYER
Gotcha Dry™ 1000, a mini-styler dryer with drying comb and styling brush that snap on unit. $7^{5}/_{8}$″ long, 14 oz., 1000 watts, two speeds, two heat settings.

**PRICE B**  From Norelco (similar, Schick Drying Stick 1200 watts)

PERSONAL CARE    33

## 2.61  HAIR DRYER, PORTABLE

Gotcha Gun™ mini compact hair dryer with folding handle. 16 oz. weight. Three settings for drying and styling. Click handle into half-open position and set unit on table for hands-free drying.

**PRICE B**  From Norelco

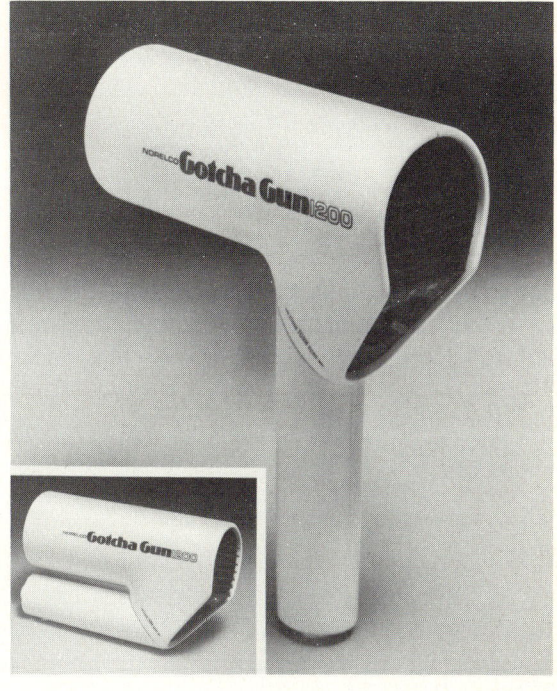

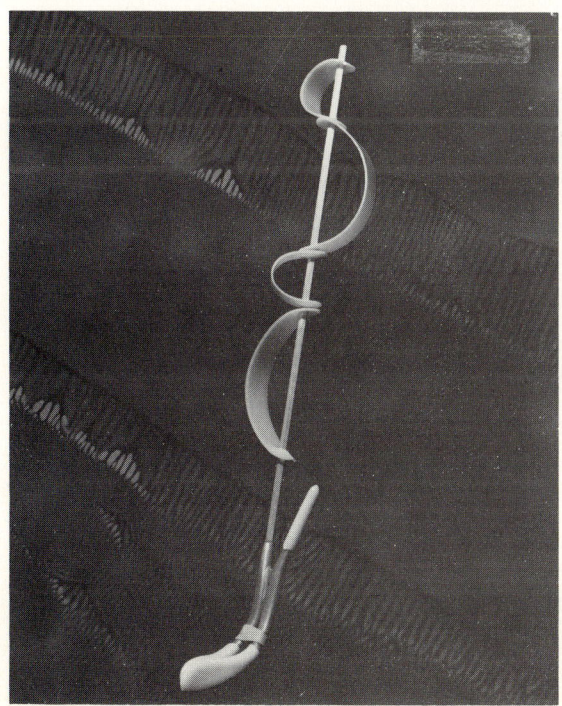

## 2.62  HYGIENE-AID

Designed to be a set of "fingers" that will hold toilet paper, fit contours of the body for cleansing desired areas, and drop soiled tissue into toilet bowl. Is also used for inserting and removing vaginal tampons. Adjustable straps. Only one moving part. 8 oz. weight, 23" long.

**PRICE B**  From Therafin

## 2.63 LIMB WARMER
Tubular, double-thick terry cloth stretchable warmers. Provides soothing warmth for joints or limbs. $8^{1}/_{2}$" long, 2-way stretch.

**PRICE A** From Maddak


## 2.64 MEDIC ALERT
An emergency life-saving medical system. Member wears bracelet or necklace with his medical problems, identification number, and a hot line 24-hour telephone number that has his computerized file with balance of information on instant recall.

**PRICE A** From Medic Alert Foundation


## 2.65 MICROLERT™
A device which enables users to get help immediately in case of emergencies such as sickness or robbery. A 1-oz. transmitter, worn like a medallion under clothing, is squeezed if help is needed. It will activate a receiver up to 300 feet away which in turn sends out telephone calls automatically to pre-programmed numbers. Tapes describe location and nature of emergency. Additional security systems are available.

**PRICE D** From Microlert Systems


## 2.66 MEDICAL SYMBOL
Custom-printed tag with red medical symbol alerts police or emergency personnel everywhere to look for medical information that can save a life. Vital information can be printed on necklace or bracelet.

**PRICE A** From National Identification Company (Emerg-Alert®)


## 2.67 BODY MASSAGER PILLOW WITH HEAT
Massage and heat treatment at same time or separately for every body area. Three settings. 20" long. Heavy-duty leatherette vinyl.

**PRICE B** From Oster (Oster Body-Tone)


## 2.68 MASSAGER
Sanyo Electropedic Massager is 2-speed with built-in frequencies that penetrate muscles. Has extra attachments.

**PRICE C** From Electropedic Products

PERSONAL CARE 35

### 2.69 FOOT MASSAGER
Starts instantly at a touch. Portable, just plug in. 7 lb.

**PRICE B** From Hammacher Schlemmer

### 2.70 EXTENSION MIRROR
Two-sided magnifying and regular mirror. Mounted arm extends 2½′. 8″ by 6″, mirror adjusts and holds any angle. Flip to regular or magnified. 7 lb. Easily mounted with two screws.

**PRICE B** From Hammacher Schlemmer

### 2.71 LOCK-ON MIRROR
Leaves hands free. Suction base attaches to any surface. Socket and swivels allow adjustment at any angle. Unbreakable. Has mirror on one side and magnifier on other. Extends 6″ to 28″.

**PRICE A** From FashionAble

### 2.72 FLEX-A-MIRROR
Hand inspection mirror for those subject to pressure sores. 4″ by 6″ plastic mirror attached to flexible shaft that may be bent to any angle. 6″ handle with strap. Soft polyethylene handgrip. Length 20½″, weight 6 oz.

**PRICE A** From Therafin

### 2.73  MIRROR, FOUR-WAY
Use around neck, freeing hands, or as a standing, hand or hanging mirror. Adjustable. One side regular; magnifying mirror other side. Mirror 5" diameter. Overall length 12".

**PRICE A**  From Cleo

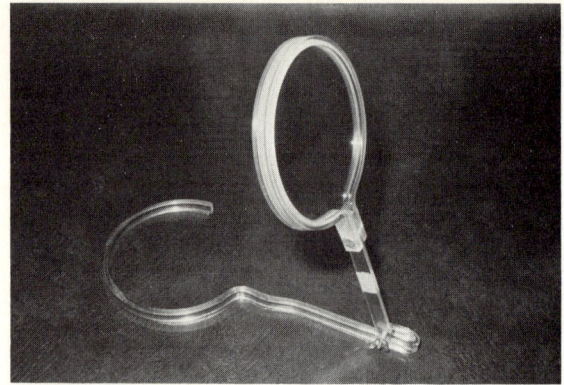

### 2.74  NAIL CLIPPER ON BLOCK
Standard nail clipper and file attached to a heavy plastic block with two suction cups to hold it on table top. Aid for those with limited finger strength or manipulative ability.

**PRICE A**  From Maddak

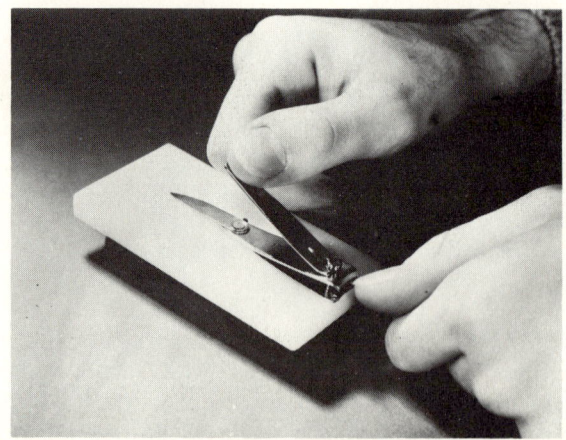

### 2.75  PILL REMINDER BOX
Seven-compartment molded plastic box with individual snap lock and hinged lid for each compartment. Each lid has molded-in letter for day of week. Small $4^{1}/_{2}$" by 1" by $^{3}/_{4}$"—Large 6" by $1^{1}/_{4}$" by 1".

**PRICE A**  From Maddak

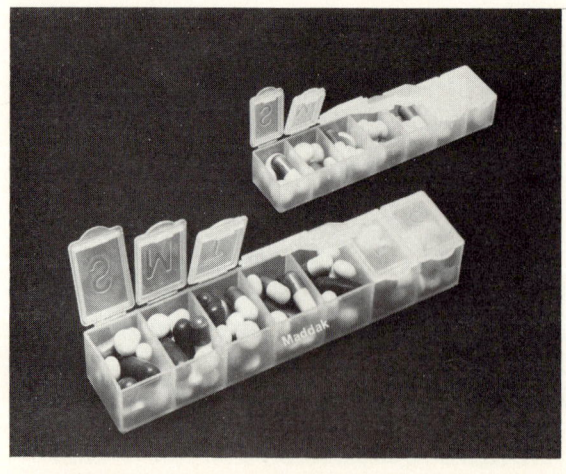

PERSONAL CARE    37

## 2.76  NAIL MACHINE
Norelco Nail Dazzler™—cordless, battery-operated manicure machine, with attachments for shaping, filing, buffing, cleaning and removing callouses. Portable, fits any size hand. Pressure-sensitive on/off rotary action or continuous speed.

*PRICE B* From Norelco

## 2.77  SAFETY TUB BAR
Aids in getting into and out of bathtub (higher portion). Aids in sitting and rising in bathtub (lower portion). Clamps securely to tub walls 4" to 7½" wide. Rust-proof. Won't scratch tub.

*PRICE B* From Invacare (similar, FashionAble; Everest & Jennings; Cleo)

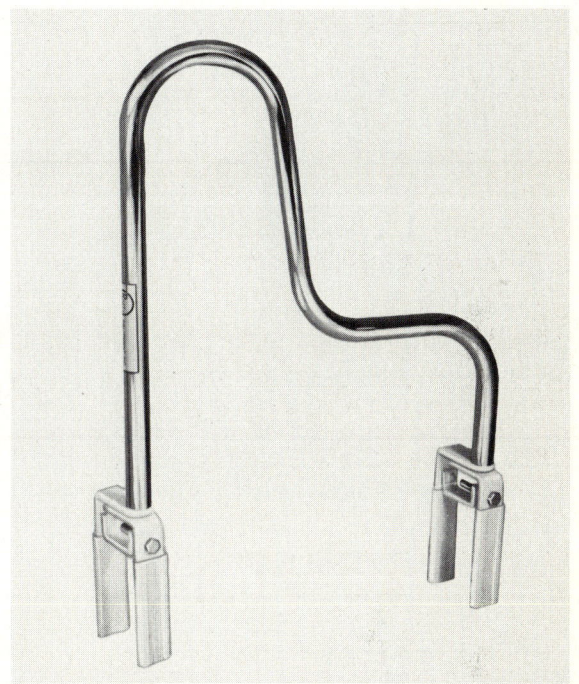

## 2.78  SAFETY TUB BARS
Hi Bar is adjustable, has lined brackets that won't mar tub. 14" high, 6" wide with crossbar. Low bar won't mar tub. 17" long. Either bar facilitates entering or leaving of tub. No tools necessary. Other models fit wider rims.

*PRICE B* From Cleo

## 2.79  SAFETY TUB RAIL
Provides safety in and out of tub. Adjusts to fit 4", 5", 6" tub wall width. All areas contacting tub are protected. Fits straight or tapered sides.

*PRICE B* From Lumex / Cleo

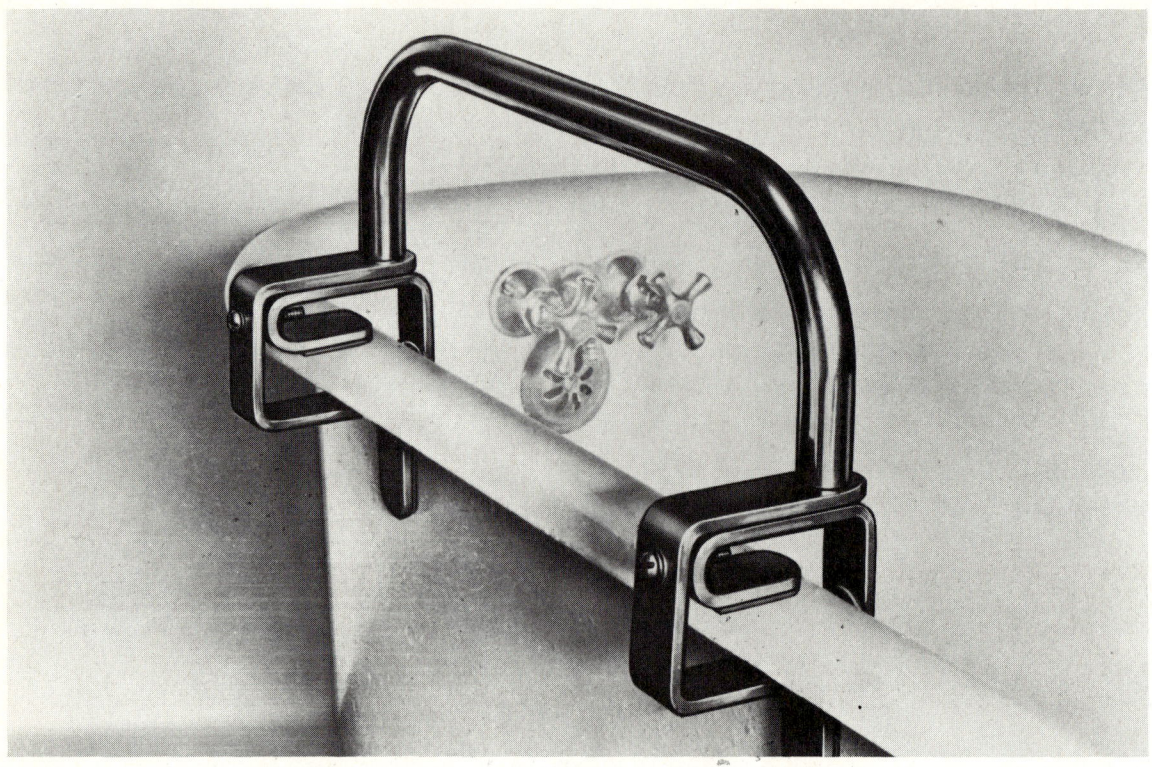

### 2.80 SAFETY TUB RAIL
Bathtub security rail for old-style bathtubs. Aids in getting into and out of tub.

**PRICE B** From Frohock Stewart Company

### 2.81 SAFETY TUB RAIL
For nonslip support. Cast aluminum encased in white vinyl. Allows unobstructed tub entry.

**PRICE B** From Everest & Jennings

### 2.82 SOAP CADDY
Keeps soap available when bathing. Hangs around the neck or over shower head. Plastic case and cover.

**PRICE A** From Camping World

### 2.83 STOW AWAY
Keeps all toilet items handy in one convenient spot. Even holds 5-oz. paper cups. Molded plastic container mounts on any wall.

**PRICE A** From Camping World

## 2.84 SAFETY SHOWER AND TUB GUARD

Apor Safety Shower and Tub Guards have thermostats that shut off too-hot water until the temperature drops to a safe level. This prevents surges of hot water which sometimes scald bathers. Shower guard can be used with any shower head. Tub guard replaces tub spout. Stops water over 110°F.

**PRICE B** From Apor Industries, Inc.

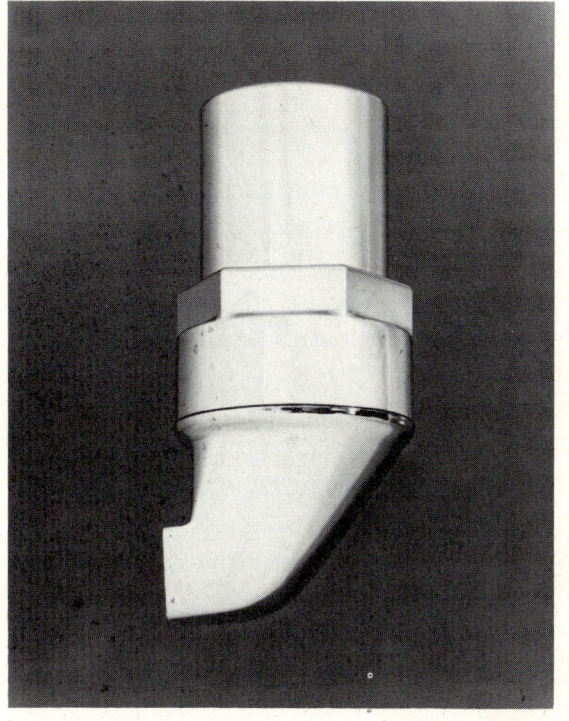

## 2.85 SWIM SNEAKS

Double rubber, treaded, nonskid bottoms. Inner sole. Protects from sharp rocks, hot sand or cement and also prevents slipping in tub or shower.

**PRICE A** From Dorsay

### 2.86 SHOWER CADDY
Hang over shower head. Avoids bending for items. Washable coated frame won't rust. Size 6¼" by 3¼" by 17".

**PRICE A** From Grayline (similar, Frohock Stewart Company)

### 2.87 RETRACTABLE SHOWER SEAT
Seat in use has stainless-steel tube legs angled to base of wall for rigid support. Folded seat lies against wall, taking up little space. Foam rubber cushion covered in Naugahyde. Seat 14" by 16" by 18" height open. Projects 16" from wall.

**PRICE D** From Tubular Specialties

### 2.88 SHOWER SEAT FOR WHEELCHAIR
Shape allows for transfer from wheelchair. Folds against wall when not in use. Cushion is foam rubber covered in Naugahyde. Size 32" by 20" by 13" by 14". Supports and frame, stainless-steel tubing.

**PRICE D** From Tubular Specialties

### 2.89 TIP-UP BATH SEAT
For bath or shower. Can fold against wall when not in use. Chrome-plated brass frame. Teakwood slats. 18½" by 13½".

**PRICE D** From Alsons (similar, Tubular Specialties)

### 2.90 FIXED SHOWER SEAT
Corner mounted. Stainless steel with satin finish. 18½" by 18½" by 36" with 1" lip.

**PRICE C** From Tubular Specialties

## 2.91 LEFT-HAND BARBER SCISSORS
Reversed blades, 7" overall length. For trimming human or pet hair. Made in Italy. Vinyl case, forged-steel scissors.

**PRICE A** From The Left Hand

## 2.92 LEFT-HAND NAIL SCISSORS
Reversed blades. Tapered scissors made in West Germany. Blades $3^{1/2}$" full length.

**PRICE B** From The Left Hand

## 2.93 LEFT-HAND TOENAIL SCISSORS
$3^{3/4}$" West German scissors. Have sturdy reversed blades, powerful leverage and fine edges.

**PRICE B** From The Left Hand

## 2.94 "TWIZZERS," LEFT-HAND
Tweezers that handle like scissors. Reverse blades enable left-handers to grasp, focus, and pull with ease.

**PRICE A** From The Left Hand

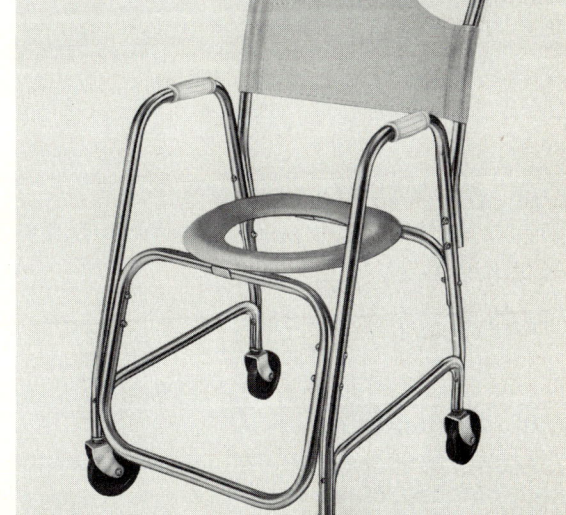

## 2.95 SHOWER CHAIR
Rolling shower chair. Complete access to body when washing. Very maneuverable. Footrest. Nylon back designed to slip out of way when washing. Seat, solid plastic. Rust-resistant chair. Can be used as commode seat. Fits over standard-height toilets.

**PRICE C** From Lumex (similar, Winfield; Invacare; Professional Convalescent Products)

### 2.96 COMBINATION SHOWER COMMODE CHAIR
Backrest folds down for ease in washing. Has footrest and plastic armrests. Corrosion resistant. Locks automatically in position. When chair is used as commode, commode bowl locks in place.

**PRICE C** From EDCO/Pasco

### 2.97 SHOWER CHAIR
Suction cup on each leg. Seat, solid plastic. Curved back. Anodized aluminum tubing chair. Plastic armrests.

**PRICE C** From Winfield

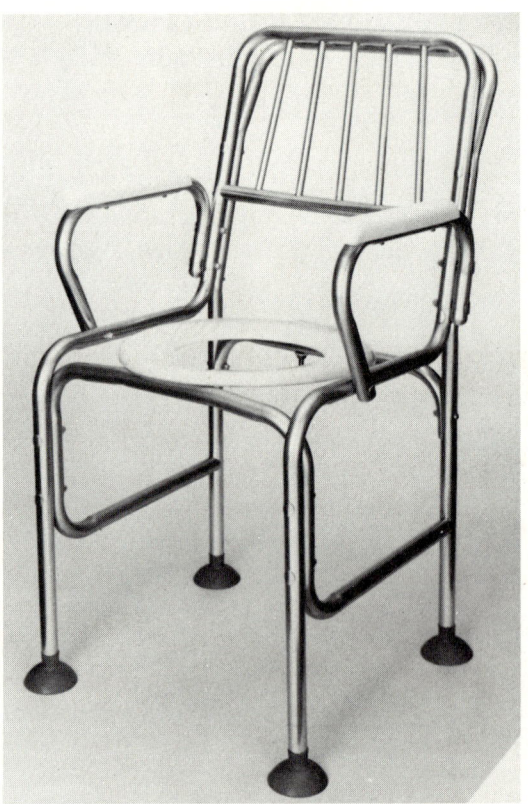

### 2.98 DIGITAL SCALE
Electronic digital scale. Bright, easy-to-read numbers that light up. Battery operated. Records weights from 25 to 300 lb.

**PRICE B** From General Electric

### 2.99 SHAMPOO IN BED
Shampoo-rinse tray set. For easy shampooing in bed. Comfortable neck opening tapered to drain into tray. Made of white polyethylene. Holds 7 quarts. Inside size 12" wide by 22" long. Has stainless-steel clip to attach hose, and 4' hose.

**PRICE B** From Raymo

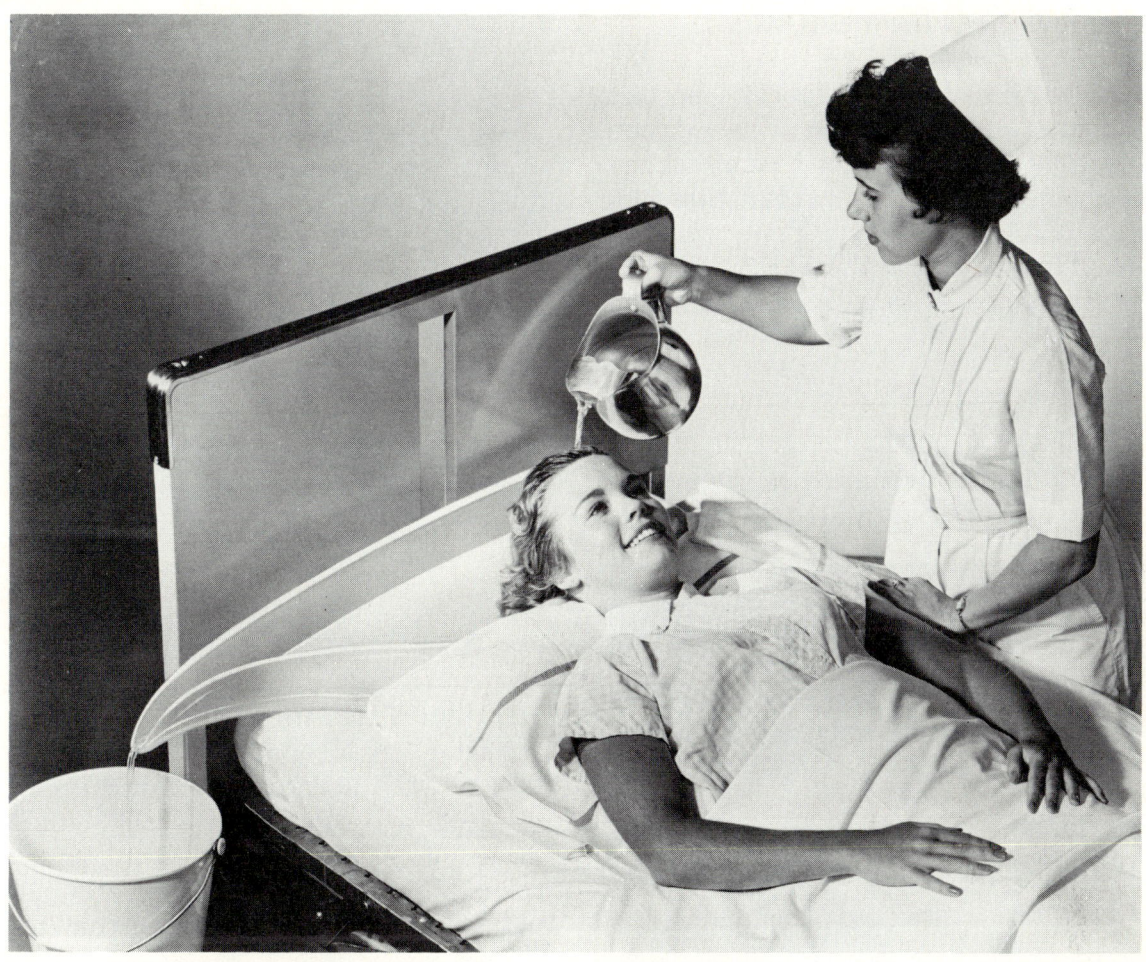

### 2.100 SHAMPOO IN BED
Wash N' Rinse tray. Plastic, comfortable, no-leak neckrest. Protects linen and mattress. Can be used with hair tints.

**PRICE B** From FashionAble

### 2.101 HAND SHOWER
Push-button hand shower allows fingertip control of water without readjusting water setting. Comes with height-adjusting bar or wall brackets. Flexible hose which allows reaching all areas of body.

**PRICE B** From Alsons Corp. (similar, Cleo; Kohler)

## 2.102 WHEELCHAIR SHOWER

One-piece Fiberglass stall. Has two soap shelves. One vertical and three horizontal grab bars. Fold-down stainless-steel seat with redwood, 18" height for easy transfer from wheelchair. Floor turning area 5' in diameter. Size floor, 63 1/4" wide by 63 7/8" long. Entry ramp, 36" wide, 18 7/8" long and 2 5/8" rise to door opening. Lipped door edge keeps wheelchair from rolling out.

**PRICE D** From Universal-Rundle

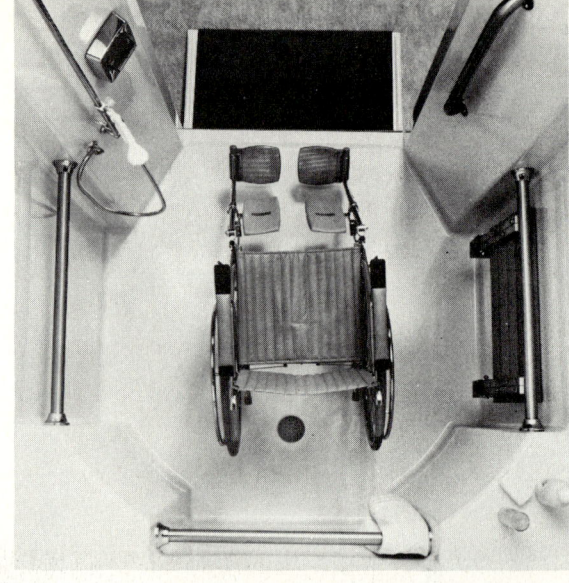

## 2.103 WHEELCHAIR SINK

Designed especially for people in wheelchairs. 20" wide by 27" front to back. Narrow width, extra depth and curved front enable wheelchair user to wheel close to basin. Provides ample legroom when installed at proper height. Gooseneck spout, 4" wrist-blade faucet handles add extra convenience.

**PRICE C** From Kohler Co. (similar, Universal-Rundle)

## 2.104 TOILET PAPER HOLDER

Snap-on commode toilet paper holder. Plastic holder has two spring clips which snap securely on any round tube or post from 1/2" to 1" diameter. Can be used horizontally or vertically.

**PRICE A** From Maddak

## 2.105 WASH-AND-DRY TOILET

A complete toilet installation. Most helpful to disabled who cannot cleanse themselves after using toilet. Push button and toilet flushes, at same time warm clean water cleans user. When button is released warm air dries user. Provides self-care on toilet.

**PRICE F** From Clos O Mat Inc. (Mfg. Joseph Muller Corp.)

PERSONAL CARE 45

## 2.106 WASH-AND-DRY TOILET

Attaches to any existing toilet. Completely self-contained. Makes its own warm water and warm air automatically. This Wash N' Dry Toilet Seat is most useful to those who, because of a disability, cannot properly cleanse themselves after using the toilet. Fingertip switch controls water and air which cleanse and dry person on toilet. Provides self-care on toilet.

**PRICE D** From American Bidet

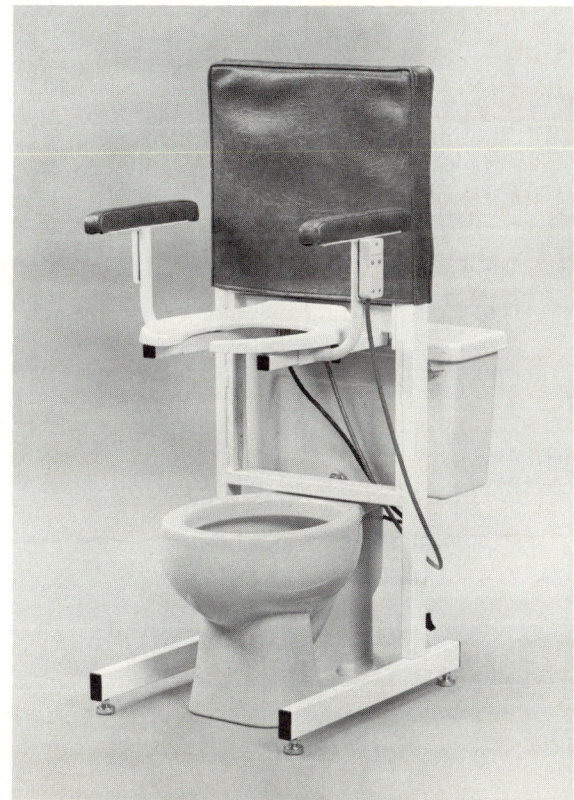

## 2.107 TOILET LIFT

Lift raises seat above toilet allowing user to assume an almost standing position before leaving the seat. Adjusts to fit over most toilet bowls. Operates electrically. Arms are adjustable and removable. Seat is hinged at back to lift up out of the way so others can use toilet conveniently. Allows independent use of toilet.

**PRICE E** From Ortho-Kinetics Inc.

### 2.108 CUSHIONED TOILET SEAT
Constructed of foam rubber in a durable vinyl cover on a base of wood composition. Fits all standard-size toilet bowls. Both seat and cover are cushioned.

**PRICE B** From Preston (similar, Wal-Jan)

### 2.109 RAISED TOILET SEAT
Padded, raised, adjustable toilet seat. Fits nearly every toilet bowl rim. Remains steady and doesn't tip even when used during wheelchair-to-toilet transfer by user. Vinyl padding. Right or left side opening to make self-care easier. Detachable splash guard.

**PRICE B** From MED

### 2.110 RAISED TOILET SEAT
Padded, raised; no side opening. Adjustable height, $4^{3/4}''$ to $6''$. Coated brackets won't mar toilet. Fits almost all toilets. No tools necessary to attach. Has plastic sanitary shield.

**PRICE B** From Lumex (similar, but not padded—Professional Convalescent Products)

### 2.111 RAISED TOILET SEAT
Elevates body so it becomes easy to rise from toilet. Tall-ette II® contoured for stability. One-piece polyethylene, open front design. Securely held, no slippage in use. Recessed handgrip. 4'' height weighs 3 lb.; 6'' height, 4 lb.

**PRICE B** From Maddak

### 2.112 TOILET SEAT CARRYING CASE
Convenient carrying case with zipper and handstrap. Gray vinyl with white vinyl lining. Various sizes for raised toilet seats of Tall-ette® models (polyethylene).

**PRICE A** From Maddak

### 2.113 RAISED TOILET SEAT WITH ARMREST
Allows user to sit down and stand up safely. Foam-padded armrests. Fits all toilet bowls. Has safety strap. Can be easily removed when not in use. White enamel seat. Splash guard. Adjustable height from 5'' to 6''. Can be purchased with padded seat.

**PRICE B** From EDCO/Pasco

PERSONAL CARE 47

## 2.114 RAISED TOILET SEAT WITH SAFETY BARS

Tall-ette® adds 4″ to seat height and gives added convenience of safety side bars to assist when arising from toilet. Seat is polyethylene, bars are epoxy coated. Fiberglass armrests.

**PRICE C** From Maddak (Tall-ette® with side bars)

## 2.115 TOILET GUARD RAILS

Helps user get up and down on toilet and acts as guard rail when user is sitting. Attach one or both. Black plastic armrests. Rubber-tipped legs. Chrome-plated tubular steel rails.

**PRICE B** From Sears (similar, Invacare; Frohock Stewart—adjustable height; Winfield—adjustable height; Lumex)

## 2.115 COMMODE CHAIR

Lightweight anodized aluminum. Adjustable legs. Seat height 18" to 22" from floor. White bucket with lid. Black plastic armrests. Can be used without bucket seat over toilet as safety rail. Used as commode with bucket attached.

**PRICE C** From Professional Convalescent Products (similar, Sears)

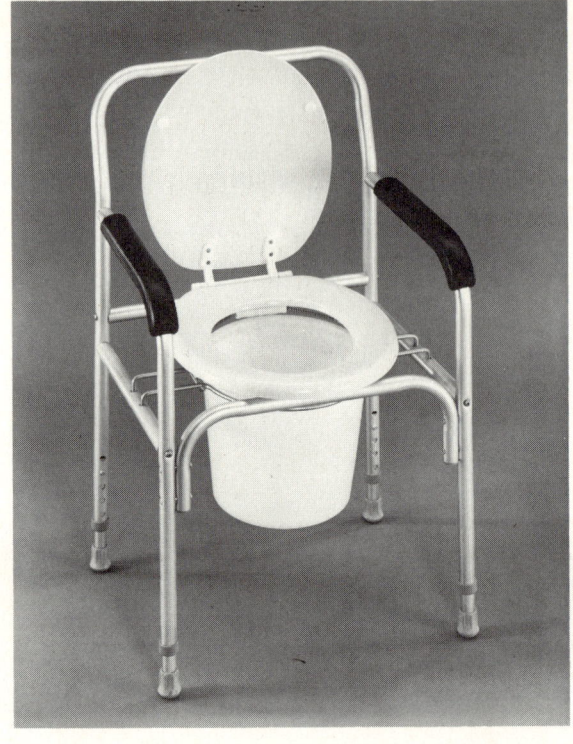

## 2.117 URINAL DRAINAGE BAG

The "Hideway" is a cover for a urinal drainage bag and can go wherever the bag goes. Made of lightweight vinyl or fabric.

**PRICE B** From Ventura (Hideway)

PERSONAL CARE    49

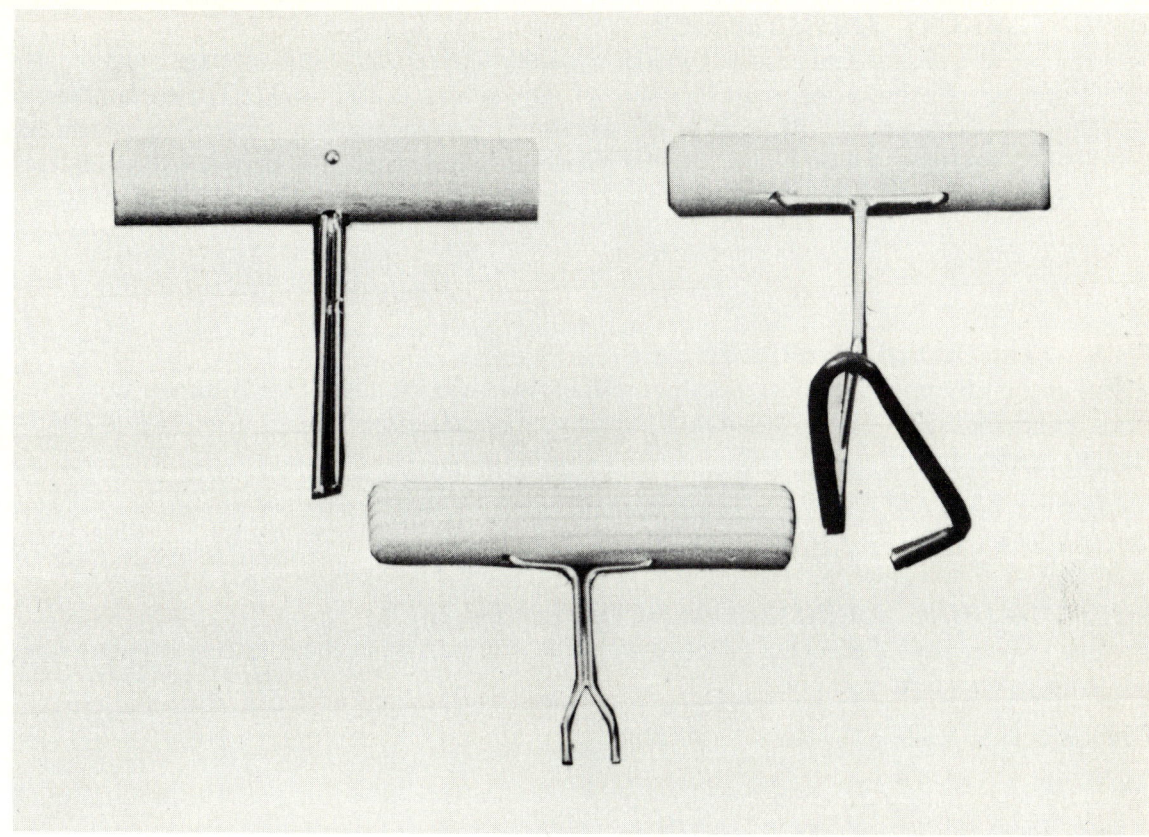

### 2.118  TUBE WINDER
Rolls up tubes of toothpaste, Vaseline, creams, etc. Has large wooden handle and two-pronged steel jaw with 2"-long opening.

**PRICE A**  From Maddak

### 2.119  STOVE VALVE TURNER
Fits various sizes of stove controls. Has wood handle and steel rod covered with soft plastic.

**PRICE A**  From Maddak

### 2.120  ALARM CLOCK WINDER
Winds alarm clocks and turns similar keys and knobs. Has large wooden handle and double-pronged steel jaw.

**PRICE A**  From Maddak

## 2.121 "TALKING" THERMOMETER

May be used as a clinical (oral or rectal), indoor or outdoor, or cooking and roast meat thermometer (with purchase of extra probe at additional cost). Range: minus 25°F to 375°F. Has removable metal-tipped plastic probe. Takes up to 60 seconds for proper reading. Has on/off switch. All temperature readings, however used, will be given via speech. Switch in back will give readings in Celsius.

**PRICE D** From American Foundation for the Blind

## 2.122 ELECTRONIC THERMOMETER

Rectal or oral thermometer. Temperature-taking time: two minutes. Dial is turned until tone stops. User reads dial by feel. Raised dots indicate temperature which reads from 95°F to 106°F. Battery operated.

**PRICE C** From American Foundation for the Blind

## 2.123 "TALKING" URINE-SUGAR/KETONE ANALYZER

Enables visually limited diabetics to test their urine, and be told of the results in concentration percentages via voice read-out.

**PRICE D** From American Foundation for the Blind

## 2.124 "TALKING" SCALE

General Electric Electronic Digital Scale EDS-1/5801/001 is connected to a voice module which speaks out the weight.

**PRICE D** From American Foundation for the Blind

## 2.125 WHIRLPOOL—FOOT OR HAND

Hand and foot whirlpool bath, lightweight and easy to use. Tub is molded plastic. Height 6½″, width 14″. Fill manually with 5 gallons of water which pump automatically recirculates at rate of 5 gallons per minute. Aerator and flow control give maximum benefit.

**PRICE B** From Professional Convalescent Products (similar, Dazy Products, Sears)

PERSONAL CARE 51

### 2.126 FOOT BATH MASSAGE
Foot saver can be used as dry foot massager or water massager. Portable. Powerful vibrating motor on/off switch.

**PRICE B** From Dazy Products Co.

### 2.127 WHIRLPOOL—FOOT OR HAND
Whirlpool foot or hand massager. Swirling air bubbles with warm water. Stimulates and relaxes. Good also for arm or wrist. Adjustable from gentle to high intensity. Durable polypropylene. Pump recirculates 8 gallons per minute after massager is filled with water.

**PRICE B** From Oster

### 2.128 PORTABLE WHIRLPOOL FOR BATH
Jacuzzi® combines stimulating action of water massage with warm bath to comfort sore muscles and help relaxation. Fits standard bathtubs. Weight, 32 lb.

**PRICE D** From Battle Creek Equipment

### 2.129 CORDLESS WHIRLPOOL
No electric cords. Self-contained, rechargeable battery. Fits any standard wall tub up to 6″. Solid state. Pumps 35 gallons per minute. Automatic timer switches off whirlpool. Directable water flow. Adjustable aerator.

**PRICE D** From Dazy (similar, Sears)

### 2.130 WHIRLPOOL
Works in any bathtub. Portable. Pumps 50 gallons per minute. Adjustable jet stream and flow direction. Resists corrosion from oils and chemicals.

**PRICE D** From Amsco

### 2.131  WHIRLPOOL

Semi-portable, weighs 30 lb. Pumps 55 gallons per minute of warm water. Pressure and direction of flow adjustable. Stand won't mar tub. Relaxes muscles. Unit is driven by a 110-volt motor which runs a built-in aerator using water already in the bathtub.

**PRICE D** From Dakon (Aquassage)

### 2.132  WHIRLPOOL—NO ELECTRICITY

Hydro-Whirl uses just water—no motors, pumps or compressors—to give whirlpool bath. Can be installed on most bathtubs. Mixes water from bath spout with air in unit to deliver jet flow of bubbly water. No moving parts.

**PRICE C** From Kohler

### 2.133  WHIRLPOOL

Therapool® generates whirlpool action by forcing air through hundreds of tiny jets in circulating panel. Has high-velocity blower, no electrical components in or near water, automatic timer, volume control, heavy-duty tub panel (15" wide, 32" long, 1" deep). Weight, under 16 lb. Electric cord plugs into motor on floor outside of tub.

**PRICE D** From Professional Convalescent Products

PERSONAL CARE 53

## 2.134 CORDLESS TOOTHBRUSH

Tooth Pro is a battery-powered tooth cleaner. Uses special cleaning cup contoured to teeth. Sits in storage unit which holds four color-coded cleaning heads and 12-volt battery-charger. Power handle holds cleaning cup. Comes with instruction book.

**PRICE B** From Chris Craft

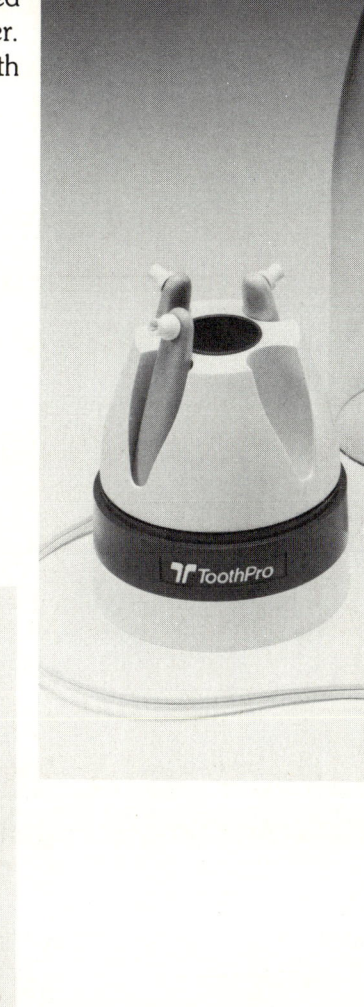

## 2.135 CORDLESS ELECTRIC RAZOR

Battery-run electric razor made in West Germany by Braun. Platinum-coated foil head. Includes long-hair trimmer. Operates on 2 "C" batteries. Comes with travel case, mirror, and cleaning brush.

**PRICE B** From Chris Craft

# ③ *Dressing*

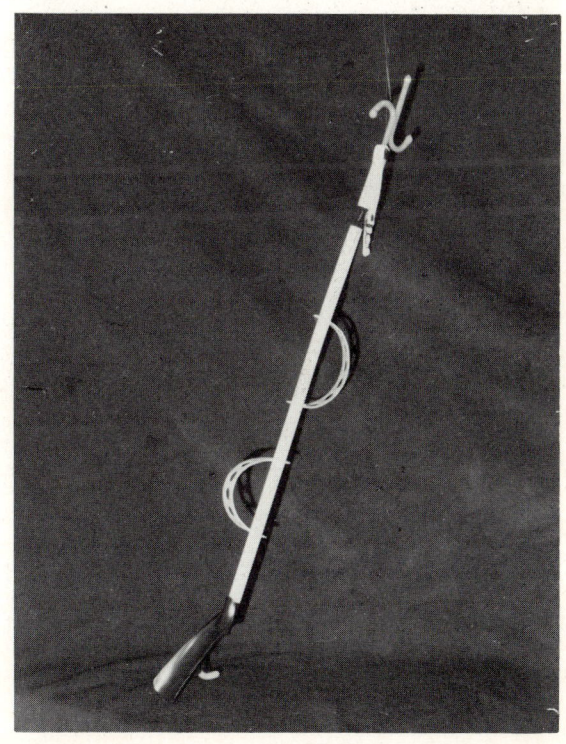

## 3.1 DRESSING AID

Do-All™ Dressing Aid helps in putting on socks, shoes, stockings, and pulling on and pushing off articles of clothing. Has a shoe horn on one end, and garter hook and push-pull pointer hook on the other end. Can be used from seated position. Has two adjustable hand loops. Length $30^1/_2$"; weight 10 oz.

**PRICE A** From Therafin Corp.

## 3.2 BUTTON HOOK — LARGE HANDLE

Large-handle button hook. Assists persons with limited dexterity. Vinyl handle with large stainless-steel wire loop.

**PRICE A** From Cleo

## 3.3 COAT HANGER AID

The aid extends the reach of those with severe loss of movement. Helpful to lift coat hangers, and sweaters, jackets, coats or other articles of clothing having loops. Helpful to push or pull small items on table or desk. A steel-wire elongated "S" hook 2½" mounted on 10"-long wooden handle.

**PRICE A** From Maddak

## 3.4 DRESSING STICK

Dressing aid with accessories that can be attached — comb, sponge, shoe horn, magnet, reaching hook, and grasping clip. They fit into an anodized aluminum master shaft 24" long, with a wrist strap.

**PRICE B** From Hausman

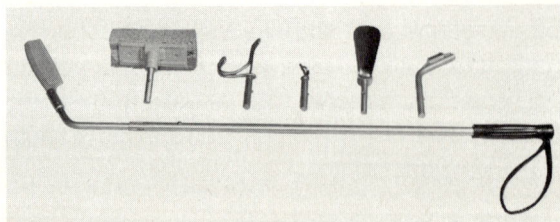

DRESSING 57

## 3.5 DRESSING STICK

An excellent aid in dressing for the disabled. Plated metal semicircular hook is opposite two-pronged fork with vinyl plastic covering. Attached to a 20"-long wooden stick. Stick has rubber tip.

**PRICE A** From Maddak

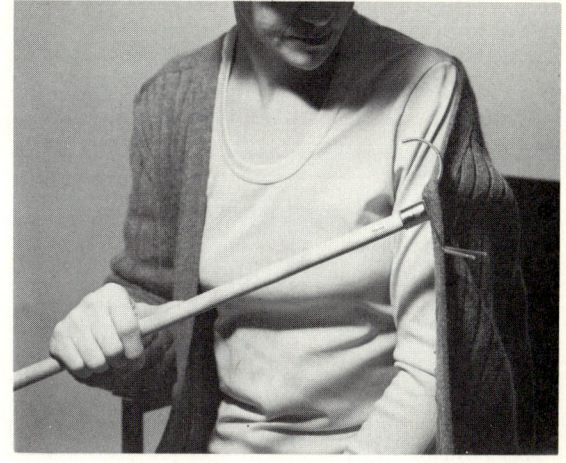

## 3.6 DRESSING STICKS WITH GARTER CLIPS

Sticks used as an aid in pulling clothes on and into place. Garter clips can be attached to clothing. Two 20"-long sticks with cloth tape extensions have garter clips sewn on.

**PRICE A** From Maddak

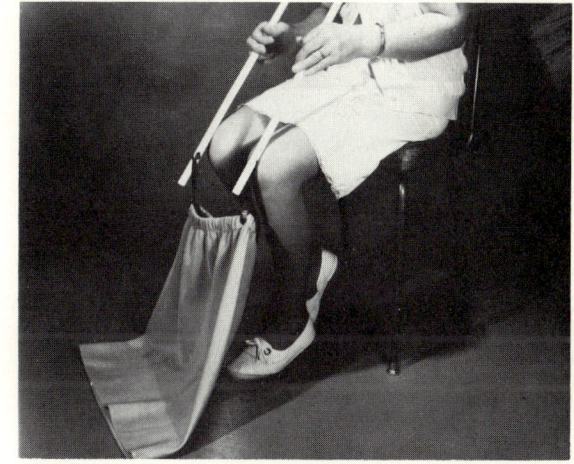

## 3.7 MONEY BELT

Safe insurance in the zippered lining for the money you carry. Fine leather belt with solid brass buckle. A money belt is the safest way to carry cash.

**PRICE B** From Orvis Company (other models available from men's clothing stores)

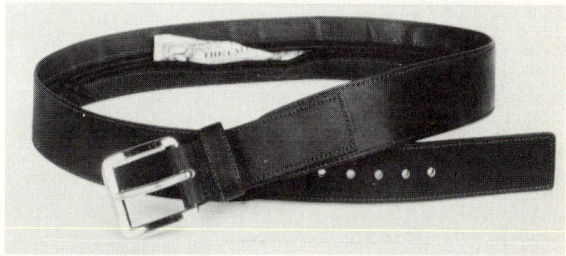

## 3.8 PANTY HOSE AID

Easy way to put on panty hose without having to bend. From sitting position, panty hose are pulled up by tapes with garter clips on end and plastic forms that hold open feet of hose.

**PRICE B** From Comfortable (also Maddak)

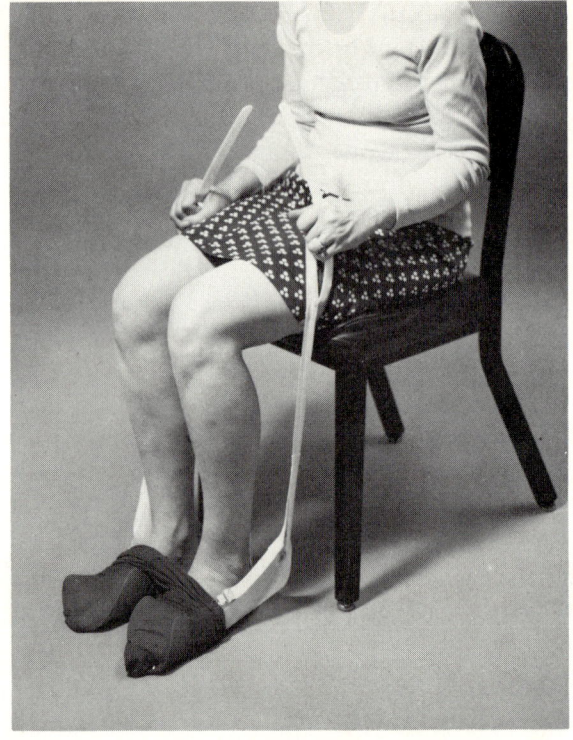

## 3.9 SHOE REMOVER

Heel grip helps remove footwear. Platform is held down by one foot. To remove opposite shoe, heel is placed in "V" of heel grip and leg is lifted. Platform can also be held down by cane, stick or crutch. Rubber pad provides nonslip surface. 12" length by 6¼" width. 18 oz. weight.

**PRICE A** From Therafin Corp. (similar, Maddak)

## 3.10 SHOE HEEL AID

A smooth plastic device that is slipped over shoe back before inserting foot. Allows foot to slip into shoe without a shoe horn and without bending back of shoe. Slips out easily after foot is in place.

**PRICE A** From Cleo

## 3.11 ONE-HANDED SHOE LACE FASTENER

No-Bows hold shoe laces tight when in place. Small light plastic blocks with spring plungers are operated by one hand; squeeze to release.

**PRICE A** From Maddak

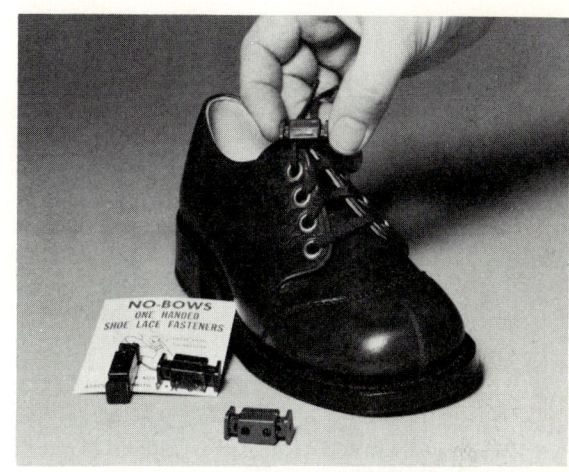

## 3.12 ELASTIC SHOE LACES

No bows to tie. Shoes can be slipped on with laces tied because laces stretch.

**PRICE A** From FashionAble / Cleo / Preston

### 3.13 SHOE-LACING AID

A hook is used to loosen or tighten shoe laces without having to stoop or bend. A 24" polyethylene rod with a right-angle brass hook on one end.

**PRICE A** From Maddak

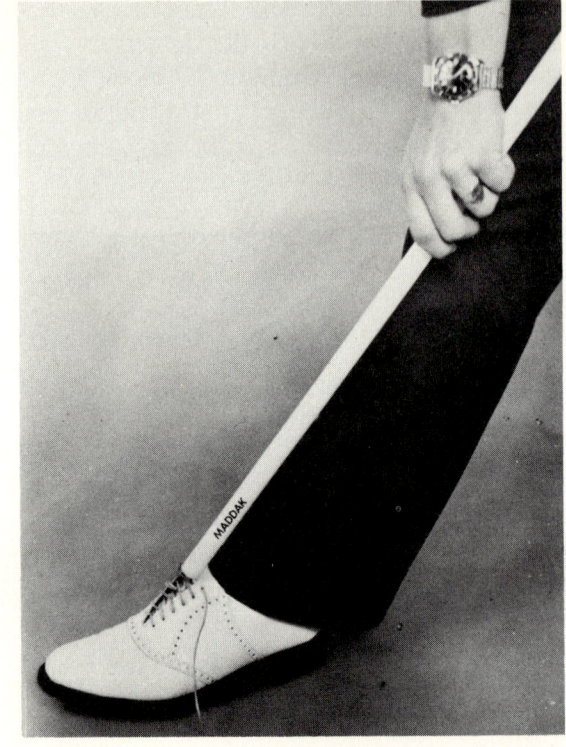

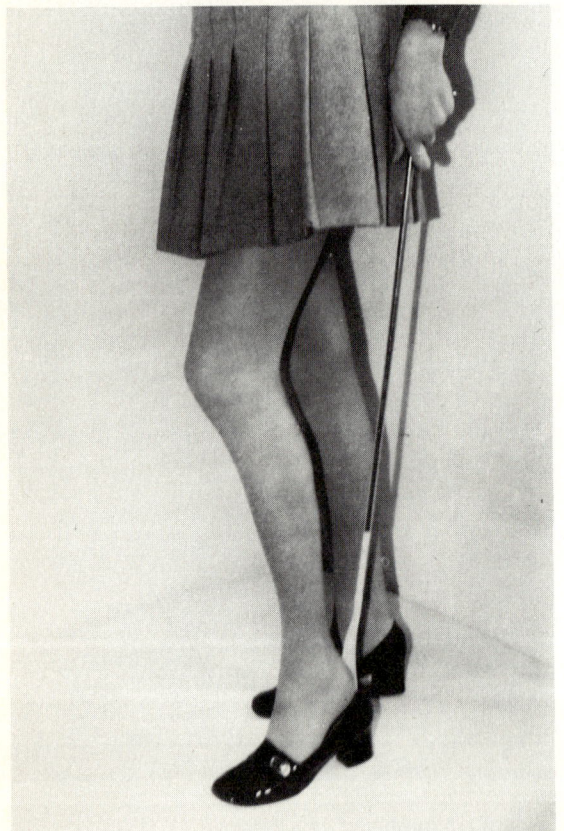

### 3.14 LONG SHOE HORN

To help one put on or remove shoes comfortably without bending down or sitting. A 24"-long shoe horn with a smooth plastic blade, round metal shaft, and wood handle grip.

**PRICE A** From Maddak

## 3.15 FLEXIBLE HANDLE SHOE HORN

24" long. Strong aluminum tubing with spring action at the end. Helps put on shoes without bending.

**PRICE A** From Cleo

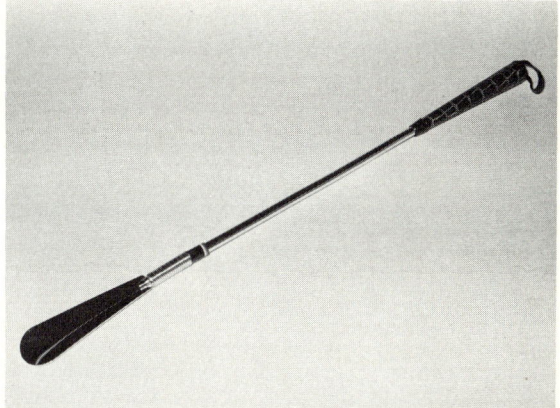

## 3.16 SHOES — WIDE OR NARROW

Women's shoes. An unusually large selection of extra-wide and extra-narrow shoes.

**PRICE B** From Selby (Get catalog)

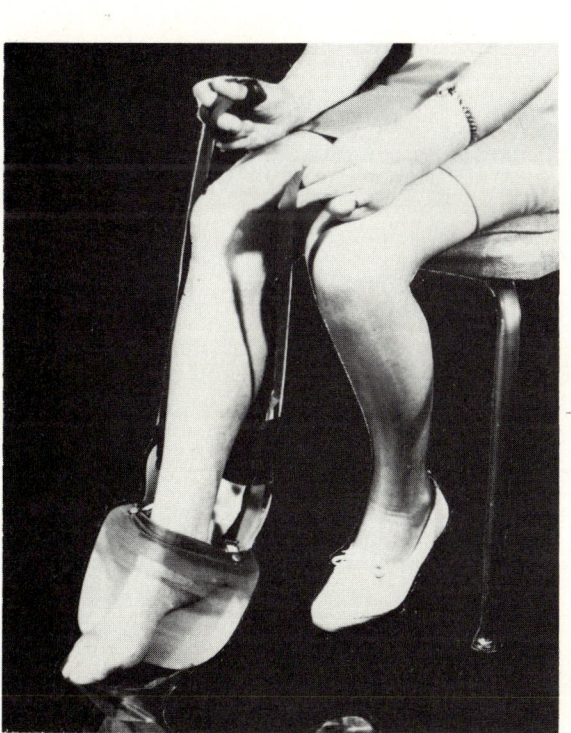

## 3.17 STOCKING AID

Helps put on stocking from sitting position without bending. When foot is inserted into stocking, a flexible plastic sheet is withdrawn and stocking pulled up by garter clips attached to cloth pull-strings.

**PRICE A** From Maddak

### 3.18 STOCKING AID

Helps person with limited hip or knee motion put on stockings.

**PRICE B** From Preston

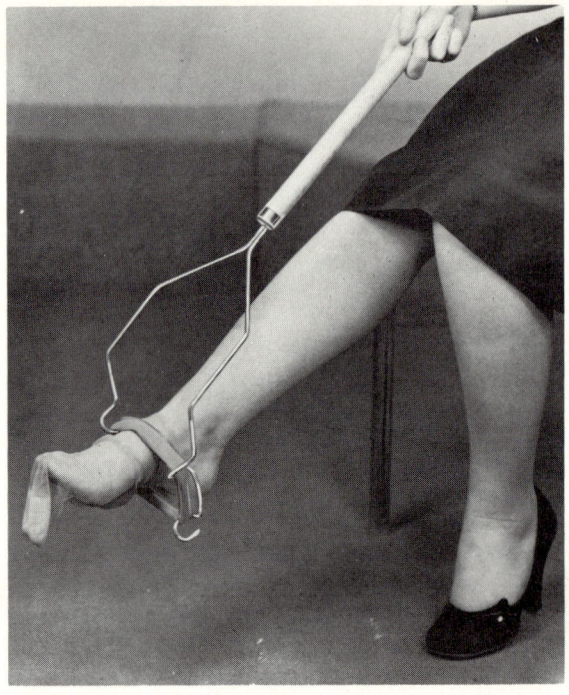

### 3.19 SOCK-AID

An aid to putting on socks without bending. A thin plastic sheet is shaped to roll into sock and keep it open for foot to enter. Cloth tapes attached to upper end permit user to pull sock on and remove aid without bending.

**PRICE A** From Comfort-Able-Aids (also Maddak)

## 3.20 TROUSER AID

To help one pull up pants. A wide, stiff plastic band has four attached clips which hold pants open. A flexible strap connected to the band in two places pulls on trousers.

**PRICE A** From Maddak

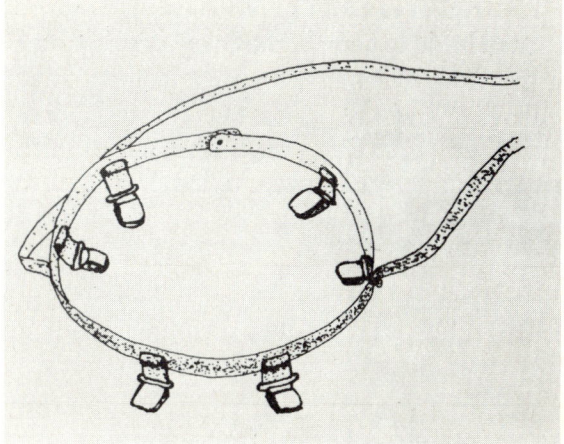

## 3.21 HEATED SOCKS

Lectra-Sox® develops heat under the toes to overcome chilled feet. They are heavy, knitted 50% wool with heating wires connected to a battery pouch which can be kept in a pocket or belt. Three sizes.

**PRICE B** From Comfort-Able-Aids (also Maddak)

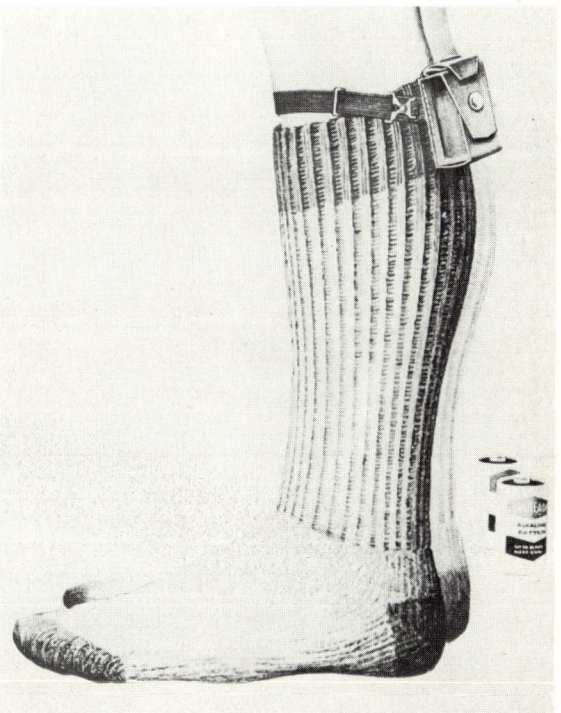

## 3.22 HEATED MITTENS

To avoid cold fingers, Lectra-Mits® develop heat at the extremities. Black suede leather, lined with 100% wool, and have heated wires connected to battery pouch on back of each mitten. Sizes: small, medium, large.

**PRICE B** From Maddak

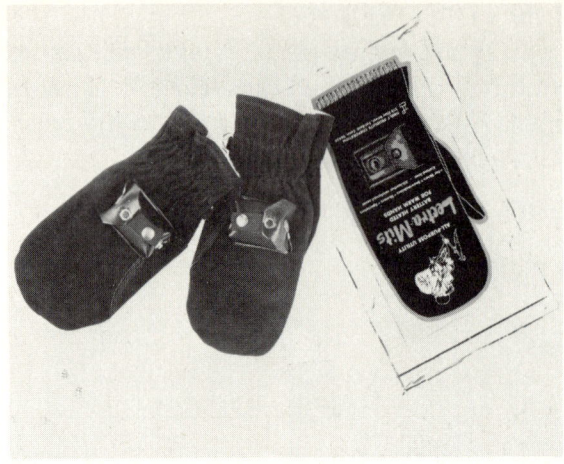

## 3.23 EASY-READ THERMOMETER

8" dial provides visibility associated with much larger thermometers. Large black numerals on white dial with bright red pointer. Rugged, weatherproof styrene case. Fahrenheit and Celsius scale. Use indoors or outdoors.

**PRICE A** From Springfield Instrument Company

## 3.24 INDOOR-OUTDOOR THERMOMETER

Matched set of thermometers mount on inside and outside of window with self-stick adhesive. See-through design permits seeing both inside and outside temperature at same time.

**PRICE A** From Camping World

DRESSING 65

### 3.25 ZIPPER PULL

Eliminates struggling with hard-to-reach zippers. 18″ coiled plastic cord with metal hook and ring enables user to hook and pull up zipper.

**PRICE A** From Cleo

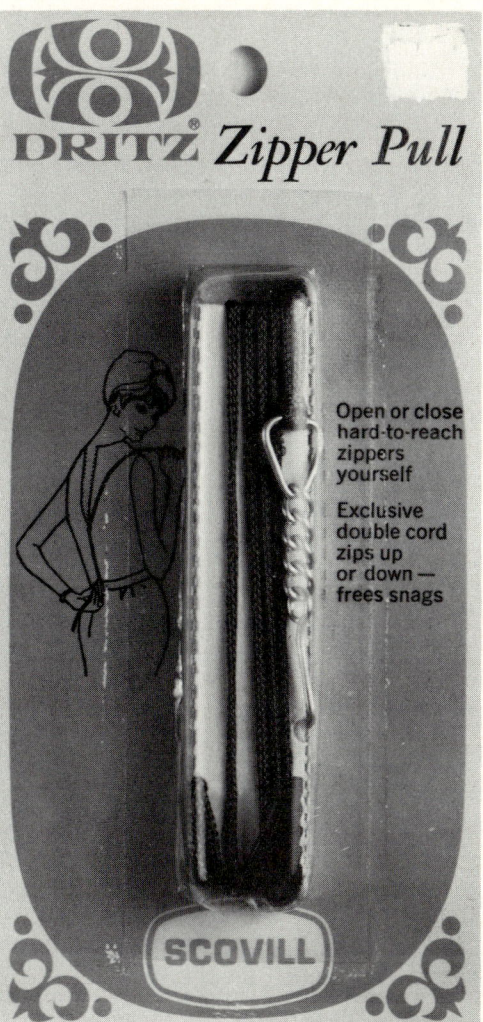

# Meal Preparation ④

### 4.1 HOOP APRON
Apron can be put on with one hand. Hoop is removable for washing. Three pockets. One size. Calico and percale prints.

**PRICE A** From Handee For You

## 4.2 BOTTLE HOLDER
Half-gallon glass bottle holder. Prevents slipping, makes pouring easier.

**PRICE A** From Evlo Plastics

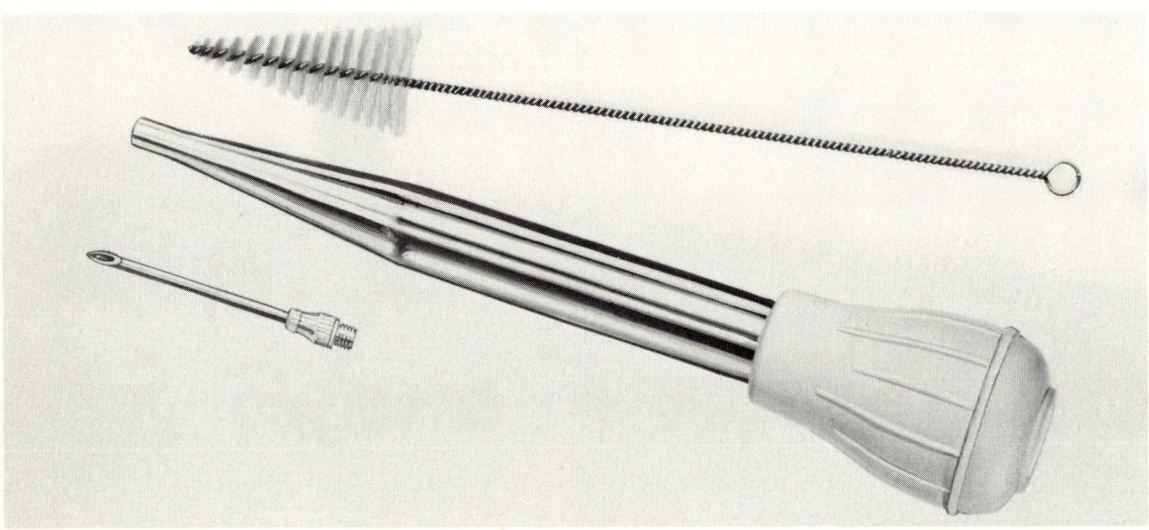

## 4.3 STEEL BASTER
Zim Ade-O-Matic Internal-External Baster. Stainless-steel baster will never crack or break. Has injector needle on Z-50 model to reinject natural juices into meat for faster cooking and tenderizing.

**PRICE A** From Zim Manufacturing Company

## 4.4 BREAD SLICE HOLDER
Holds a slice of bread and prevents it from moving when being buttered. Hard plastic board with rubber feet and two raised sides. Aid to those with use of only one hand.

**PRICE A** From Maddak

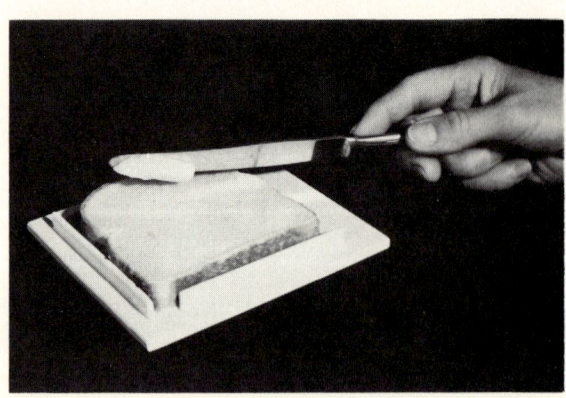

## 4.5 BLENDER FOR FOOD

Oster blender prepares food easily, including liquefied meals for those who cannot swallow solid food. Will also chop, grate or grind to convenient sizes. Opens at both ends for easy emptying and cleaning. Comes with cookbook.

**PRICE B** From Oster Corporation

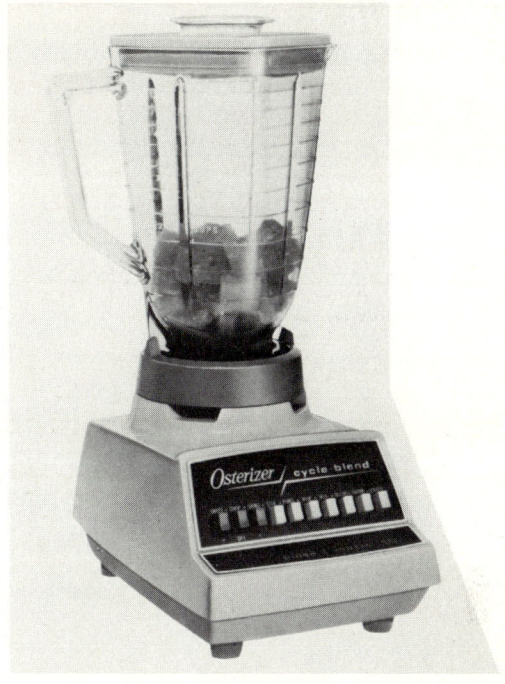

## 4.6 CARTON HOLDER

Gallon holder and carrier. Easy to carry. Keeps carton from slipping, easy to pour from.

**PRICE A** From Evlo

## 4.7 CONTAINER HOLDER

Handi Holder® prevents slipping container, makes pouring easier. Changes milk and juice containers into easy-to-handle-and-pour pitchers. Comes in heavy-duty polyethylene. Dishwasher safe. Sizes: quart, half-gallon.

**PRICE A** From Evlo Plastics (similar, Grayline Housewares; Comfort-Able-Aids)

## 4.8 COOKBOOK — BRAILLE

Rival Crock Pot® Cookbook for visually impaired. Recipes to be used with Crock Pot® cooker. In Braille.

**PRICE FREE** From Beth Shalom

## 4.9  COOKBOOK — BRAILLE
"Easy 'N Thrifty Recipes for Two." For visually impaired. Fourteen recipes with precise instructions for timing and measurement. In Braille.

**PRICE FREE** From Rice Council of America

## 4.10  COOKBOOK — BRAILLE
"Osterizer Blender Spin Cookery Cookbook" for visually impaired. Recipes use blenders as aid to meal preparation. In Braille.

**PRICE A** From Oster Corporation

## 4.11  LARGE PRINT COOKBOOK
Betty Crocker Cookbook contains package directions and simple recipes for many Betty Crocker products. For visually impaired. In large print.

**PRICE A** From Betty Crocker Kitchens ("Cooking with Betty Crocker Mixes," Large Type Edition)

## 4.12  LARGE PRINT COOKBOOK
Campbell Soup Company Book of Recipes using canned or frozen foods. In large type for visually impaired.

**PRICE FREE** From Volunteer Service for the Blind ("Easy Ways to Delicious Meals," Large Type Edition)

## 4.13  TWO-CUPPER OR HOT WATER MAKER
Makes two cups of drip-brew coffee or makes enough hot water for instant soup, cocoa, tea, etc. Fill stainless-steel tank with water. Pilot light goes on when water is heated. Push lever for hot water.

**PRICE B** From Farberware®

MEAL PREPARATION 71

## 4.14 CAN DISPENSER
Beverage-can dispenser is easy way to store cans conveniently. Holder is cushion-coated. Loads from front. Remove one can, others roll forward. Has handy top shelf 13 1/2" long by 6 7/8" high.

**PRICE A** From Grayline

## 4.15 ROLLING CAN RACK
Racks for different-size cans. Racks are cushion-coated vinyl. Remove one can, next rolls forward. 11 3/8" long by 7 3/4" high. Available in two different widths for small cans and large.

**PRICE A** From Grayline

## 4.16 REVOLVING CUP RACK
Spins any of eight cups right to you. Smooth turning, no wobble; soft cushion-coating protects china.

**PRICE A** From Grayline

## 4.17 CUP STACKER

Convenient way to store cups. Vinyl coated. Space saver. Holds up to six cups. 3⅛" by 3⅛" by 7¼" high.

**PRICE A** From Grayline

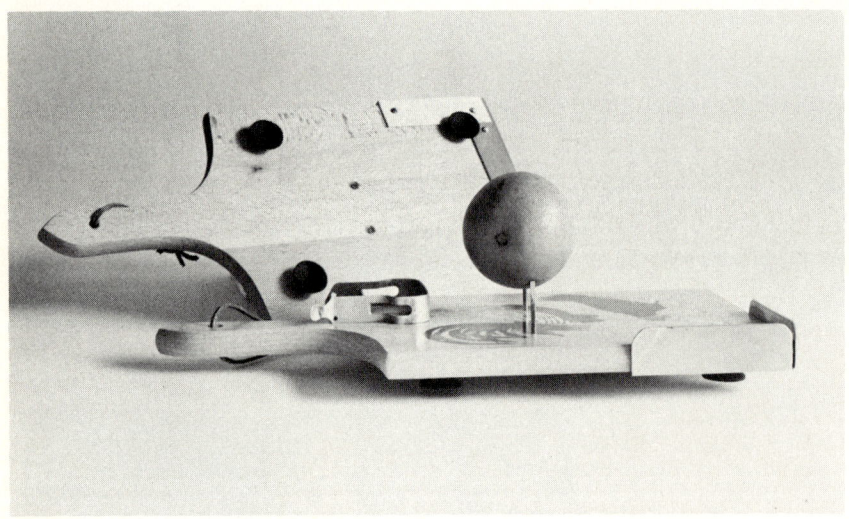

## 4.18 CUTTING BOARD

Handy helper with peeler. Stainless-steel nails hold vegetables and fruit for peeling and slicing, meat for carving. Suction cups anchor it. Corner ledge to spread and cut sandwiches with one hand. 7" by 14" laminated ½" hardwood, with U-handle peeler. Just hook fingers through handle. Aluminum and steel blade.

**PRICE A** From FashionAble

MEAL PREPARATION 73

## 4.19 FOOD CUTTING BOARD
A white plastic ½" thick easily cleaned cutting board. A 2" high stop block with nails on one end is used to hold bread, meat, cheese, etc. For one-hand cutting. Four vertical pins can be used to hold a slice of bread for buttering. Four suction cups on bottom keep board from sliding. Size 9½" by 18½" by 2½".

**PRICE B** From Maddak

## 4.20 CROCK POT
Rival 3½-quart Crock Pot®. Slow cooker with automatic shift—shifts from high to low heat automatically. 92-page (200 recipes) cookbook comes with pot. It cooks all day without attention. Uses very little electricity. Can cook complete meals in one pot at the same time.

**PRICE B** From Rival Manufacturing Company (similar, Farberware®; Hamilton Beach)

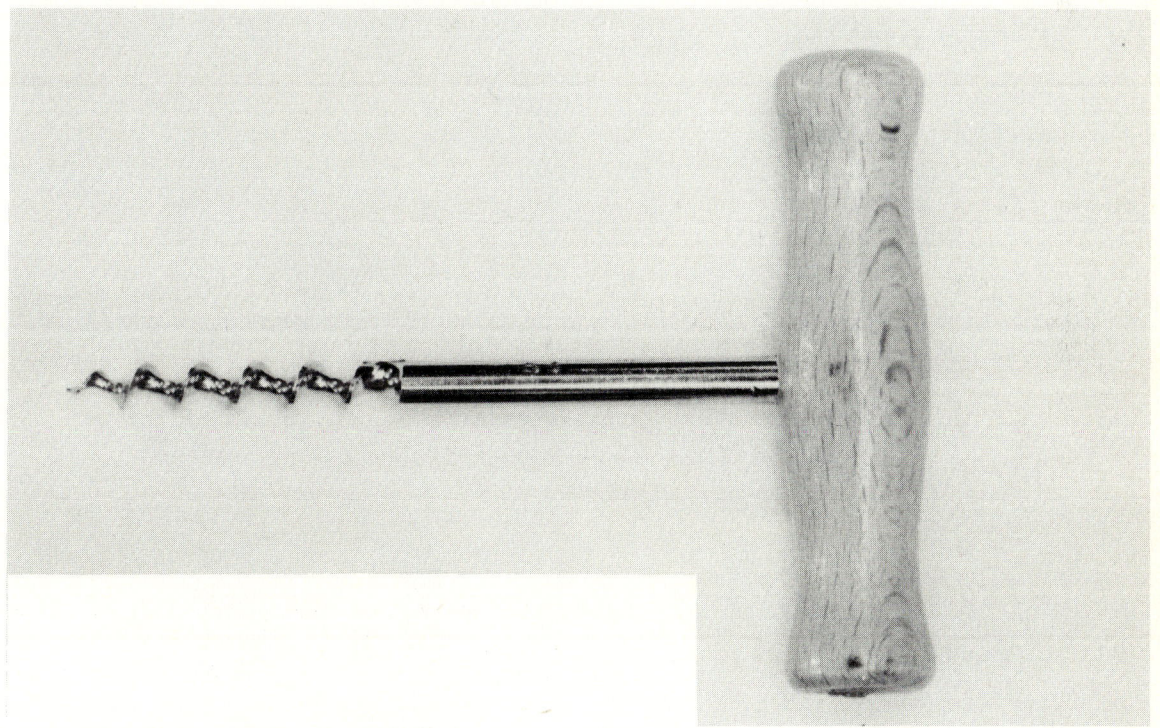

## 4.21 LEFT-HAND CORKSCREW
Special counter-clockwise corkscrew is nickel plated, has wooden handle and 2" spiral.

**PRICE A** From The Left Hand

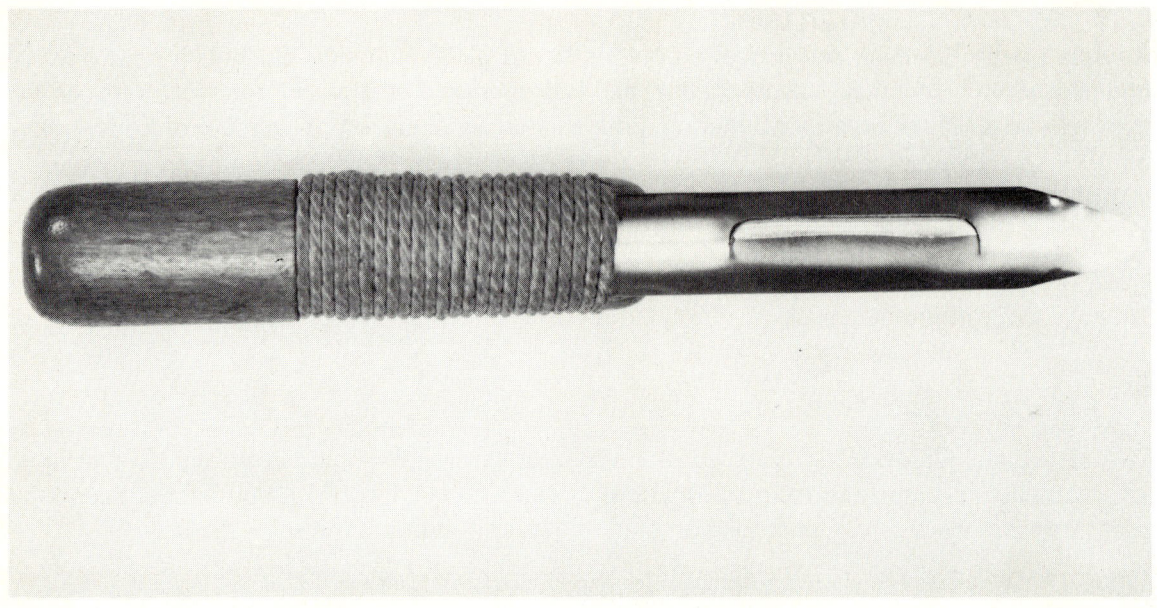

### 4.22 LEFT-HAND PEELER
Stainless-steel blade cuts toward you.

**PRICE A** From The Left Hand

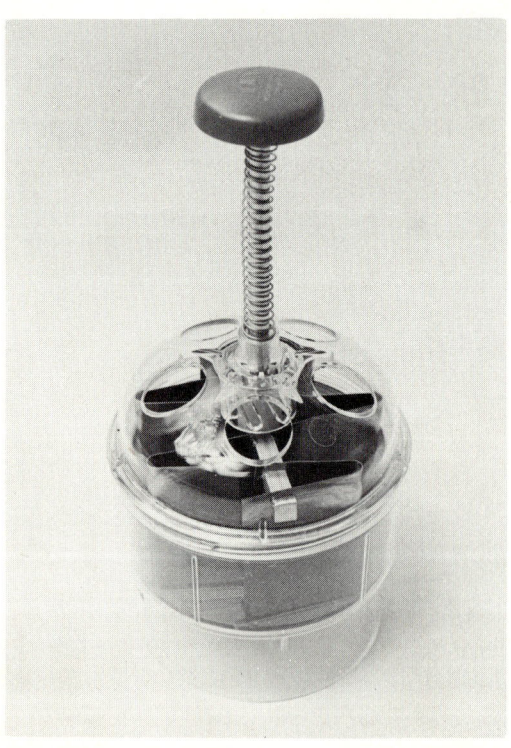

### 4.23 FOOD CHOPPER
One-hand food chopper. Chops almost any solid or leafy food, raw or cooked vegetables and meats, etc. Just tap knob with flat of hand a few times and chopping is done. Six stainless-steel blades. Self-cleaning.

**PRICE A** From Cleo

## 4.24 ONE-HAND CAN OPENER
Ronson Can-Do®. Electric one-hand can opener. Simply by squeezing lever, any can from sardine to gallon-size may be opened. Use with either hand. Lightweight.

**PRICE C** From Preston (also FashionAble)

## 4.25 AUTOMATIC EGG COOKER
Oster electric egg cooker makes up to eight hard- or soft-cooked eggs or three poached eggs at one time. Cooker signals when eggs are ready. All parts coated with nonstick, nonstain surface. Glass cover.

**PRICE B** From Oster

## 4.26 HALF RUBBER GLOVE
Soft rubber half-glove protects fingers and nails. Use with steel wool, soap pads, etc.

**PRICE A** From Aparco

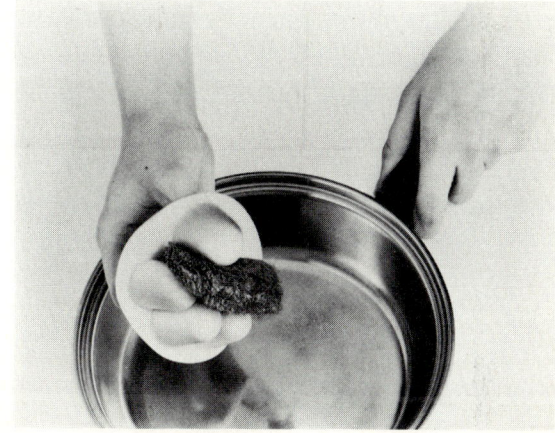

## 4.27 GRIPPER
Nonslip both sides. Use on tables, kitchen counter, trays. Can be used as jar opener. For one-hand use put jar on gripper and use other gripper to open. Flexible rubber 5″ in diameter.

**PRICE A** From FashionAble

## 4.28 AUTOMATIC HOT DOG COOKER
Electric cooker turns out six franks in less than two minutes. Convenient, quick and simple to use. White with smoke-tinted cover.

**PRICE B** From Hamilton Beach

### 4.29 JAR OPENER
Zim Jar Opener attaches to wall and folds flat when not in use. One slight twist opens anything with a cap, screw, pry-up, friction, vacuum, or crown. Heat-treated steel jaws, all-steel construction.

**PRICE A** From Cleo / Zim Manufacturing Company

### 4.30 JAR OPENER
Adjust-A-Grip opens the smallest screw cap. Adjusts up to $4^{1/2}''$-diameter lids.

**PRICE A** From Swing Away Manufacturing Company (similar, Foley)

### 4.31 JAR OPENER
Un-Skru® is a compact opener for screw caps from $1/2''$ to $5''$ in diameter. It attaches to underside of any cabinet, counter, table, shelf. It requires no adjustment and can be used with one hand. Made of nylon with hardened steel gripper.

**PRICE A** From Multi Marketing, Inc. / Comfort-Able-Aids

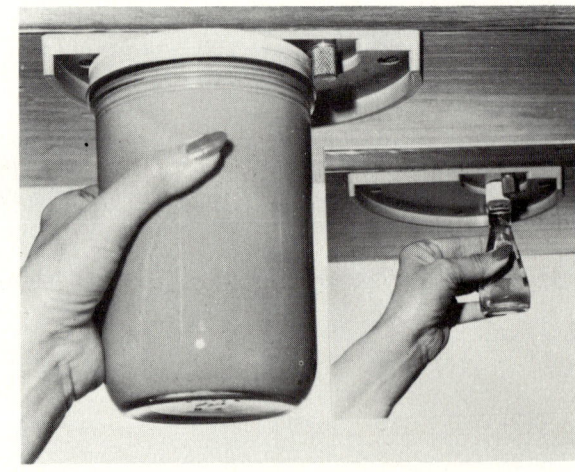

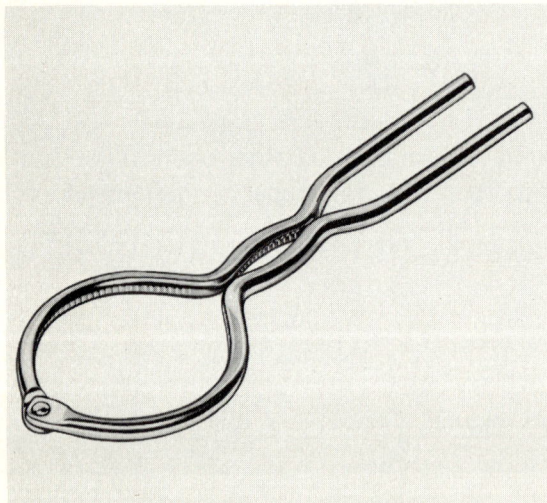

### 4.32 JAR WRENCH
For removing any size jar or bottle lid easily. Just squeeze around lid and turn.

**PRICE A** From Aluminum Housewares Company (Jar Wrench) (similar, Foley)

# MEAL PREPARATION

## 4.33 JAR LIFTER
Lifter grips any canning jar or similar object in either vertical or horizontal position. Can be operated with one or two hands. Plated metal frame, wooden handles and cushion grip.

**PRICE A** From Comfort-Able-Aids (similar, Aluminum Housewares, Foley)

## 4.34 LEFT-HAND WONDER KNIFE
A slicing machine in the palm of your hand. Stainless-steel blade is serrated on the correct side for left-handed users. Special blade guide can be set for carving, cutting or slicing anything to desired thickness.

**PRICE B** From The Left Hand

## 4.35 BREAD KNIFE, LEFT HAND
Scalloped serrations on correct side for left handers to cut properly. $7^{1}/_{2}''$ stainless-steel blade with black handle.

**PRICE A** From The Left Hand

## 4.36 ELECTRIC KNIFE
Rival® Knife allows effortless precision slicing and carving with one hand. Stainless-steel blades with serrated edges. Positive safety blade lock. Blade release. Lightweight. 8-foot cord, push-button control, 32-page carving guide.

**PRICE B** From Rival Manufacturing Company (similar, Hamilton Beach)

## 4.37 ELECTRIC KNIFE
Knife with easy-grip handle. Has 90° rotating blade for vertical or horizontal carving. Built-in counter rest. Detachable cord. Stainless-steel blade. Safety switch. Good for user with limited hand grip.

**PRICE B** From Hamilton Beach

## 4.38 ONE-HANDED BUTCHER KNIFE
Rocking motion permits one-handed cutting of meat and vegetables. $4^{1}/_{2}''$ hardwood handle. Curved 6" blade. Well balanced. Dishwasher safe.

**PRICE A** From FashionAble

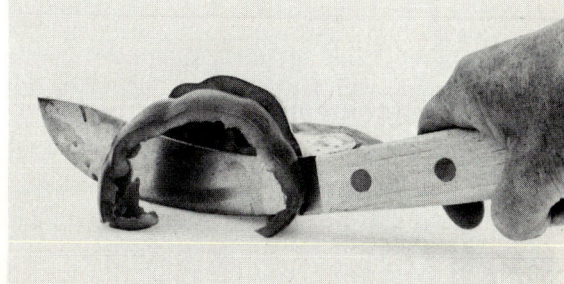

### 4.39 BOWL WITH HANDLE

Grip 'N Mix Bowls feature handles sized for a firm grip when mixing and pouring. Bowls have drip spouts, and soft rubber rings on base to keep them from skidding. Volume calibrations are both metric and U.S. equivalents. In 1½-quart and 3-quart capacities.

> **PRICE A** From Rubbermaid, Inc. (similar models, available in most good housewares departments and hardware stores made by other manufacturers)

### 4.40 OVEN MITT

17" oven mitt, elbow-length. Offers maximum protection. Flame-retardant.

> **PRICE A** From American Foundation for the Blind

### 4.41 CONVECTION TURBO-OVEN™

Saves time and energy. Roasting time reduced by one-third. Broiling uses one-half energy of conventional oven. Lower baking temperatures required. Electricity cycles on and off, saving energy. 18-lb. turkey capacity. Fan circulates hot air resulting in even browning, sealed-in flavor, little shrinkage. Can be taken anywhere. 28-lb. weight. Convenient for countertop use. Heating unit concealed behind a screen. Keeps kitchen cool. Continuous-clean interior walls. Automatic timer 15 minutes to 4 hours.

> **PRICE D** From Farberware®

### 4.42 CROCK-OVEN

Rival™ Crock-Oven™ slow cooks an entire meal in separate dishes all day without tending and timing. Fat-free roasting. Holds 12-lb. turkey. Bakes, dehydrates, saves energy. Countertop level. Little or no clean-up. Comes with 180-recipe cookbook.

> **PRICE D** From Rival®

MEAL PREPARATION 79

### 4.43 CONVECTION OVEN
Maxim™ countertop convection oven. Bakes, broils, roasts with fan-forced circulating air. Reduces cooking time and uses less electricity than conventional stoves. Self-cleaning. Not a microwave oven. 17½" wide by 18¼" deep by 13¾" high overall. 1 cu. ft. capacity. Comes in other sizes.

**PRICE D** From Maxim Company™

### 4.44 POTATO PEELER
One-hand operation. User holds potato in hand and slides it against blade. Double-edged potato peeler mounted in durable metal clamp for temporary attachment to a table or cutting board.

**PRICE A** From Maddak

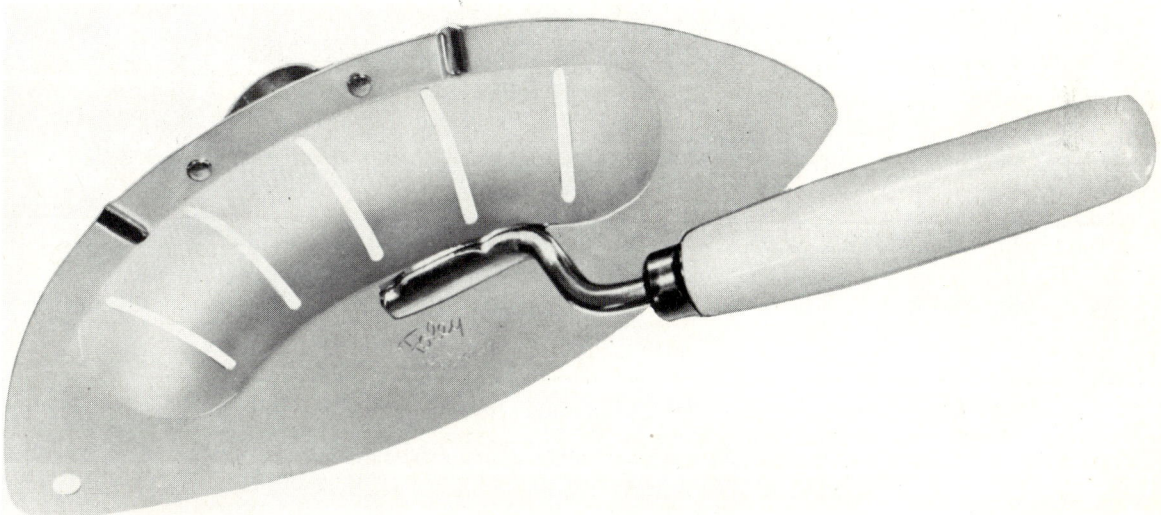

### 4.45 PAN DRAINER
Drains without scalding the cook. Holds food back while liquid drains through slots. For vegetables, fruits, spaghetti. Aluminum. 11" long.

**PRICE A** From Foley (similar, FashionAble — no handle)

### 4.46 ELECTRIC PEELER
New Peeling Wand™ electric peeler makes peeling fruits and vegetables less of a chore. A gentle touch guides peeler. Peels potatoes, carrots, apples, cucumbers, squash, tomatoes, peaches, etc. Has "Eyertip" for removing blemishes and potato eyes and a splatter shield. Unit can be used under running water.

**PRICE B** From General Electric

### 4.47 PEELER
Grip for hand makes handling easy. Peels, slices, shreds. If used with cutting board, only one hand needed.

**PRICE A** From Cleo (also FashionAble)

### 4.48 PAN HANDLER
Placing handle of cooking pot into vertical slot keeps pot from moving during stirring. Suction cups hold pan handle firm. Stirring can be done with one hand.

**PRICE A** From FashionAble

### 4.49 PAN HOLDER
Stirring can be done with one hand. Epoxy-coated steel wire frame attaches to stove top with suction cups. Placing handle of pot into vertical slot keeps pot from spinning during stirring. Various pot heights can be accommodated. Size of holder: 16" wide by 4$^1$/$_2$" high.

**PRICE A** From Maddak

### 4.50 FOOD PROCESSOR
Processor simplifies food preparation tasks. Can be used for shredding, slicing, grating, grinding, mincing, mixing, chopping, and blending.

**PRICE C** From General Electric

### 4.51 LOCK LID SAUCE PAN
Eliminates messy "boil-overs." Lid locks in place for "cook" or "drain," sets over guide pins inside pan. When turned to "drain" (clockwise) position, holes are exposed to simplify draining off liquids. 3-quart capacity. Teflon inside, porcelain outside.

**PRICE A** From American Foundation for the Blind

## 4.52  SLIDING POT AND PAN RACK

Convenient for storing pots and pans. Just pull out telescoping rack to get pots. Holds eight utensils. 18" long.

**PRICE A**  From Grayline

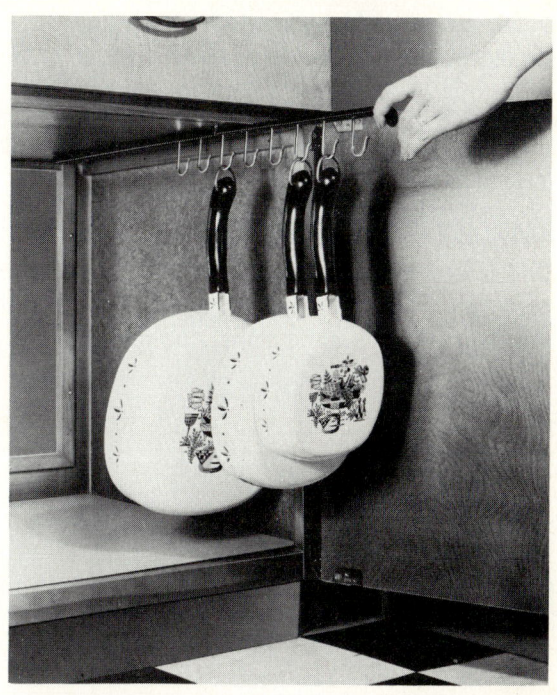

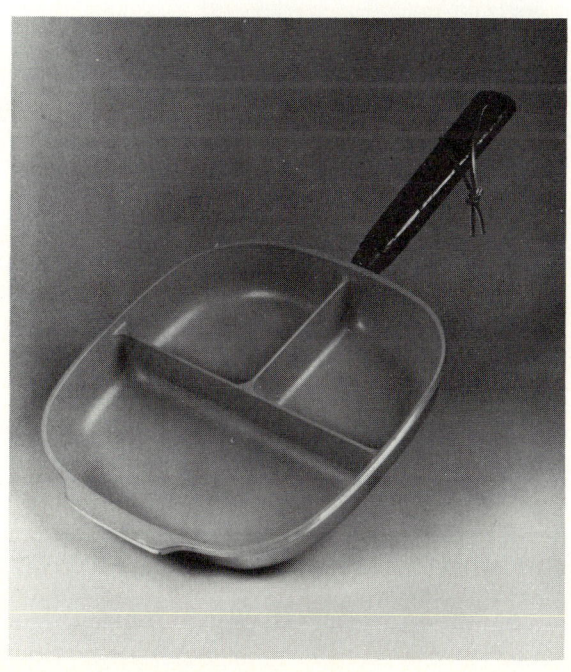

## 4.53  TRI-PAN

Three pans in one make meal preparation simple. Cook complete meal in one pan. Non-stick surface makes clean-up easy. Heavy cast aluminum with wooden handle. Size $10^{1/4}"$ by $17^{1/2}"$ by 2".

**PRICE B**  From Northland Aluminum

### 4.54 RUBBER SUCTION
Suction base permits disabled to secure bowls and dishes on table or tray without using hands.

**PRICE A** *(set of 3)* From Preston

### 4.55 CORDLESS BEATER
Whisk beater is cordless (uses two "D" cells). Easy to use, clean, store. Ideal for beating light mixtures. Safe for children. Durable plastic beaters withstand high temperatures and will not damage nonstick surfaces of cooking pans.

**PRICE A** From Camping World

### 4.56 CORDLESS JUICER
Can be used anywhere. Operates on "D" cell batteries. No electric cords. Quick and easy to use.

**PRICE A** From Harper-Lee International, Inc.

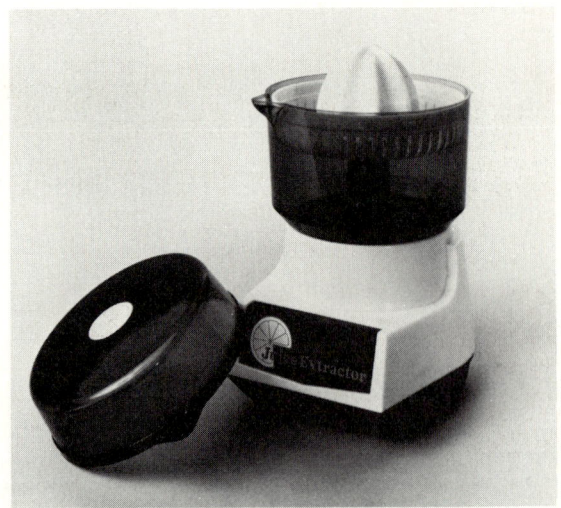

### 4.57 HANGING SPOON
Kitchen spoon for hanging inside of cooking utensil. Hooks on inside edge of pot. Stainless steel. Keeps spoon from falling into pot when not in use.

**PRICE A** From Aluminum Housewares

### 4.58 STOVE VALVE TURNER
Fits various sizes and types of stove controls. Has large wooden handle and shaped plated-steel rod with soft plastic covering. (See Tube Winder, Chapter 2.)

**PRICE A** From Maddak

MEAL PREPARATION 83

### 4.59 FOOD MILL
Foley Food Mill mashes and strains vegetables and fruits with little effort. Three sizes: 3½ quart, 2 quart, ¾ quart.

**PRICE A (each)** From Foley

### 4.60 SINK CUTTING BOARD AND STRAINER
Sink cutting board with strainer. Fits sink conveniently, has extendable handles and 5" strainer inserted into cutting surface to catch food being cut for easy washing or serving. Strainer with handle slips out for cleaning. 1" by 12" by 13".

**PRICE A** From Foley

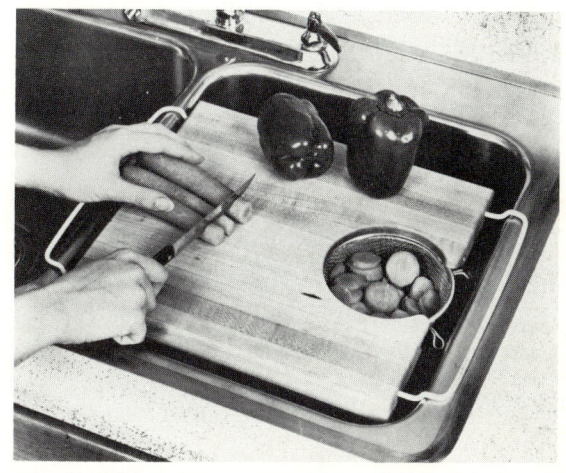

### 4.61 RANGE BUTTONS IN FRONT
Many modern stoves are made with controls at the back to keep small children from reaching them easily. Cooks with limited mobility may prefer range buttons in front for easy accessibility. On this model the oven door comes off easily. Storage drawer underneath.

**PRICE D** From Whirlpool

### 4.62 SURFACE STOVE UNIT
Built-in surface units with controls on side. Regular or ceramic surface (which may crack if objects are dropped on it). Prevents burns incurred by reaching over burners to controls in rear.

**PRICE D** From Whirlpool

### 4.63 RANGE, SELF-CLEANING, FRONT CONTROLS
Whirlpool set-in range offers easy oven cleaning, convenient front controls. A digital automatic clock and timer are in front of unit for easy access. No burns from reaching for controls in rear.

**PRICE D** From Whirlpool

### 4.64 SPECIAL RANGE KNOBS
Braille knobs are available for ranges, except for microwave products.

**PRICE FREE** From General Electric Servicenters. Give model and serial number of range

### 4.65 STRAINER/COLANDER
For washing and draining vegetables or to thaw frozen foods. Designed to rest on rim of a saucepan. Twin spouts allow flexible, no-drip pouring. Handy handle. 8" by 12 1/4" by 3 1/2" high.

**PRICE A** From Rubbermaid

### 4.66 SLICING GUIDE
Slicing guide and roast holder made of durable aluminum. Has curved tines that hold roast firmly. A standard slicing knife is inserted in grooves which act as guides and allow even slices to be cut. Has locking device in closed position for easy storage. Can also be used to cut bread, salami, etc.

**PRICE A** From American Foundation for the Blind

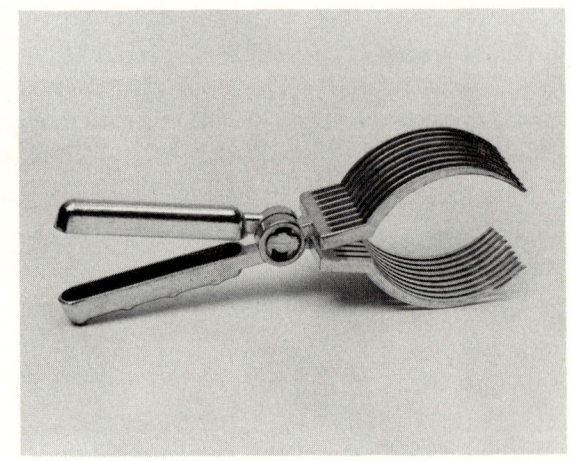

### 4.67 FOOD SLICER
The slicer adjusts for thickness from thin to 3/4". The cutting blade comes off easily for cleaning. Entire unit folds up for easy storage. Unit only operates when "push and hold" button is depressed.

**PRICE C** From General Electric

### 4.68 CORDLESS ONE-HAND SIFTER
Sifter vibrates automatically with one "C" battery. Holds three cups. Stainless screen is removable.

**PRICE A** From Harper-Lee International, Inc. (also Hammacher Schlemmer)

### 4.69 TURKEY OR ROAST LIFTER
Easy, safe way to lift turkey. Metal turkey lifter sling is centered and laid across inside of pan with handles hooked on side of pan. Turkey goes on top of the sling and when cooked handles are lifted to remove the bird from the pan.

**PRICE A** From Aluminum Housewares Company, Inc.

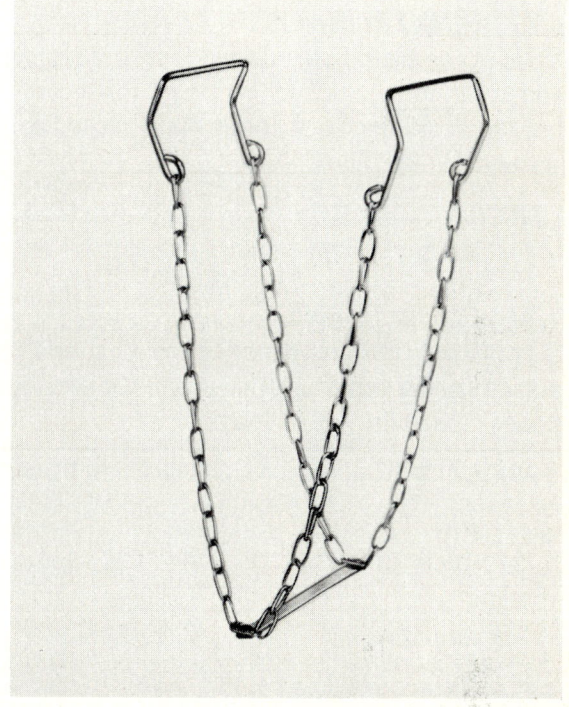

### 4.70 TOASTER TONGS
Wood tongs make lifting bread out of toaster easy and safe. Magnet on tongs attaches to side of toaster for convenient storage.

**PRICE A** From Aluminum Housewares Company, Inc.

### 4.71 BIG TIMER
Times from 1 to 60 minutes. 6" diameter with large numbers and bold minute markers that can be seen across a room. Hang it or set it on a counter.

**PRICE A** From American Family Scale Company, Inc.

### 4.72  LONG VERTICAL TONGS
Very useful for reaching down into narrow-necked containers or retrieving small items from boiling water, etc. Can be used with one or two hands. Plastic handles with plated metal tongs. Length 11".

**PRICE A**  From Maddak

### 4.73  FOOD TURNER
11" chrome-plated spatula-type tongs with flat and wide surfaces ($2^{1}/_{2}$" by $3^{1}/_{2}$") for turning hot foods. Sliding lock keeps blade closed for storage. Weight 8 oz.

**PRICE A**  From American Foundation for the Blind

### 4.74  FOOD TURNER
Scissors-style chrome-plated tongs. One side is a spatula, the other a fork. Useful for serving salads, spaghetti. $15^{1}/_{2}$" long.

**PRICE A**  From American Foundation for the Blind

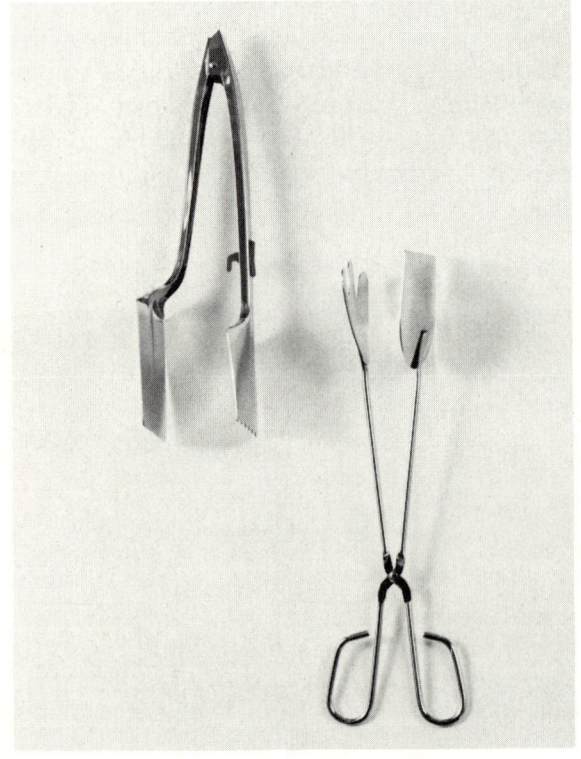

### 4.75  GAS LIGHTER
Handispark® is safe way to light gas grill, heater, stove or any gas appliance with propane, natural gas or alcohol flame. Saves fuel on gas cooking stoves since pilot lights for top-of-stove burners can be turned off. Just squeeze trigger handle and multispark action lights flame. No batteries or flint to replace. Lifetime piezo electric crystal. Adjustable nozzle. Water- and shock-resistant and windproof. $11^{1}/_{2}$" by 5".

**PRICE A**  From Chris Craft

# 5
# *Eating*

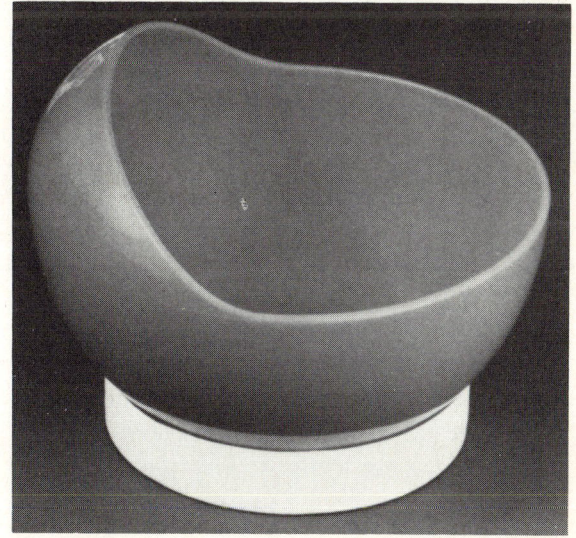

Unique, specially curved rim guides food onto spoon. Tommee Tippee Bowl® has nonslip base, is unbreakable, heat- and scratch-resistant. Aids those with poor hand control.

**PRICE A** From Westland Plastics (also Glenco)

## 5.2 SCOOPER-PLATE

Tommee Tippee Plate® has specially curved rim to guide food onto fork. Nonslip base, unbreakable, heat-resistant and scratch-resistant. Aids those with poor hand control.

**PRICE A** From Westland Plastics (also Glenco)

## 5.3 TWO-HANDLE CUP

Tommee Tippee® cup makes it easier for users with weak grip to drink without spilling. Has two handles to grip.

**PRICE A** From Westland Plastics (also Glenco)

## 5.4 PLASTIC CUP-HANDLE

Provides a 3½" handle extension for easy grip. Strong plastic handle in two parts with plated metal rivet and screw for tightening onto standard cup handle. Help for those with weak grip.

**PRICE A** From Maddak

### 5.5 MANOY CUP
Unique design of cup reduces wrist and finger movement due to special stem and careful balance. Cup holds 6½ oz. Made of Melamine plastic. Aid for those with weak grip.

**PRICE A** From Maddak (also Everest & Jennings)

### 5.6 MANOY PLATES
Oval-shaped plates with gentle slope leading to a lip which helps guide food onto cutlery. There is a wide flange around the perimeter. Made of Melamine plastic. Help for those with poor hand control. Two sizes: Small, 9" by 6"; Large, 11" by 8".

**PRICE A** From Maddak (also Everest & Jennings)

### 5.7 MANOY KNIFE AND SPOON
Cutlery consists of a knife with a rocker-type blade and a spoon with angled head. Aid to those with weak hands or poor hand coordination. Spoon available in right-handed or left-handed model.

**PRICE A** From Maddak (also Everest & Jennings)

## 5.8 FEEDING DISH — ELECTRIC

Sturdy dish has two warm compartments and one cool. Each holds 4½ oz. No-slip suction base. Detachable cord. Fully immersible in water and dishwasher safe. Unbreakable, safe, nontoxic. Aid in feeding young children or those confined to bed.

**PRICE A** From Evenflo® Company (Big Mouth Singers™ Electric Feeding Dish)

## 5.9 EGG CUP — SUCTION

A plastic egg cup with suction cup on its bottom for temporary grip on plate or table top.

**PRICE A** From Maddak

## 5.10 FOOD BUMPER

The sanitary snap-on "Food Bumper" is a curved rail designed to keep food from sliding off the plate. Made of polyethylene with strong clips of the same material. Fits plates 9" to 11" in diameter.

**PRICE A** From Maddak

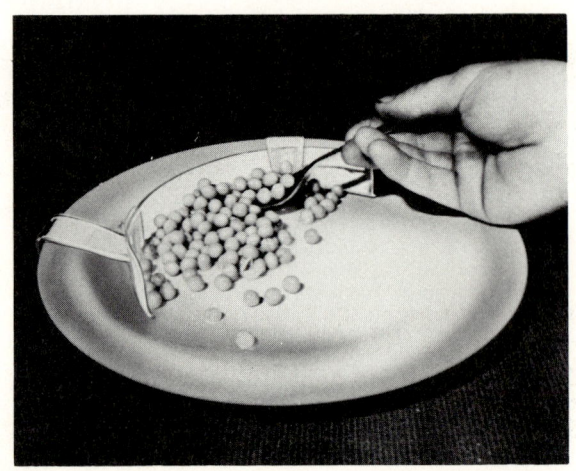

## 5.11 COLLAPSIBLE DRINKING CUP

Collapsible drinking cup with built-in pill box in cover. Convenient, compact, made of plastic. Aid for wheelchair or other travelers, backpackers, campers.

**PRICE A** From Aluminum Housewares

## 5.12 GLASS HOLDER

Clip-on attaches to upright of wheelchair. Clamp has rubber grommets and is adjusted with thumb screw.

**PRICE A** From Cleo

## 5.13 GLASS HOLDER

Holder has a spring clip which can be snapped onto a wheelchair upright, commode, or tubular pole having a diameter of 3/4" to 1". Easily attached or removed. Can be used on walkers, canes, and crutches. Welded-steel wire holder coated with baked-on epoxy.

**PRICE A** From Maddak

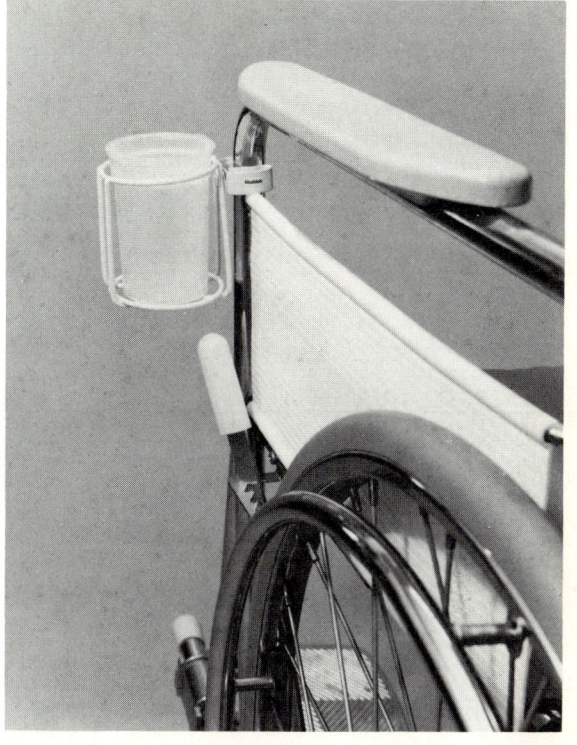

## 5.14 SNAP-ON GLASS HOLDER OR ASH TRAY

Easily attached to any vertical chair leg or table leg. Can be used as a coaster or ash tray. Excellent for wheelchairs, lawnchairs, bridge tables, etc. Made of plated metal with strong spring clip.

**PRICE A** From Maddak

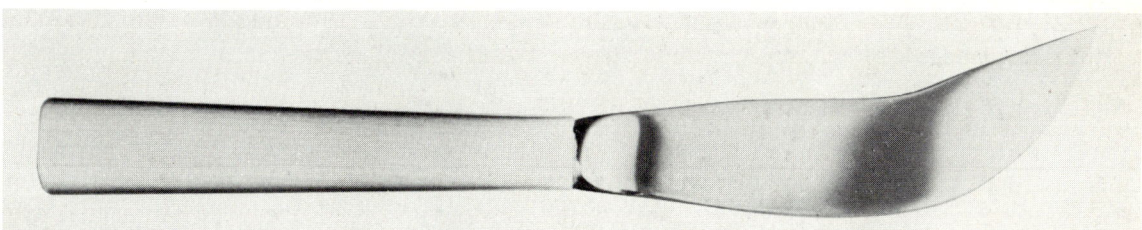

## 5.15 ROCKER KNIFE

Can be used with one hand. Rocker motion allows easy cutting. Stainless handle. Good for those with limited hand strength.

**PRICE A** From Lamson & Goodnow

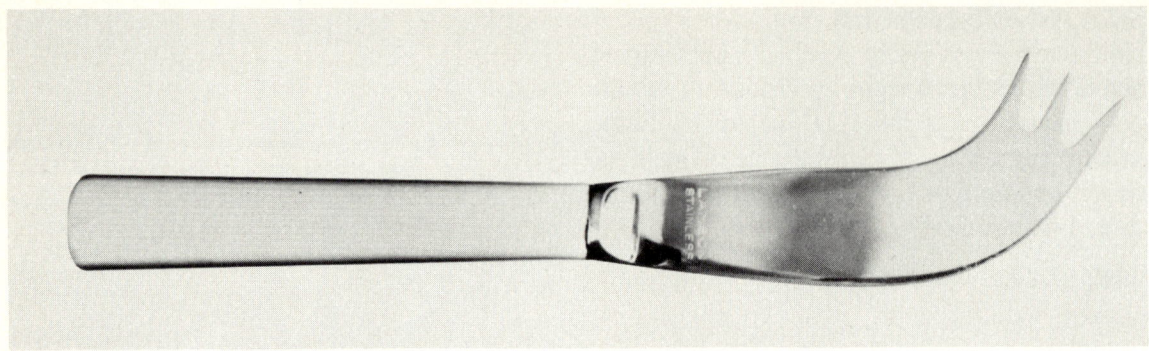

### 5.16 ROCKER KNIFE-FORK
Has curved blade and three deep prongs to serve as fork or knife. Helpful for those with use of only one hand. Overall, 8".

   **PRICE A** From Lamson & Goodnow (similar, Maddak, 4 prongs; Single Hander, 3 prongs)

### 5.17 NONSLIP DISC
Nonslip, flexible Vikem® vinyl surface provides an excellent cushion, a surface on which glassware and other items will not slip. It is easily cleaned, non-conductive, adheres to tables or other surfaces.

   **PRICE A** From Maddak

### 5.18 NONSLIP LINED TRAY
Prevents any items on tray from slipping. Stainless tray 15 1/8" by 10 1/2" by 5/8" deep with rounded corners and rolled top edge. Inside of bottom surface lined with easily cleanable Vikem® cushion.

   **PRICE B** From Maddak

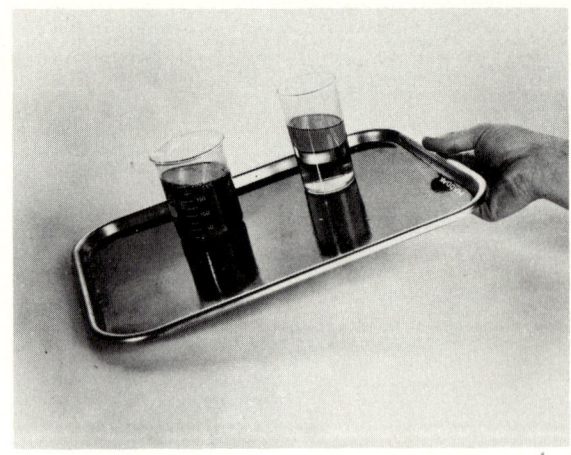

### 5.19 NONSLIP PLACE MAT
Nonslip flexible Vikem® vinyl surface cushions and prevents objects from slipping. Easily cleaned. Will not slide on table or other surface. 15¾" by 10¾" by ⅛", weight 12 oz.

**PRICE A** From Maddak

### 5.20 LARGE STRAWS
Washable, reusable natural polyethylene drinking straws. 1/16" thick, 18" long. Packed twelve to package. Available with 3/16" hole or ¼" hole.

**PRICE A** From Maddak

### 5.21 STRAW HOLDER
A simple plastic clip which mounts on edge of a glass and keeps a drinking straw in position.

**PRICE A** From Maddak

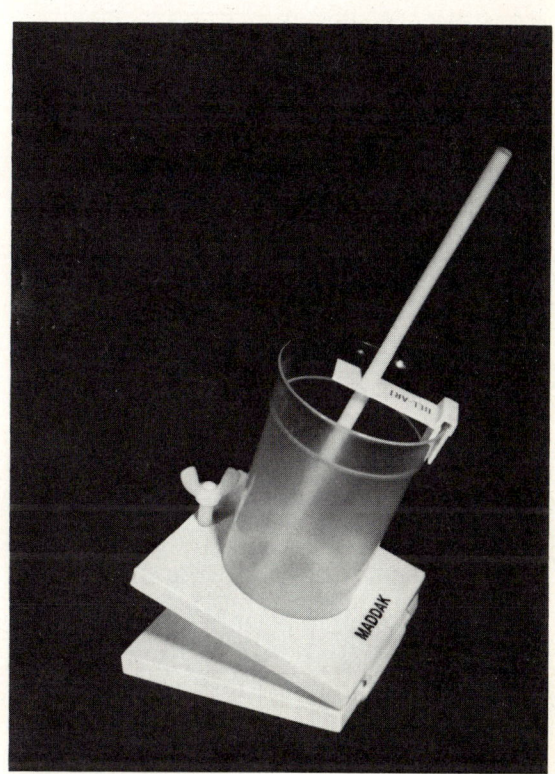

### 5.22 STACKING TRAY AND FRAME
Is helpful in feeding conditions when coordination is poor. Rugged construction of Zylonox®. Light, muffles sound of utensils, boilable to 275°F. Comes with suction-foot tray holder. Additional items available: soup bowl, cup, safety spoon.

**PRICE A *(each)*** From Jones-Zylon

## 5.23 BUILT-UP UTENSILS

Stainless-steel eating utensils. Built-up handles with finger grips. Made of resilient vinyl. Withstand dishwasher heat. Aid to those with poor grip or problem closing hand.

**PRICE A** From Maddak (also Comfort-Able-Aids)

## 5.24 OVERSIZE HANDLE UTENSILS

Built-up utensils with special $1^{5}/_{16}$"-diameter handles for those with limited ability to grip.

**PRICE A (each)** From Cleo

## 5.25 UNIVERSAL CUFF

An adjustable leather pocket for various utensils is attached to a $^{3}/_{4}$"-wide elastic strap. Small, medium, and large sizes.

**PRICE A** From Maddak

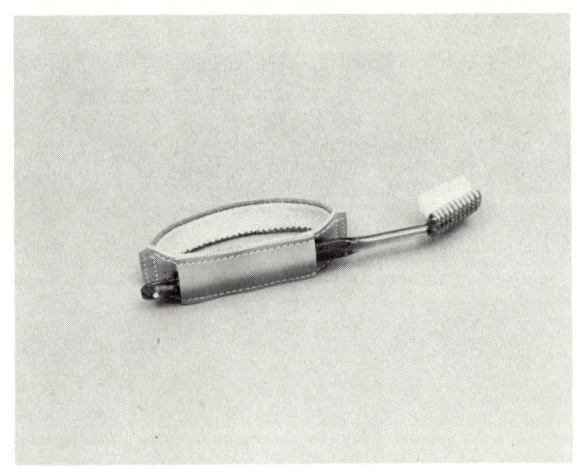

## 5.26 WEIGHTED SPOONS

Plastic handles that have added weight. Weight is completely enclosed in plastic. Plastic cap over ends. Has 8 oz. of weight. Aids those with poor hand coordination to hold spoon steadier.

**PRICE A** From Cleo

## 5.27 ANGLE HANDLE FORK AND SPOON

Stainless-steel fork and large spoon with built-up vinyl handles. They have comfortable feel and finger grips. Choice of left or right utensils. Aids those with poor coordination.

**PRICE A (each)** From Maddak

## 5.28 SELF-LEVELING TEASPOON

The L-shaped utensil handles are mounted on a swivel which permits utensil to remain level even though handle is rotated up to 60°. Double stops prevent excessive swing for left or right hand. Stainless-steel in soft vinyl handles. Withstands dishwasher heat. Weight 2.1 oz. Aids those with poor coordination to keep spoon steadier.

**PRICE A (each)** From Maddak — Swivel Fork, Swivel Teaspoon, Swivel Soup Spoon

## 5.29 THREE-FUNCTION EATING UTENSIL

Stainless-steel combined knife-fork-spoon. Assists those with limited hand function, or use of only one hand. Available in left- or right-handed models.

**PRICE A (each)** From Maddak

## 5.30 HORIZONTAL GRIP UTENSILS

A plastisol-covered hand grip is bendable for adjusting to hand size. Aid for those unable to grip utensils.

**PRICE A (each)** From Cleo

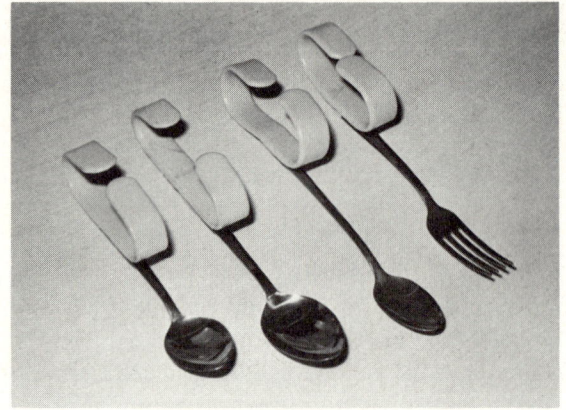

## 5.31 SPORKS

Combination spoon and fork with some of the advantages of each. Stainless steel. The teeth help in getting food into the bowl of the utensil. The bowl holds semi-liquids better than a fork. Aid to those with weak hands or use of only one hand.

**PRICE A (each)** From Cleo

## 5.32 SIDE CUTTER FORK

A special eating utensil which provides an edge along the side of the fork. The blade is only semi-sharp, so there is no danger of cutting oneself. Will cut average food but not all meats. Aids those with functional use of only one hand.

**PRICE A** From Cleo

## 5.33 WATER FILTER

Invento tap water filter. Charcoal filter removes offensive taste, odor, discoloration. Disposable filter lasts up to six months. Won't interfere with faucet use. Weight 4 lb.

**PRICE B** From Hammacher Schlemmer

## 5.34 WATER FILTER

Eco-Filter® cleans tap water of repellant tastes, chlorine, pesticides, fluorides (use Eco-Filter® filter type cf), noxious odors. Cleans at least 600 quarts before new filter replacement necessary. Fits any tap. No special plumbing needed. Eco-Filter® with eco-char has no oily aftertaste, leaves no black on container.

**PRICE A** From Eco-Filters (water filter) / S. Margolis

# Getting Around 6

## 6.1 CLIP-ON ASH TRAY FOR WHEELCHAIR
Clips on wheelchair or table leg of similar diameter.

**PRICE A** From Amigo

## 6.2 WALKER BAG
Two sturdy pockets that fasten securely to walker bar with three Velcro tabs. Provides lots of carrying space. Size 12″ by 16″.

**PRICE A** From Handee For You

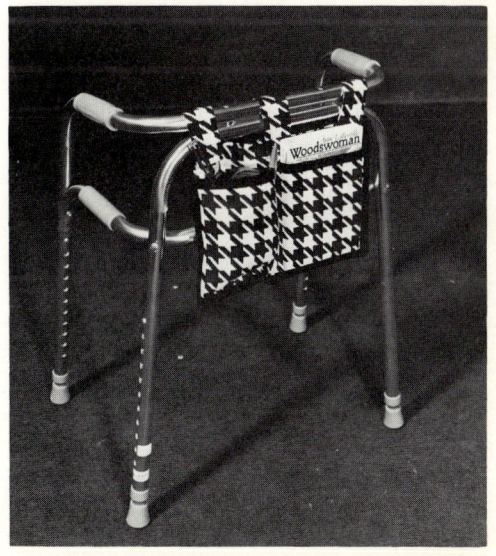

### 6.3 WALKER BAG
Utility apron attaches to walker by adjustable snap tabs that fit around top rung. Four large pockets. Made of blue washable canvas.

**PRICE A** From Camp

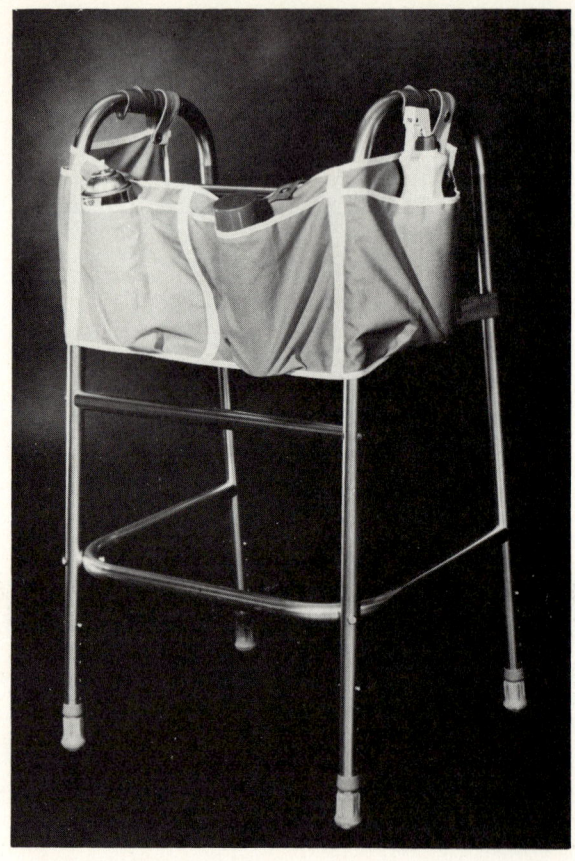

### 6.4 WALKER BAG
Two pockets back-to-back fit over side hand bars, secured by Velcro patches. Stays firmly in place without swinging. Size 9" by 10". Convenient for necessary items.

**PRICE A** From Handee For You

### 6.5 WALKER BAG
Strong plastic net carrier bag has six swivel hooks and rings for attachment to most walkers. Bag opening can be on inside or outside of frame.

**PRICE A** From Maddak

### 6.6 WALKER BAG
Fits top bar of walker. Has two pockets, one on each side of bar for balance. Secured over top bar of walker. Size 12" wide, 8" deep. Available in vinyl or tapestry.

**PRICE A** From Ventura (Comrade)

## 6.7 WHEELCHAIR OR RAIL BAG

All-purpose open-topped carry-all, for back of wheelchair, walker, or bed rail. Size 15″ by 15″. Fully self-lined.

**PRICE A** From Ventura (Collegiate)

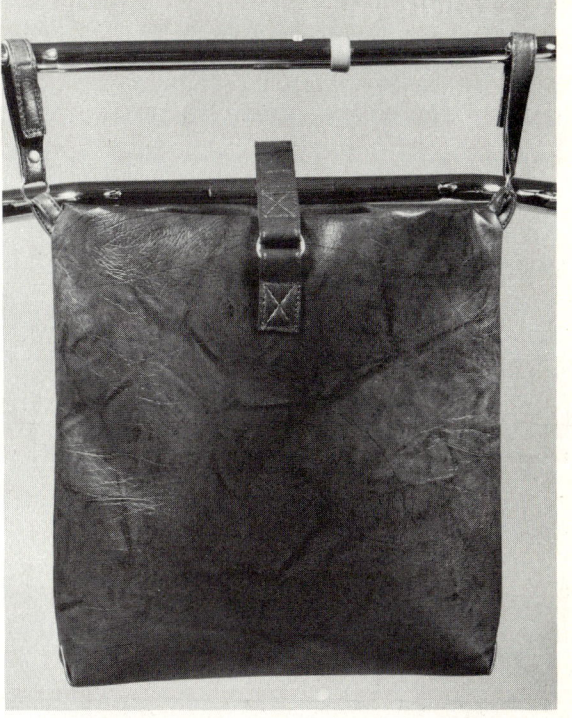

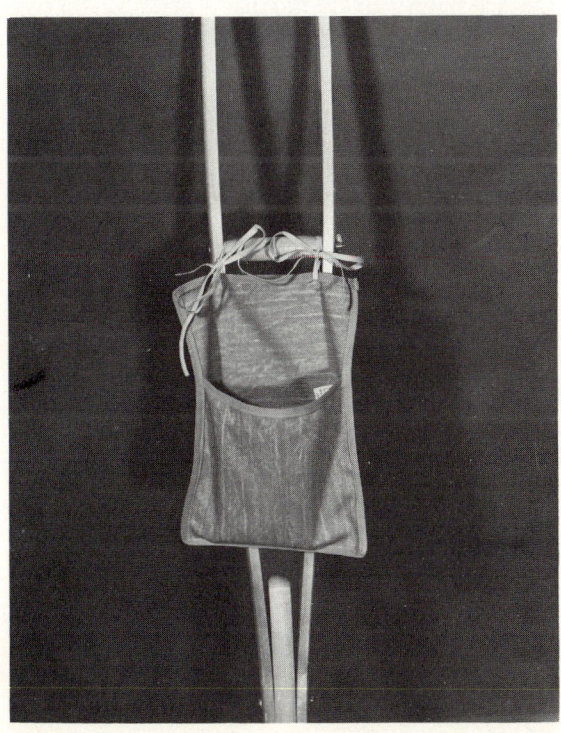

## 6.8 CRUTCH BAG

Crutch pocket fastens to hand bar of crutch with two sets of ties. Tab on back keeps pocket from swinging. Slips on from bottom. Also works on some canes. Size 8″ by 11″. Helpful to keep desired items easy to reach. No need to put crutch down.

**PRICE A** From Handee For You

### 6.9 CRUTCH BAG
Can hang on regular crutches, canes and Canadian crutches. On regular crutches bag is placed over additional hand grip beneath one normally used. Made in soft vinyl. Size 7" wide, 9" deep. Makes items easy to reach. No need to put crutch down.

**PRICE A** From Ventura (Stash)

### 6.10 CANE BAG
Pocket can be secured tightly to shaft of cane by plastic no-release band. Ample room. Tab keeps pocket from swinging out. Size 7½" by 8½". Makes items easy to get without putting cane down.

**PRICE A** From Handee For You

### 6.11 WHEELCHAIR BAG
Can be used over or under wheelchair armrest, also on walkers, many bed rails, over a rod or the open arm of a chair. Size 10" by 7". With Velcro-secured flap. Holds desired items conveniently.

**PRICE A** From Ventura (Charlie)

### 6.12 WHEELCHAIR BAG
Fits inside either arm of wheelchair, on walker bars or bed rails. Has zippered top or flap with Velcro closure. Securing strap at either end and outer pockets.

**PRICE B** From Ventura (Slim Jim)

### 6.13 WHEELCHAIR CARRY-ALL
Convenient to carry many items needed for daily activities. Attaches to upholstered or tubular type armrest. Made of heavy duck material.

**PRICE A** From Preston

### 6.14 WHEELCHAIR CARRY-ALL
Fastens securely to chair arm by two Velcro straps. Use on either side. Full-length zipper top, six inside pockets, four outside pockets—two on each side. 14″ by 7¼″. Fits full length of wheelchair arm.

**PRICE B** From FashionAble

### 6.15 WHEELCHAIR BAG
Two expansion pockets tie on arm of wheelchair. Size 8½″ by 14″. Sturdy construction.

**PRICE A** From Handee For You

### 6.16 WHEELCHAIR BAG
For back of wheelchair. Detachable carrying pocket. Convenient for carrying daily-use items.

**PRICE B** From Everest & Jennings

### 6.17 WHEELCHAIR BAG
For back of wheelchair or walker. Large inner capacity, top zipper or flap with Velcro closure. Outer pockets for easy access to small items. Vinyl securing straps. Can be used on bed rail.

**PRICE B** From Ventura (Continental)

### 6.18 WHEELCHAIR BAG
Tote bag for back of wheelchair. Made of heavy-duty blue canvas. Closes with Velcro fastener. Can be personalized with three initials. Size 14″ by 14″ by 4″.

**PRICE A** From Gorman Products (Wheelchair Tote Bag)

### 6.19 WHEELCHAIR BRAKE EXTENSION
Fits over standard brake levers. Extends height, increases leverage for those with limited arm movement.

**PRICE A** From Everest & Jennings

### 6.20 WHEELCHAIR ATTENDANT BRAKE

The brake is designed for anyone pushing a wheelchair to go up or down inclines safely and effortlessly. Fits most wheelchairs. Made of stainless steel. Chair can be used as a walker when user is standing in rear. Brake needs pressure of only one finger to operate.

**PRICE C** From KGB Research & Development (Justa Finger)

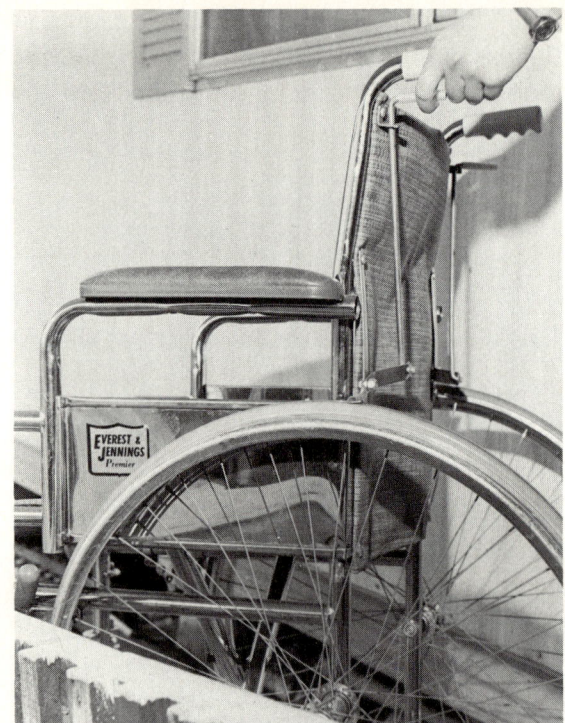

### 6.21 WHEELCHAIR PUSH CUFF

Used over hands as protection and an aid in pushing wheels of wheelchair. Tough, all crepe, gives maximum traction. One size fits most hands. Velcro fastener. Thumb flap gives extra protection.

**PRICE A** From Alimed (Quad Push Cuff)

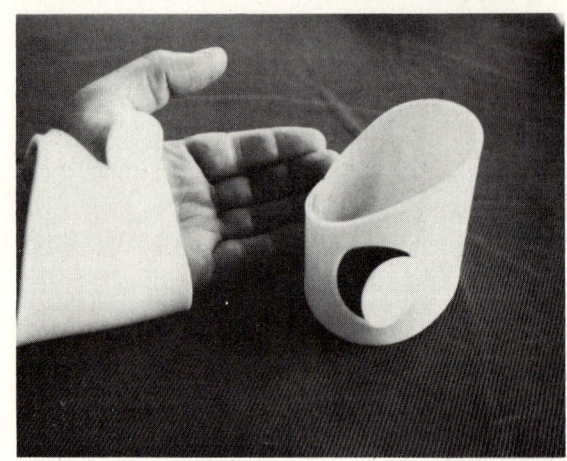

### 6.22 CANE CLIP

Can be clamped to any open-edge flat surface such as table, chair arm, or shelf. Rubber tip prevents marring of surface, and cane-holding spring clip fits most cane diameters. Keeps cane upright and within easy reach. Fits any surface from $1/4''$ to $1 3/4''$ and has a $1 1/2''$ throat. Aluminum C-type clamp with steel screw and plastic adjusting knob.

**PRICE A** From Maddak

GETTING AROUND    105

## 6.23  WHEELCHAIR CANE AND CRUTCH HOLDER
Clamp-on design permits mounting on either side behind back. Convenient for carrying cane or crutch while in wheelchair.

**PRICE A**  From Everest & Jennings

## 6.24  WHEELCHAIR CRUTCH HOLDER
Receptacle bolts to lower part of chair frame and web. Strap attaches to upper part of back upholstery. Convenient for storing crutches or cane while using chair.

**PRICE A**  From Preston

## 6.25  FOLDING CANE
Aluminum sections heat-treated for strength and durability. Self-opens by action of heavy-duty elastic cable. Hardwood handle form-fits hand. Comes in gold, silver, or black finish. 30", 33", 36" lengths. Folds to $12^{1}/_{2}$" length, $4^{1}/_{2}$" width. Helpful for part-time cane users. Fit in purse or pocket. Excellent for full-time use also.

**PRICE A**  From Cleo / Professional Convalescent Products.

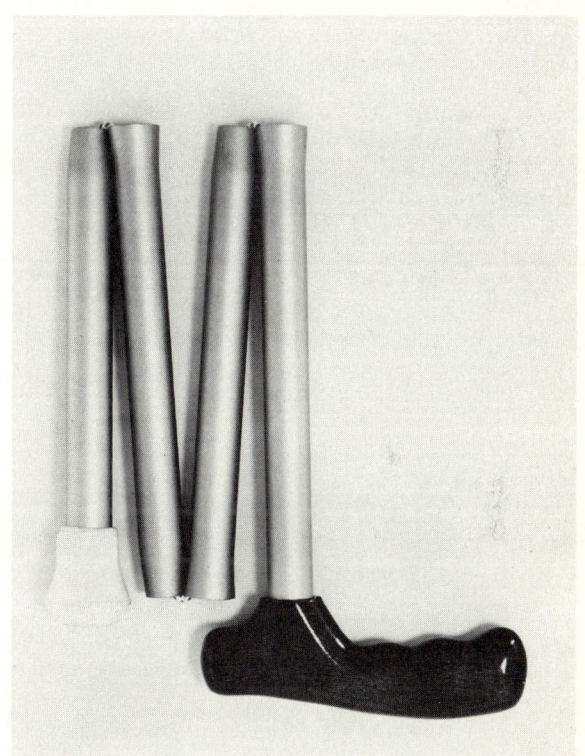

## 6.26  ADJUSTABLE CANE
Adjustable from 32" to 39", using double push button for adjusting and positive locking. Plastic grip aluminum cane. Design places hand grip centered over shaft for better support. Ortho-Rect™ cane.

**PRICE B**  From Camp

### 6.27 CANE, FLASHLIGHT, AND WHISTLE

Combined cane, flashlight, whistle, and wrist strap. Cane of anodized aluminum is adjustable in height, has curved handle over center for maximum balance. Flashlight of high-impact plastic, easy-slide switch, special lens for rectangular beam, adjustable position on cane. Wrist strap has stretch-type adjustable loop. Has police whistle for emergency alarm signal. Safety staff prevents falls due to dim lighting. Allows use of two hands without dropping cane.

**PRICE B** From Easy Riser (Safety Staff)

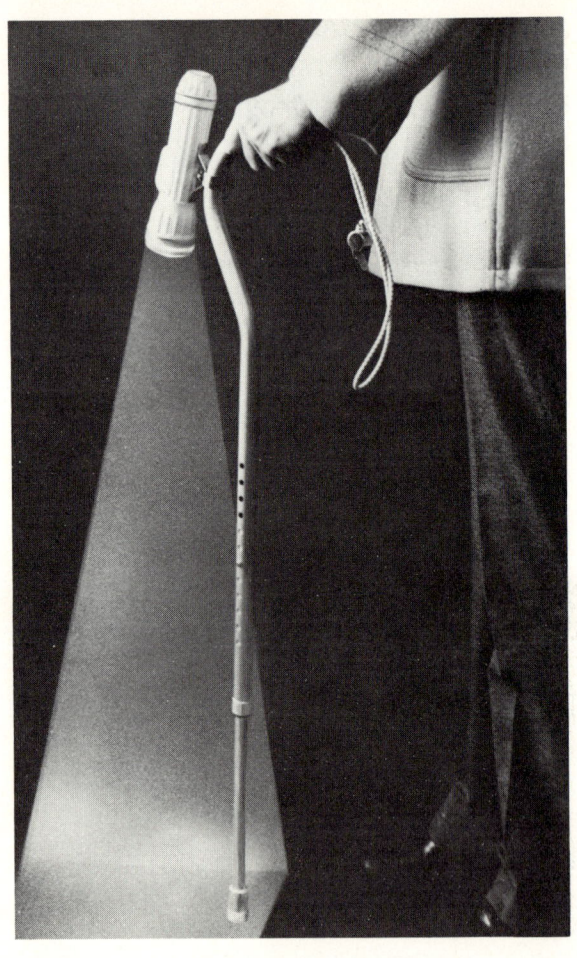

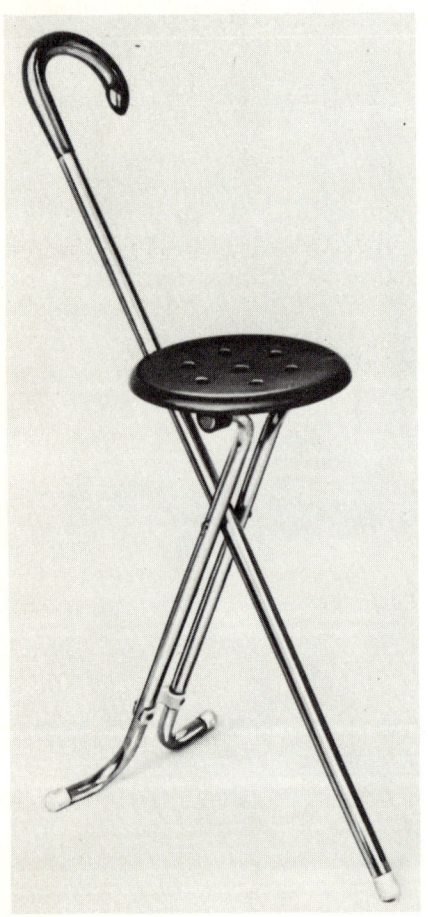

### 6.28 CANE SEAT

Tripod chair—fold down and sit, fold up and go. Lightweight, 4 lb. Nonrusting aluminum. Cane converts to seat in an instant.

**PRICE A** From Hammacher Schlemmer (similar, Wal-Jan; FashionAble; Preston)

## 6.29 CANE-CONE BASE

For use on ⁷/₈" to 1" diameter canes. Tripod base. Gives more stability to cane user. Center tip can be flexed.

**PRICE A** From Camp (similar, Wal-Jan)

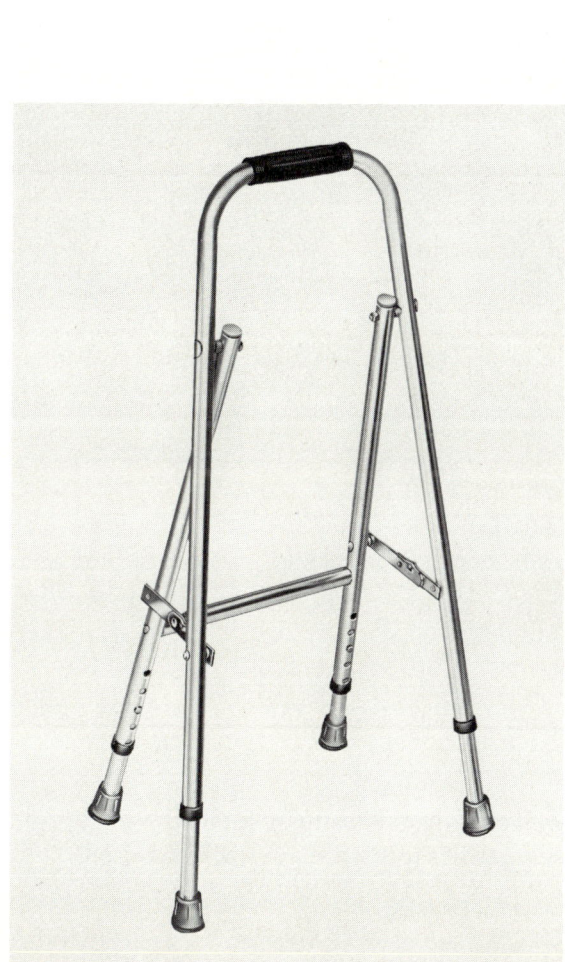

## 6.30 WALKANE, ADJUSTABLE

Lighter than a walker, more stable than a cane. Folds flat for storage. Push-button height adjustment 28" to 32" or 33" to 37".

**PRICE B** From Cleo (also Lumex)

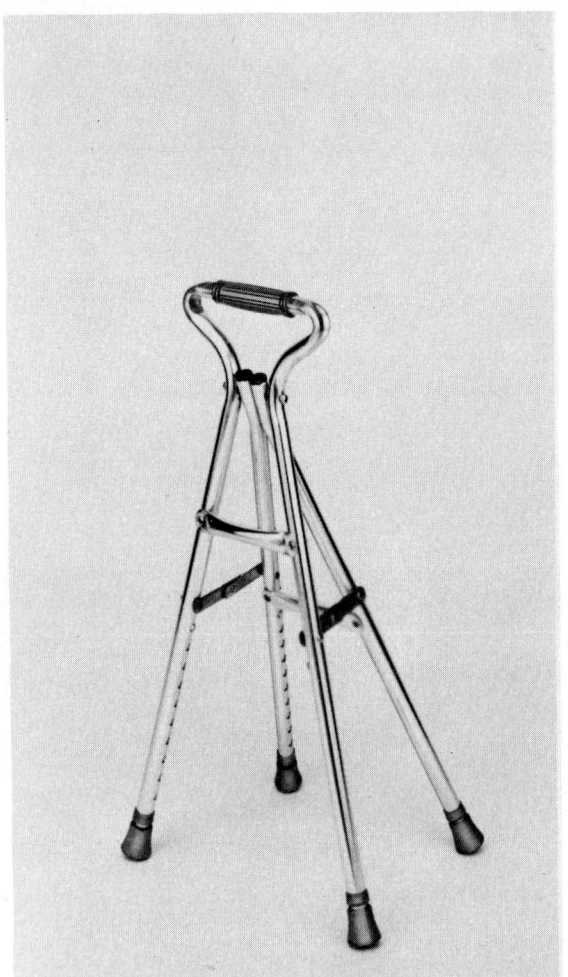 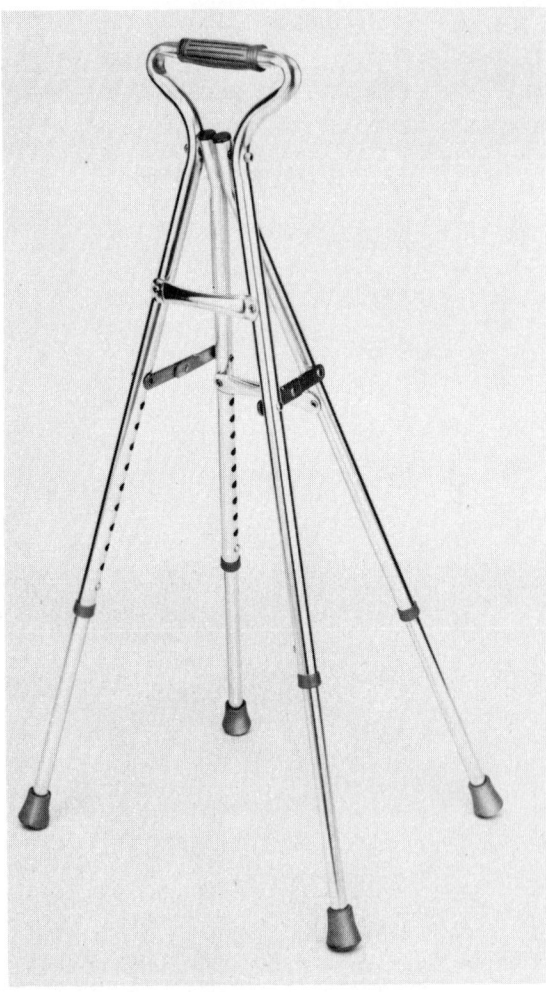

### 6.31 PYRAMID™ FOLDING CANE, ADJUSTABLE

As height of cane increases, base width and depth increase, providing greater support and stability. Closed handle concentrates user's weight over center of base of cane. Push button for height adjustment from 28¾" to 37¼". Weight 3 lb. Folds to 2".

**PRICE B** From EDCO/Pasco

### 6.32 LARGE BASE CANE, ADJUSTABLE

Has four legs, padded grip and Vibra-Lok™ for positive holding adjustment for length. Just push button for nine adjustments in 1" increments. Gives stability to user. Base size 12" by 18".

**PRICE B** From EDCO/Pasco (similar, Professional Convalescent Products)

GETTING AROUND 109

## 6.33 SMALL BASE CANE, ADJUSTABLE
Has four legs, padded grip, and Vibra-Lok™ for positive holding adjustment for length. Just push button for nine adjustments in 1" increments. Gives better stability to user. Base size 7½" by 5¼".

**PRICE B** From EDCO/Pasco (similar, Professional Convalescent Products)

## 6.34 CUSHION, DRY FLOTATION
Roho cushion design prevents and promotes healing of pressure sores from users who must sit for long periods of time in beds, wheelchairs, autos, etc. Air is used to support user's body uniformly and in comfort. Allows air to circulate under and around user. Size 15" by 17" by 4". Added sections and accessories available. Also various sizes of cushion.

**PRICE D** From Roho Research & Development

### 6.35 CUSHION, WATER FLOTATION, WHEELCHAIR

Water-filled, comes in four sizes. Reduces pressure on critical areas to prevent pressure sores. Cutout design offers even greater pressure reduction. Body heat is dissipated by water in cushion. Standard size 16" by 18" by 3".

**PRICE C** From Jobst Institute

### 6.36 CUSHION, WATER FLOTATION

Medpro cushion gives relief from pressure sores. Spreads user's weight and distributes pressure over larger area. Fills with water. Heavy-duty heat-sealed vinyl. 16" by 18"; 15 lb. when filled.

**PRICE C** From Medpro, Inc.

### 6.37 CUSHION, FOAM, WHEELCHAIR

Synergistic tri-pad designed to distribute pressure away from main pressure points. Center is "cored" at three main pressure areas and filled with low-density foam. High-quality, fire-retardant foam. Washable cover. Pad weight 1½ lb.

**PRICE B** From Everest & Jennings

### 6.38 CUSHION, AIR, TWIN REST

For wheelchair or regular chair. Gives relief to sensitive areas. Adjusts in height. Air-filled. Deflates to pocket-size for travel. 16" by 17" size.

**PRICE A** From Better Sleep, Inc.

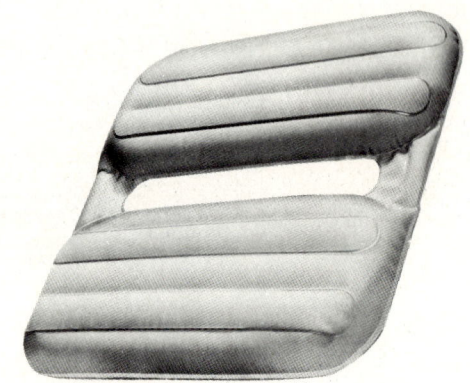

### 6.39 CUSHION, LIQUID, WHEELCHAIR

For prevention and treatment of pressure sores. Eliminates pressure points when sitting. Contains chemically treated liquid. Covered with special vinyl with carrying handle, wipes clean. Weighs 7 lb. Size 17" by 17". Safety liner prevents leaks.

**PRICE C** From Aquatherm (Aqua-Seat®)

## 6.40 CUSHION, "T" FOAM, WHEELCHAIR

Relieves pressure-sore problems. Cushions available in various sizes, thicknesses and densities. "T" foam flows and molds itself, to distribute user's pressure. "T" foam breathes. Comes siliconized to make cushion waterproof. 16" by 18" by 3".

**PRICE B** From Alimed

## 6.41 CUSHION, AIR, WHEELCHAIR

Six models and sizes of air cushions for individual problems to prevent or heal pressure sores. Fits all types and sizes of wheelchairs. These rubber cushions equalize pressure when sitting. Can also be used in bathtub, shower, or auto. Odorless. Sizes range from 13" by 14" by 3" to 17" by 17" by 4".

**PRICE A** From Ken McRight

## 6.42 CUSHION, GEL, WHEELCHAIR

Cushion helps prevent and relieve pressure sores and fatigue caused by incorrect support. Contains Spenco gel emulsion. Will not leak if punctured. Naugahyde cover. 17" by 17". Back for chair also contains gel. 13" high by 16" wide with nylon straps for height adjustment.

**PRICE B (seat) A (back)** From Cleo

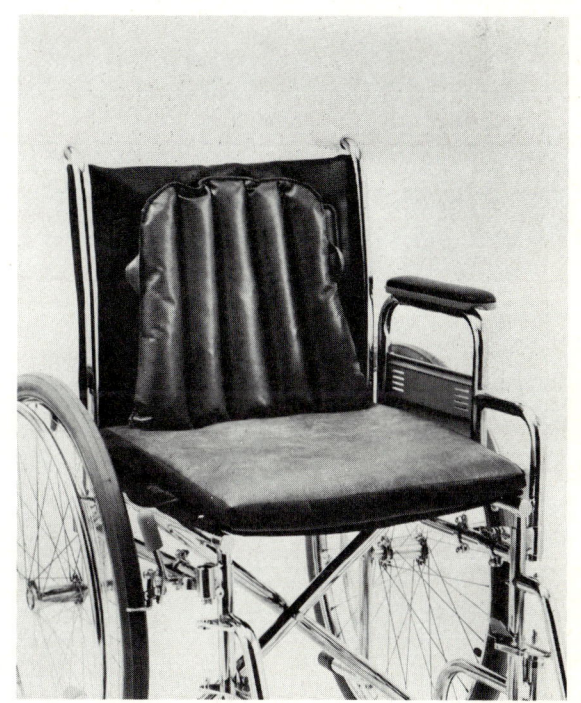

## 6.43 BACK CUSHION, WHEELCHAIR

Back support rolls up for easy carrying. Available in two back heights with or without cut-out. Raises back height of wheelchair 2" to 4" to give firm support. Takes up only ¾" space in back of chair. 14" wide, 2" rise above chair back. Comes in other sizes.

**PRICE B** From MED

### 6.44  CUSHION SEAT, WHEELCHAIR

An entirely new concept in seating for wheelchair users. A complete, one-piece seat and back which is individually contoured to fit user. Prevents or aids in healing of pressure sores. Helps balanced sitting. Various sizes available. Standard size 18" wide by 19" long seat, back 17" high. Weight 12 lb. Can be used in car, office, plane, etc.

**PRICE D**  From Contourpedic Corp. (Contourpedic™ Seat)

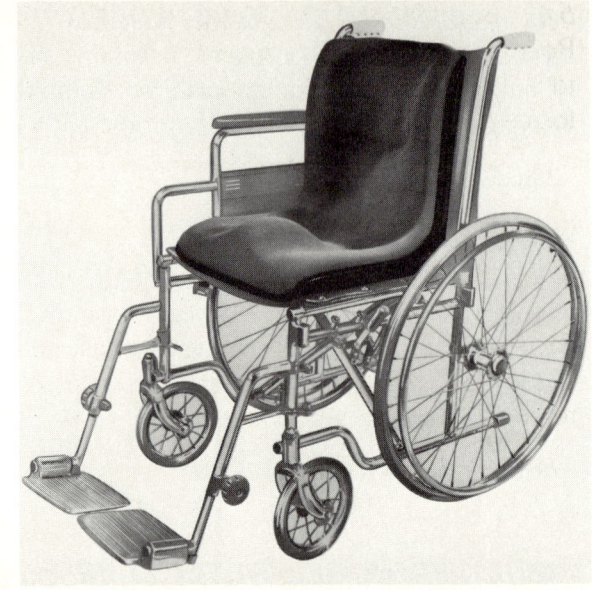

### 6.45  CUSHION-LIFT® TRADITIONAL CHAIR

Chair that assists user to standing position. User controls rate of rising to his feet, and height to which he rises. Lifts up to 500 lb. Gives complete independence to user, who can get up from chair without help.

**PRICE F**  From Ortho-Kinetics

### 6.46  CUSHION-LIFT® RECLINER CHAIR

Chair that assists user to his feet. User controls rate at which he rises to his feet, controls height to which he is raised. Gives feeling of independence to user, who can get up unassisted. Angle of back of chair adjustable. Single control makes back recline and footrests elevate. Electrically operated. Lifts up to 500 lb.

**PRICE F**  From Ortho-Kinetics

## 6.47 ELEVATING SEAT CHAIR—SWIVEL ROCKER

Rocking chair user can get into and out of unaided. Push button and seat slowly elevates one to standing position. To sit, lean against seat and turn air release valve. User is gently lowered to seated position. Swivel base allows for turning in any direction.

**PRICE E** From Burke

## 6.48 ELEVATING SEAT CHAIR— RECLINER

Easy-to-use control elevates user slowly and safely to standing position. To sit, one leans against seat and turns valve. User is lowered gently to seated position. Electric recliner permits effortless reclining. Footrest automatically rises as back reclines.

**PRICE E** From Burke

## 6.49 WHEELCHAIR CADDY

Convenient carry-all for snacks, beverages, etc. Folds compactly on side of chair. Fits most chairs.

**PRICE A** From Everest & Jennings

### 6.50 WHEELCHAIR CADDY TRAY
Snaps over side of wheelchair arm. Size 4″ by 7″ by 2″ for desk arm, or same size for full-arm wheelchair.

**PRICE A (each)** From Raymo

### 6.51 COMBINATION CUP, TRAY, ASH TRAY FOR WHEELCHAIR
A holder lug attaches to 1″ tubular vertical furniture—walkers, beds and wheelchairs. Connected to holder lug is ash tray or cup holder or utility tray.

**PRICE A (each)** From Physical Aids

### 6.52 WHEELCHAIR CUP
"Handi-Cup" beverage carrier for wheelchairs. Molded plastic. Attaches to arm of wheelchair without tools. Can also be used to carry ash tray. Available in left or right models for full-length arm or desk arm of wheelchair.

**PRICE A** From Wal-Jan

### 6.53 TRAVEL CHAIR
Chair eliminates transfer to and from wheelchair, in and out of common carrier and facilities such as theaters, auditoriums, terminals (airplane, bus, train). Handles on back and under foot pedals allow disabled to be carried up steps by two helpers. Chair can be slid onto seat in auditorium, train, plane, or wheelchair. Chair wheels by pushing on front wheels and holding back handles. Holds 210 lb. Folds for carrying and storage. Weight 39 lb. 12″, 14″, and 16″ widths.

**PRICE E** From YAD ("DIT-C")

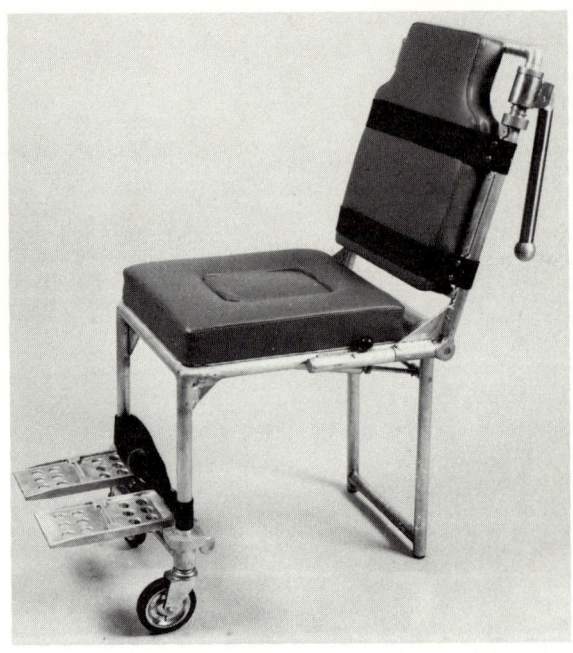

### 6.54 WHEELCHAIR DESK
Provides space to write, or read book, yet doesn't occupy full width of wheelchair. Slips out of holder for quick storage on side of chair or in a bag. Size 10″ by 12″.

**PRICE B** From MED

## 6.55 LOADING CHAIR

For transporting disabled through narrow spaces such as aisles of planes, trains, or buses. 6" rubber-tire wheels provide smooth passage on ramps, through door frames. Upholstered seat and back are vinyl-impregnated nylon. Width 14³/₄", length 33", height 54¹/₄". Seat height 20¹/₂". Weight 17 lb.

**PRICE D** From Everest & Jennings

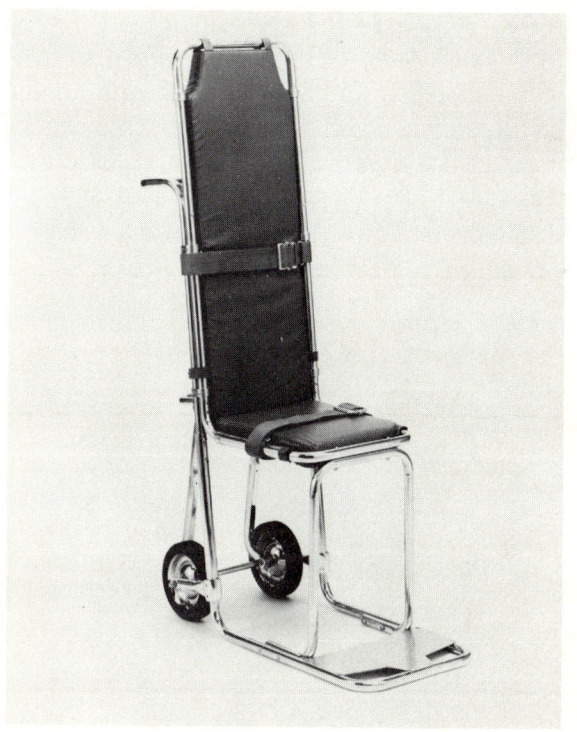

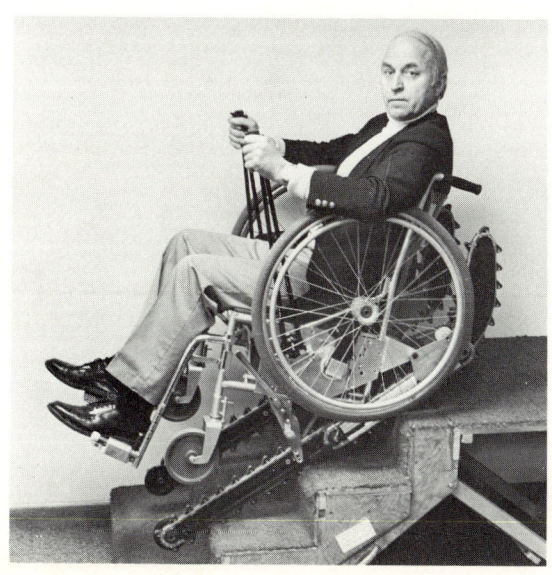

## 6.56 STAIR-CLIMBING WHEELCHAIR

First practical, stable, portable, stair-climbing wheelchair. No need for attendants. As good on level ground as best conventional chairs. Folds fully. No battery—climbing is accomplished through adjustable-ratio arm levers. Requires as little as a few pounds of pressure to operate. Weight 42 lb. Seat width 16" to 20". Various other options available.

**PRICE F** From Staircat™, Inc. (StairCat)

## 6.57 POWER-LIFT WHEELCHAIR

Stair chair easily enables one person to take another person up or down stairs with a minimum of effort. Switch for up or down movement actuates battery power, pulls unit up or lowers it onto each step. Applies vertical thrust, allowing unit to be used on wet, carpeted or highly waxed stairs.

**PRICE F** From Escalera, Inc.

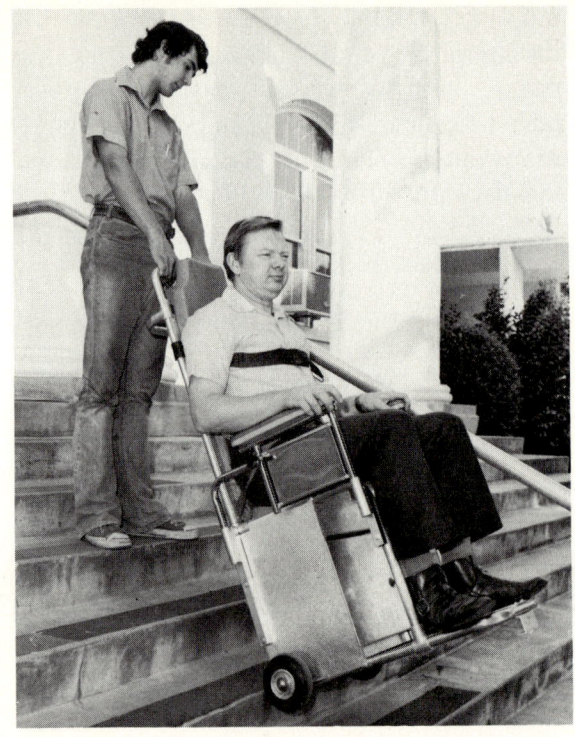

## 6.58 STAND-UP WHEELCHAIR

The unique mechanism of the Levo Stand-Up™ wheelchair enables user to rise to a standing position with the simple touch of a switch. Lifts up to 185 lb. Chair can be folded.

**PRICE F** From American Stair-Glide

## 6.59 ELECTRIC WHEELCHAIR

Exceptionally narrow (18") wheelchair—easy to operate, and maneuver. It is portable, and powered by a battery recharged by plugging into any household outlet. It dismantles into three parts. Has low center of gravity making it very stable. The seat swivels. Weight 78 lb. Comes in three models. Has 50 accessories.

**PRICE F** From Amigo (Amigo Stability)

## 6.60 WHEELCHAIR CARRYING VEHICLE

Amigo wheelchair is driven onto "boots" and locked into place so the combined vehicle is ready to go over grass, packed snow, gravel, etc. Powered by two 12-volt batteries, it travels up to $4\frac{1}{2}$ mph and is controlled with a "Joystick" operated by user's fingertips.

**PRICE F** From Amigo, Inc.

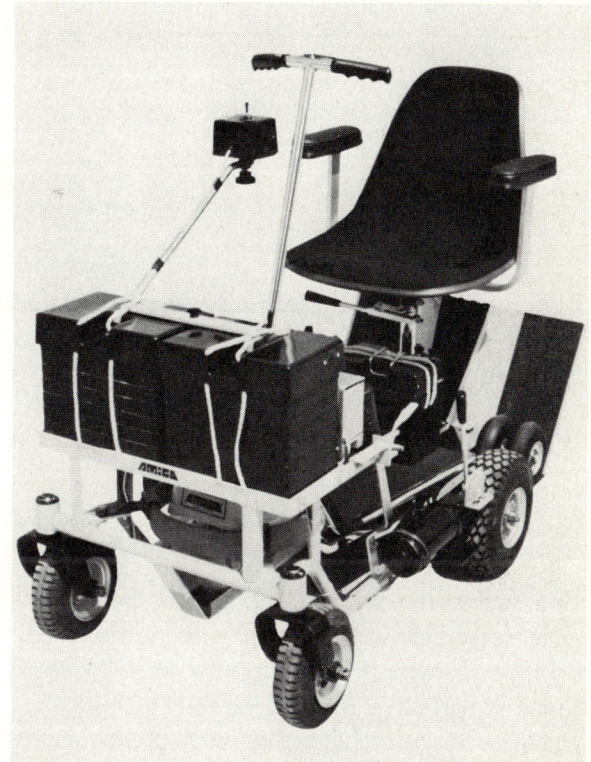

## 6.61 PORTABLE POWER WHEELCHAIR

Folds to $9\frac{1}{2}$" in seconds, has easily removable battery pack. Has built-in battery charger. Drive disengage lever allows manual operation. Weight 81 lb. (less footrest and battery). Width $22\frac{3}{4}$" (removable arm model).

**PRICE E** From American Stair-Glide Corp.

### 6.62 PORTABLE ELECTRIC WHEELCHAIR

Portascoot® goes forward or reverse in two speeds. Handle-bar steering. Seat swivels 360° and adjusts front to back to get closer to steering handles. Height adjusts from 17½" to 21" from floor. Bicycle-type hand brake. Powered by 12-volt battery. Two- or three-day normal use without recharging. 42½" by 23½" by 37½" high.

**PRICE E** From Sears

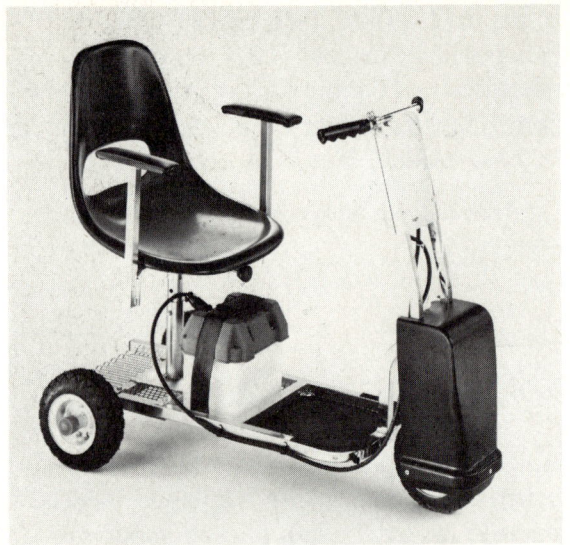

### 6.63 POWER RECLINER FOR WHEELCHAIR

Powered reclining system which elevates folding head rest, leg rests, and lowers back of chair. This system installs on full recliner frame models of some Everest & Jennings wheelchairs.

**PRICE F** From Falcon Research & Development

### 6.64 ELECTRIC SELF-RECLINING WHEELCHAIR

The Independence is a self-contained, electrically powered, reclining wheelchair. It is operated by three motors powered by two 12-volt batteries. It will run a full day without recharging. Batteries can be recharged overnight by plugging into conventional house outlet. Has accessories. Weight 300 lb.

**PRICE F** From Falcon Research & Development

### 6.65 POWER-DRIVE WHEELCHAIR

Has range up to twice that of competitive chairs. Lightweight steel frame, battery charger, small cushioned tires. Top speed 3.5 mph. Right- or left-hand drive.

**PRICE F** From Everest & Jennings

### 6.66  POWER WHEELCHAIR SYSTEM

Insta Gaiter® portable power system can be installed on nonpowered wheelchairs, both folding and nonfolding. Complete wheelchair installation with power can also be purchased.

**PRICE F**  From Theradyne Corp.

### 6.67  ELECTRO-MATIC POWER DRIVE FOR WHEELCHAIR

Can be installed on wheelchair or purchased with a chair. Folding, finger-tip control, battery powered. Has automatic brakes, plug-in battery charger and full maneuverability. Travels 10 to 20 miles between charges.

**PRICE D**  From Rosenthal Manufacturing Company

### 6.68  PORTABLE ELECTRIC WHEELCHAIR

Separates into three pieces for portability. Backrest adjusts from 12″ to 18″. Back handles; joystick control. Width 23½″, length 33″ (with footrests open). Has accessories. Swivels 360°. Charger uses wall outlet. Arms lift up. Goes up 7% grade. Footrests fold and adjust from 3″ to 8″.

**PRICE F**  From Fimco

### 6.69  INDOOR-OUTDOOR ELECTRIC WHEELCHAIR

Tri-Wheeler "Equalizer" can go through grass, sand, mud, and snow—up to 7 mph. Forward and reverse with two high and two low speeds. 15-mile range on single charge. Automatic charger. Width 24″, length 38″.

**PRICE F**  From RJ Mobility Systems

### 6.70 INDOOR-OUTDOOR ELECTRIC WHEELCHAIR
Tri-wheeler fits on van lifts and small apartment elevators. Travels on sand, gravel, grass, snow, and up 30% grades. Seat swivels. 25" wide, 41" long. Speed 8 mph. Up to 20 miles per battery charge.

**PRICE F** From Voyager, Inc. (Voyager IV)

### 6.71 INDOOR-OUTDOOR ELECTRIC WHEELCHAIR
The Elektra is easily maneuverable indoors. When used outdoors, it climbs 40% grades, attains 16 mph speeds, has 25-mile range, and also has an internal battery charger. Goes over rough terrain. Has optional equipment available. 28" wide, 39" long, weight 300 lb.

**PRICE F** From Sherry Products

### 6.72 TRI-WHEELED ELECTRIC WHEELCHAIR
Chair steered by single rear wheel connected to control. Built-in charger. Footboard raises for easier entry or exit. Width 28", length 49", weight 180 lb. (less batteries). Climbs 25% grade. Top speed 6 mph.

**PRICE F** From Steven Motor Chair (The Steven Motor Chair)

### 6.73 ELECTRIC WHEELCHAIR
Chairmobile® is electrically powered chair for indoor use. It will go forward, backward, and pivot in its own length. Rechargeable battery provides power for miles of traveling. Controls can be raised or lowered. Seat and backrest are adjustable. Seat pivots on its stem. Width $24^{1/2}$", length $29^{1/2}$".

**PRICE F** From Rubery Owen

### 6.74 CHAIR LEG EXTENDERS
Four leg extenders make almost any chair 3" to 7" higher. Strong metal brackets lock in place with a screwdriver. Fit round or square legs. Rubber feet keep chair from slipping. All parts plated to prevent rusting.

**PRICE A** From Cleo

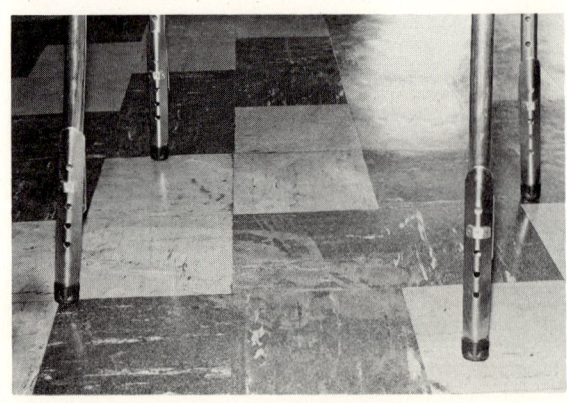

### 6.75 FURNITURE LEG EXTENDER
Raises furniture up to 8" (chairs, sofas, beds). Fits majority of leg styles (square, round, rectangular). Made of steel. Colors tan, dark brown.

**PRICE A** From Easy Riser

### 6.76 GLIDER CHAIR
Rolls easily across floors, through narrow halls and doorways. Naugahyde upholstery. Folds to 5" wide. Overall width 19$\frac{1}{2}$". Length 24". Weight 28 lb.

**PRICE D** From Everest & Jennings

### 6.77 WHEELCHAIR LEG REST
Provides calf support on chairs with footrests. Hook-on design.

**PRICE B** From Everest & Jennings

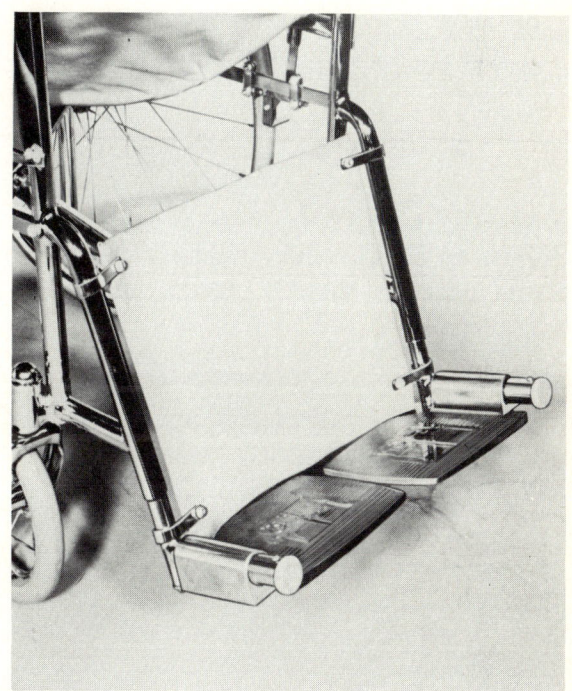

### 6.78 WHEELCHAIR HEEL STRAP
Swivel fasteners on one side. For use with removable footrest. Keeps legs from sliding off footrests.

**PRICE A** From Everest & Jennings

### 6.79 ICE GRIPPERS, CRUTCH OR CANE

This attachment is designed to provide positive gripping and nonskid support on snow and ice. Grippers are easily retracted for indoor use of cane or crutch.

**PRICE A** From Monadnock (also Preston)

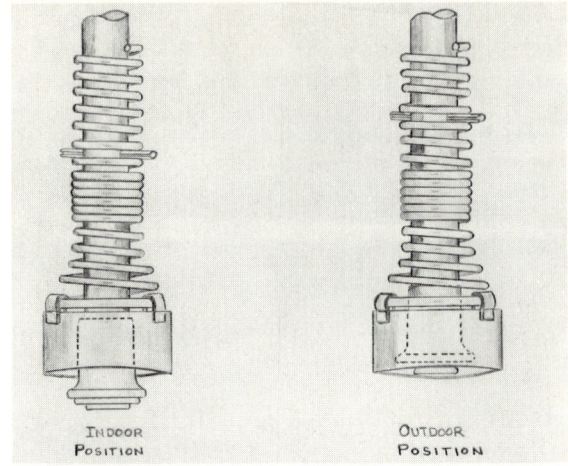

### 6.80 ICE GRIPPERS

Attach to bottom of cane or crutches. Spikes cut into ice and snow to give positive support.

**PRICE A (small) B (large)** From EDCO/Pasco

### 6.81 ICE GRIPPER

Rubber tip fits all standard aluminum and wood canes. Has screw-in steel plate with spikes. Useful in ice and snow to prevent slipping. Spike plate removes for indoor use.

**PRICE A** From Cleo

### 6.82 CANE ICE GRIPPER

Pull lever by cane handle and grippers slide out on ice. Use cane indoors and out. Grippers prevent slipping on ice and snow. When spikes are retracted, large rubber tip is used indoors or outdoors. Positive lock holds steel spikes in position. 33" long. Other sizes 35" or 37" long.

**PRICE B** From Cleo

### 6.83 KNEE SEPARATOR
Made of heavy-gauge plastic, it provides spring-like pressure to keep knees apart for wheelchair users. Comes in three sizes.

**PRICE A** From Maddak

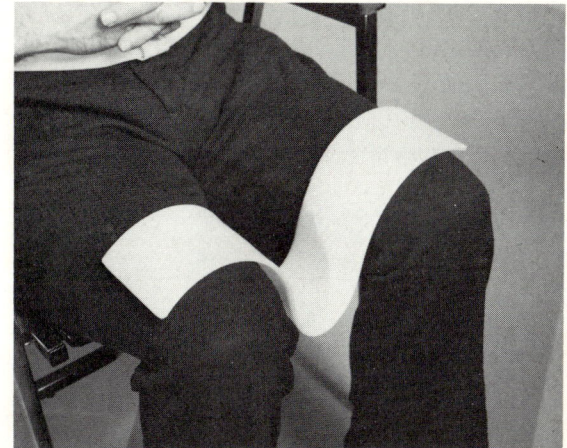

### 6.84 WHEELCHAIR STAIRWAY LIFT
Makes most stairs accessible to wheelchair users. Fits on stairways as narrow as 36" clear width. Platform is 42" long and 28" or more wide. Platform folds to $12^{1/2}$" wide when not in use, so clear stairway is available. Carries up to 350 lb.

**PRICE F** From The Cheney Company

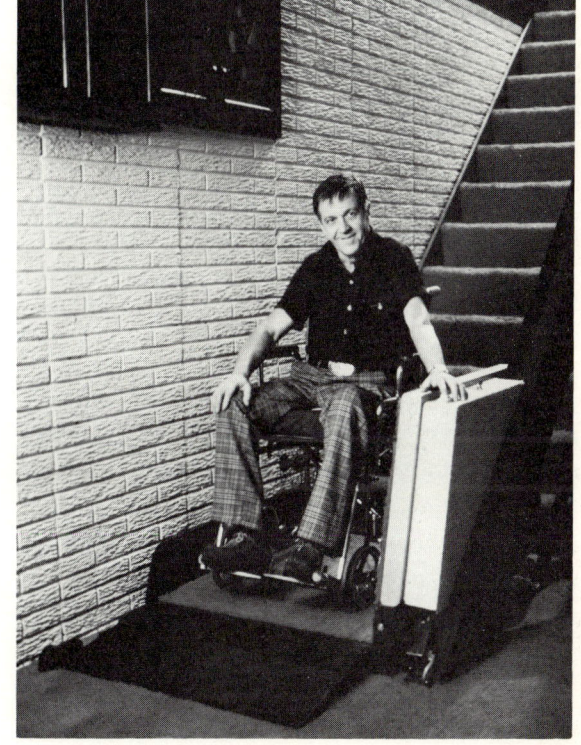

### 6.85 EARL'S STAIRWAY LIFT
Econo-Lift is ideal for individuals using wheelchairs or unable to climb stairs. If one desired, it is available with two automatic folding seats. 42" width between stairway walls required to accommodate a 28"-wide platform.

**PRICE F** From Earl's Stairway Lift

## 6.86 WHEELCHAIR STAIRWAY LIFT

Can lift 500 lb. (if an attendant to accompany the occupant is needed). Fits stairway with 34" width. Safety bar stops lift if it hits any object on stairs. Butler lift is designed to be unobtrusive.

*PRICE F* From Flinchbaugh (Butler Wheelchair Lift)

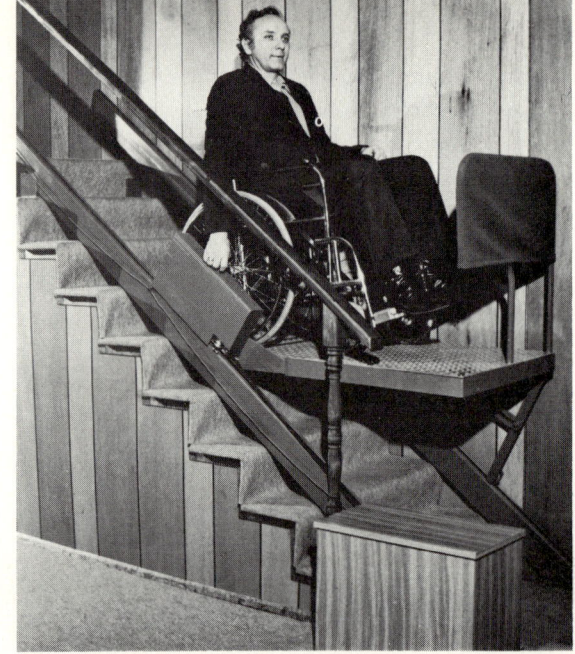

## 6.87 OUTDOOR WHEELCHAIR STAIRLIFT

Safest way for wheelchair user, or disabled not able to use steps, to go between house and ground. Just press up/down switch, lift stops when switch released. Has standard 42" lift and 60" lift height above ground. Also 72" lift. Wheel-O-Bridge also available to use from top of stairs to top position of lift. Lift platform 31" by 48" rain- and snow-proof. Lifts 350 lb. Can be operated manually.

*PRICE F* From Toce Brothers (Wheel-O-Vator 60" lift model)

## 6.88 STAIRWAY LIFT

Single seat Inclinette® with motor located in closet under stairs or in basement. Includes swivel seat with back and armrest that folds against back of car when not being used, allowing normal use of stairs. For people who can't climb stairs.

*PRICE F* From Inclinator Company of America

GETTING AROUND    125

## 6.89  STAIRLIFT
Adaptable for either side of stairs, with passenger riding sideways or facing front. Can be mounted on a straight staircase up to 17' 11" long.

**PRICE F** From Inclinator Company of America (Economy Stairlift)

## 6.90  STAIRLIFT
Can be made to adapt to almost any type of stairway. It is a complete self-contained unit resting on the stairway. Carries up to 300 lb. Travels 25' per minute. Chair folds to within $12^{5/8}$" from wall. Can be installed indoors or outdoors.

**PRICE F** From The Cheney Company (Wecolator)

## 6.91  STAIRLIFT
Butler can be installed in less than two hours on either side of stairway, and can be removed simply. Has swivel seat and armrests.

**PRICE F** From Flinchbaugh (Butler Stairclimb)

## 6.92  PORTABLE LIFT
Base adjusts from 22" to 40" width, to get through narrow doors and halls. Hydraulic lift transfers to bed, wheelchair, bath, and auto. Has various accessories.

**PRICE E** From Invacare

## 6.93 PORTABLE LIFT

Lifts user to bed, bath, wheelchair, auto. Hydraulic lift can lift 300 lb. from floor to 4' height. Fingertip control gently lowers lift. Has foot-operated adjustable base, width 22" to 40". Various accessories.

**PRICE E** From Porto Lift

## 6.94 BEACH LIFT

Two-passenger lift has luggage rack. Maximum 70' travel with 30° grade. Power unit enclosed below top landing.

**PRICE F** From Inclinator Co. of America

## 6.95 ELEVETTE

Can accommodate small wheelchair, user, and aide. Can be kept at upper landing when not in use.

**PRICE F** From Inclinator Company of America

### 6.96 PORTABLE LIFT

With help of an aide, lifts person in or out of bed, wheelchair, bath, or car. Moves easily through any door opening. Disassembles quickly without tools for transportation. Has bath adapter and other options.

**PRICE E** From Trans-Aid Corp. (Lift Aid)

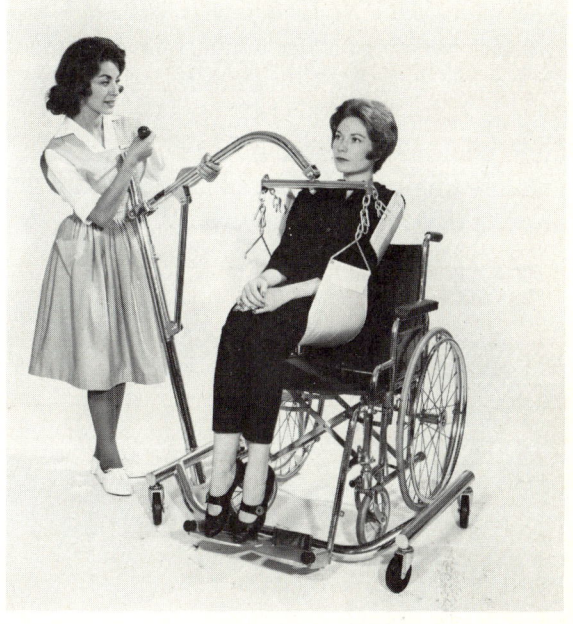

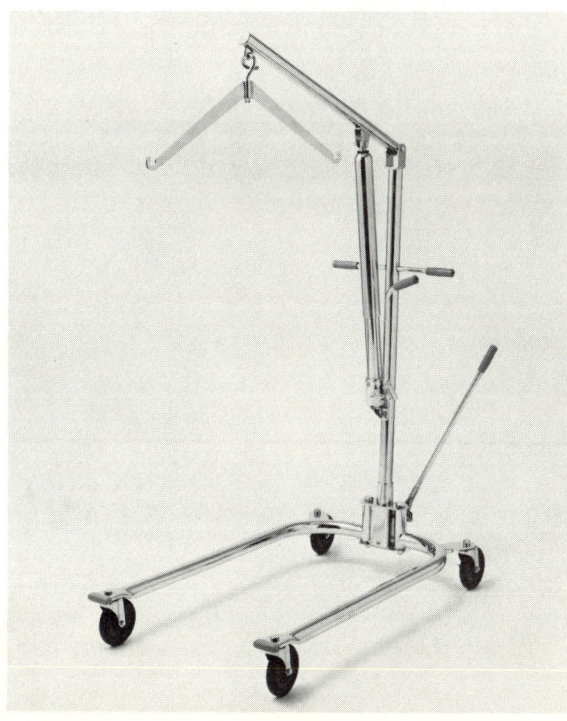

### 6.97 PORTABLE LIFT

Base and mast can be locked together or mast can be unlocked from base to enable one to transport lift in the car or store under bed. Base legs fit under low beds. Brakes on two casters at mast end of lifter. Lifts in and out of bed, wheelchair, bath, car, etc. Has various options.

**PRICE E** From Everest & Jennings / Ted Hoyar & Company

### 6.98 OUTDOOR WHEELCHAIR LIFT

Outdoor two-story lift for wheelchair. Designed for heights over 5′. Comes in raised platform heights of 8′, 10′, 12′, 14′, 16′, 18′, and 20′ (as in photo). Controlled by user with constant pressure on switch. Upper-limit switch stops lift at exact upper-level position. Lifts 750 lb.

**PRICE F** From Fred Scott & Sons (Invalift)

### 6.99 WHEELCHAIR NARROWER

Reduce-A-Width reduces wheelchair width as much as 4″. Permits user to go through narrow doorways unassisted. Self-operated. Fits most chairs.

**PRICE C** From Everest & Jennings / Preston

### 6.100 RAILING, FOLDING

Rails for getting up stairs. Permanent or fold-away. For wheelchair users or ambulatory persons needing aid in climbing steps.

**PRICE B & C** *(custom-made to order)* From Handi-Ramp (HR Custom Railing)

### 6.101 PORTABLE RAMP

Nonskid, safety-wheel guides, self-cleaning. One-man operation, folds in half. For indoor or outdoor use. Fits in trunk of auto. Size 26″ by 60″, 49 lb. Comes in other lengths—7′ and 10′.

**PRICE D** From Handi-Ramp / Cleo

### 6.102 VAN RAMP
Folding, fits all vans, one-man operation. Lightweight, safety-wheel guides, nonskid treadway. Size 26" by 84". Various other lengths available.

**PRICE E** From Handi-Ramp

### 6.103 ACCESS RAMP
Fits all vans. Three-bolt installation. Nonskid steps. Folds in half for vertical storage (wheel guides). Steps. One-man operation. 26" width, 60" length. Comes in various lengths, with or without steps.

**PRICE D** From Handi-Ramp

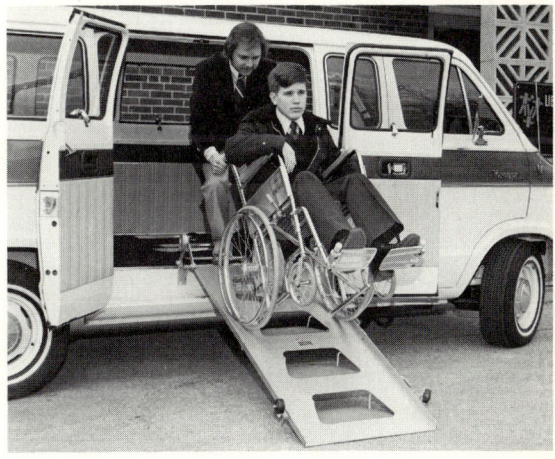

### 6.104 WHEELCHAIR RAMP

Allows electric wheelchair to go up ramp. Fits all vans. No vehicle modification necessary. Nonskid steps. Folds for vertical storage only 5" wide. One-man operation. Size 26" by 70".

**PRICE D**  From Wieland & Tanner

### 6.105 FORWARD STABILIZER FOR WHEELCHAIR

Keeps wheelchair from tilting forward. Fits most wheelchairs. Improves forward stability.

**PRICE B**  From Everest & Jennings

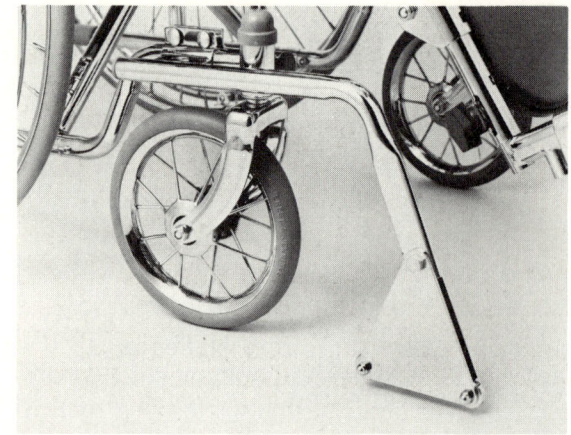

### 6.106 PORTABLE SEAT

Port-A-Seat provides a back for persons sitting for long periods of time at sporting events, picnics, on boats, etc. Has 2" padded seat and backrest. Hook secures seat to existing bench for safety. Compact and light. Made of aluminum and vinyl.

**PRICE A**  From FashionAble

### 6.107 ELEVATING SEAT

Aids user in rising from chair. Seat locks in position when weight is put on it. Raises to 45° when released. Assisto-Seat® operates by lifting levers to release seat. Seat is portable. Comes in two-spring (up to 150-lb.) and three-spring (up to 250-lb.) models.

**PRICE D**  From Maddak

## 6.108 FLIP SEAT
Holds both wheels of any wheelchair securely during transport (regardless of wheel width or tire size) and releases with flick of a wrist. Flip the seat down for additional seating. Self-contained unit with seat belt and wheelchair locks. Folded is 12" wide. Seat holds 300 lb. and has padded back and seat. 16" by 16".

   **PRICE D**  From Collins Industries

## 6.109 SAFETY BELT
Wheelchair safety belt, 2" wide. Velcro fastener.

   **PRICE A**  From Everest & Jennings

## 6.110 WHEELCHAIR RADIO
Small, lightweight, transistorized AM/FM radio clamps on any wheelchair on either side. Dials, and easy-to-read large numbers for fine tuning. 6" long by 2½" diameter.

   **PRICE B**  From Preston

## 6.111 SHOCK ABSORBERS
E-Z wheelchair shock absorbers provide smooth ride, absorb bumps, and reduce jolts to back and spine. Extend life of chair.

   **PRICE B**  From Physical Aids (comes with either 7/16" or 5/8" axle)

### 6.112 MOTORIZED WALKER

For those who need to be able to maintain a standing position and be mobile in this position with a minimum expenditure of energy. Speed 1.6 mph on level, hard surface.

**PRICE E** From Falcon (Independence)

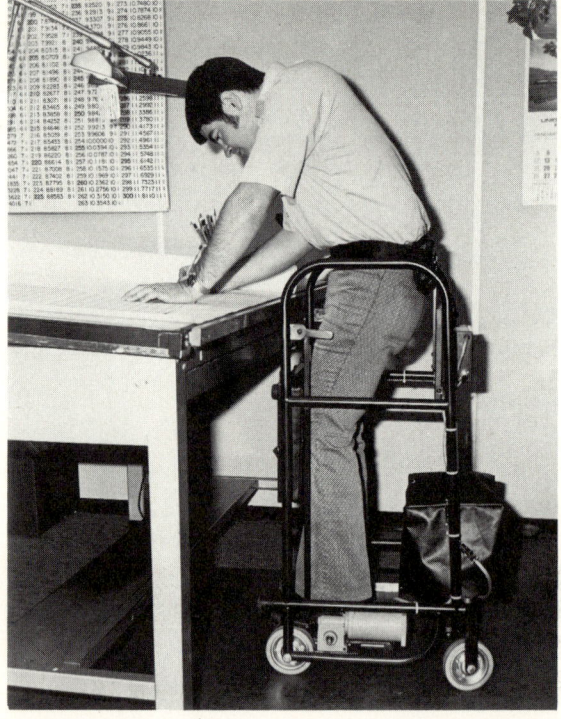

### 6.113 TRAVEL AID FOR VISUALLY IMPAIRED

The Mowat sensor is a compact, hand-held electronic travel aid. It operates by sending out a beam of ultra sound. When beam hits an object, it reflects back to sensor, causing it to vibrate silently. Rapidity of vibrations indicates distance from object. Mowat is designed to complement use of long cane or guide dog. Its use simplifies location of landmarks, doorways, mailboxes, marks a path through congested area, locates items dropped on floor. Simplicity of use of device enables all ages to benefit by it.

**PRICE E** From Telesensory Systems

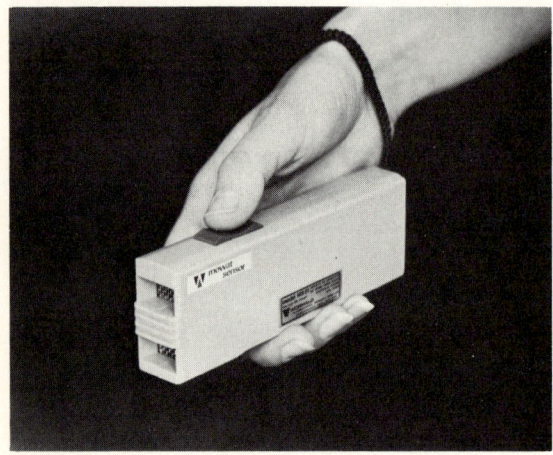

### 6.114 THREE-WHEELED UTILITY VEHICLE

Holds two adults. Has full front and rear suspension. Options available. Available in various horsepowers. Travels on sand, snow, or trails.

**PRICE E** From Carl Heald ("Super Trike")

### 6.115 TRANSFER BOARD FOR WHEELCHAIR

Chair-holder transfer board with telescoping rod is held secure, when rod is inserted into receiver for detachable arm on a wheelchair. 16" long or choice of other sizes. Made of high-gloss birch plywood.

**PRICE B** From MED (similar, Therafin)

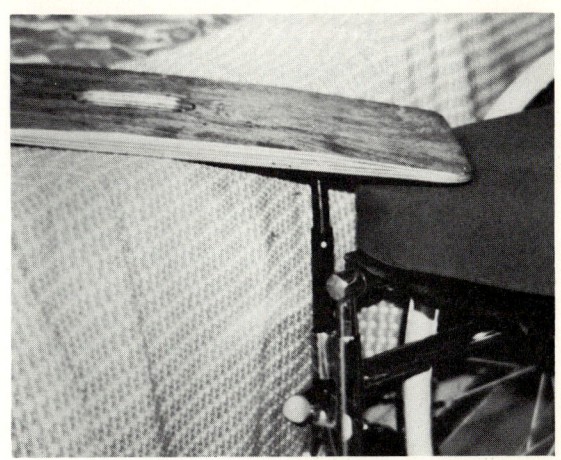

### 6.116 PLASTIC TRANSFER BOARD

For transferring from wheelchair to chair, car, bed, or toilet. Made of smooth plastic. Won't chip, crack, or warp. 8" by 27".

**PRICE B** From Cleo (similar, G. E. Miller; PCP)

### 6.117 THERAPY STROLLER

Compact folding umbrella stroller with therapeutic adaptations and firm seat and back support. Adjustable for child growth. Adjustable seat depth. Weight 12 lb.

**PRICE B** From Convaid

### 6.118 FOLDING TRANSFER BOARD

For more convenient portability when used in car or carried in wheelchair. Hinged in center, folds in half when not in use. 29″ long (open), 14½″ long (closed). Weight 62 oz.

**PRICE B** From Therafin

### 6.119 NOTCHED TRANSFER BOARD

With hand holds and stability notches for extra security. Hooking notches attach to wheelchairs with nonremovable armrests. 30″ long, 8″ wide, 9/16″ thick, weight 50 oz. High-gloss birch plywood.

**PRICE B** From Therafin

### 6.120 TRANSFER BOARD, WOODEN

Transfers user from wheelchair to bed, chair, toilet, car, etc. Highly sanded for smooth sliding surface. Tapered at both ends to make transferring easier.

**PRICE A** From Hausman

### 6.121 ANTI-TIP ATTACHMENT, WHEELCHAIR

Prevents wheelchair from tipping backward. Fits most wheelchairs. Detachable.

**PRICE B (for 2)** From Everest & Jennings

## 6.122 LAPBOARD, WHEELCHAIR

Fits any adult wheelchair. Formica top with friction attachment so lapboard will hold firm. 3/8" thick. Useful for reading, writing, eating, etc.

**PRICE B** From Cleo

## 6.123 ANTI-THEFT DEVICE, WHEELCHAIR

Prevents wheelchair from being folded and carried away when not in use.

**PRICE A** From Everest & Jennings

## 6.124 LAPBOARD, WHEELCHAIR

Plastic tray with rim, and cut-out for body. For most wheelchairs up to 20" wide. Useful for reading, writing, eating, recreation games, etc. For full-length wheelchair arms. Also available for desk-length arms.

**PRICE B** From Everest & Jennings (Ajusto Tray) (similar, MED adult or child width; similar, Cleo; similar, Raymo; similar, Hausman)

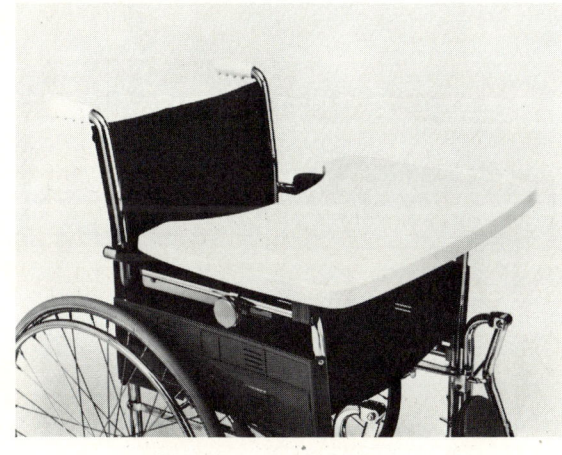

## 6.125 TRANSPARENT LAPBOARD

Clear, strong, transparent plastic panel 3/8" thick, with front and side rim. Contoured for the body. Held on to wheelchair arms by Velcro straps. Size 24" by 21 5/8". Good for performing many daily activities: reading, writing, eating, playing games. Has unobstructed view of feet and obstacles.

**PRICE C** From Maddak (similar, Invacare; Cleo)

### 6.126 TRAPEZE BAR

Has a floor base. Helps user pull up to standing position or let down to sitting position, on chair or bed. Adjusts to height of 64″. Made of chrome-plated square tubular steel. 30″ wide base.

**PRICE D** From Sears

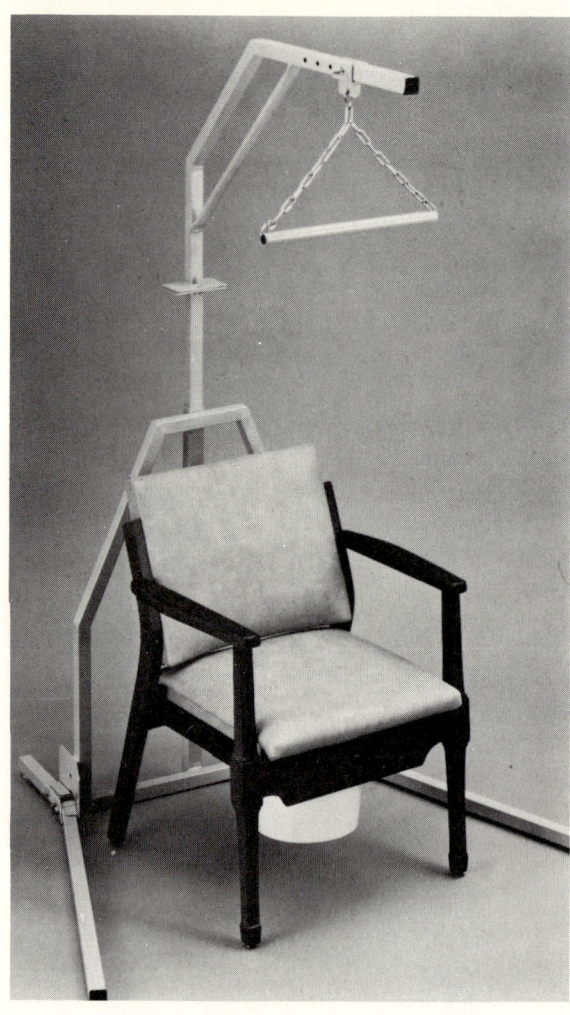

### 6.127 MOBILITY AID

Aids in walking, transporting food, carrying necessary items. Needs use of only one hand leaving the other free to put food, drinks, etc., on tray. Has stabilizer on base for better support of user. Has detachable tray, cup holder and basket. Use at home or shopping. Rolls smoothly on nonmarking rubber wheels.

**PRICE D** From Anik (Personal Mobility Aid)

### 6.128 WHEELED WALKER

User never has to raise unit to walk. Rollator has adjustable height. Helps those with difficulty in walking. Width 23½", height 29" to 34¾", adult model. Available in three smaller sizes.

**PRICE C** From Everest & Jennings / PCP

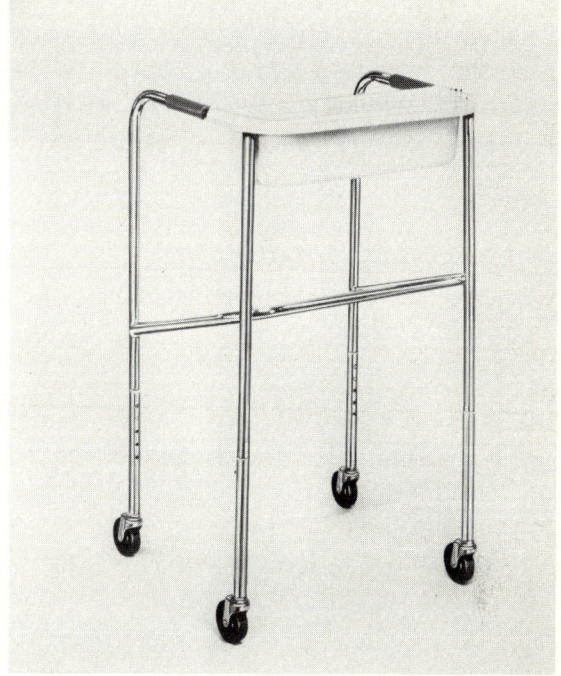

### 6.129 FOLDING SEAT WALKER

This folding wheeled walker assists those who need safe support in walking. Has seat which swings open for entering. Seat may be used from either inside or from end to sit at table. Folds to 6" width. Adjusts in height 30" to 39". Width 20½", length 34½". Seat height 18" to 23". Weight 31 lb.

**PRICE D** From Professional Convalescent Products

### 6.130 ROLLING WALKER AND CADDY

Rolling aid for use in narrow halls and bathrooms. Lightweight. High front cross-brace straddles toilets. Height adjusts 32" to 36" in 1" increments. Removable tray.

**PRICE C** From Everest & Jennings

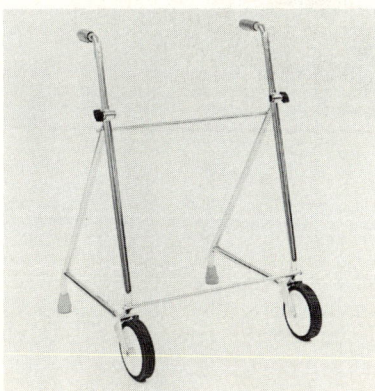

## 6.131  ROLLING WALKER

Dual-wheeled folding walker. No lifting when using. Dual wheels have "roll and glide" action. Auto-stop engages when user applies weight. Folds for transporting to 4" wide. Adjusts height 32" to 36". Width 22½". Small size available.

**PRICE C** From Lumex (also Cleo)

## 6.132  ONE-HAND WALKER

Center handle can be moved for right- or left-hand use. Walker balanced at center handle. Wide nontip base—11 height adjustment positions—27" to 37". Width 24", depth 20".

**PRICE C** From EDCO/Pasco (similar, Cleo)

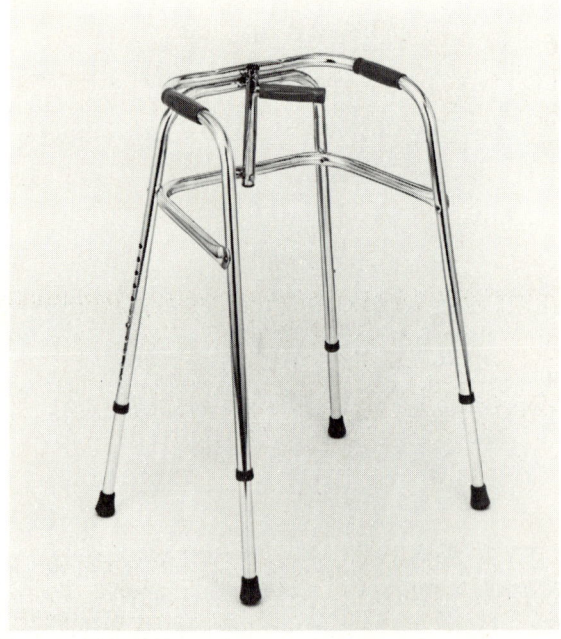

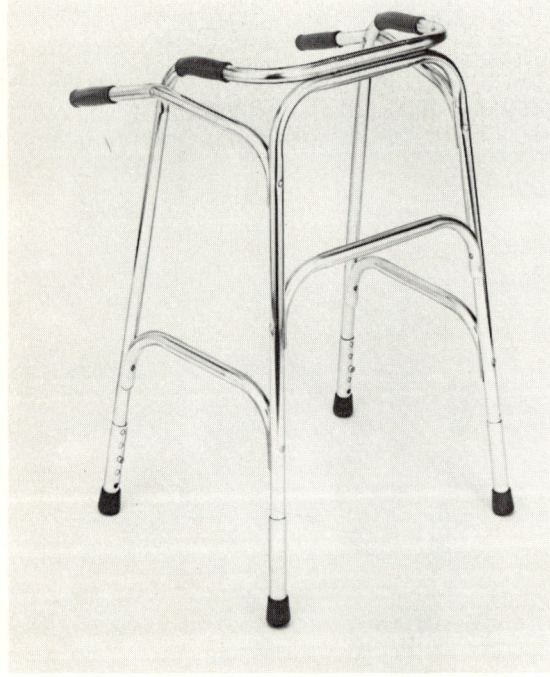

## 6.133  STAIR WALKER

Supports user's weight and maintains balance under all conditions without assistance. Height adjusts 33" to 37". When user bears down on handgrips, body weight is automatically balanced for stability. Handgrips in front to climb stairs, crossbars in rear of user. Handgrips in front to descend stairs, crossbars in front of user.

**PRICE C** From EDCO/Pasco (also Preston)

### 6.134 FOLDING WALKER

Adjustable height. Folds for easy travel or storage. Palm-pusher release (for limited finger use) to fold. Angled front legs eliminate side wobbling. Height adjusts 31" to 38" in 1" increments. Bar location allows walker use over toilet. Folds to 3¾" wide. Width 24", depth 19", weight 5¾ lb.

**PRICE B** From EDCO/Pasco (similar, Comfort-Able Aids; Prof. Conv. Prod.; Sears)

### 6.135 ADJUSTABLE SEAT WALKER

Lightweight, requires little effort for movement. Has seat of polyester that folds down with one hand. Walker height adjusts from 31" to 36". Weight 5½ lb.

**PRICE C** From Winfield

### 6.136 RUNABOUT WHEELCHAIR

Acts as both wheelchair and car seat with user remaining in chair. Also use as stroller. Rear wheels retract. Height 36". Seat 12" wide by 13" deep. Width 16". Optional attachments.

**PRICE D** From Stainless Medical Products (similar, Ortho-Kinetics Travel Chair)

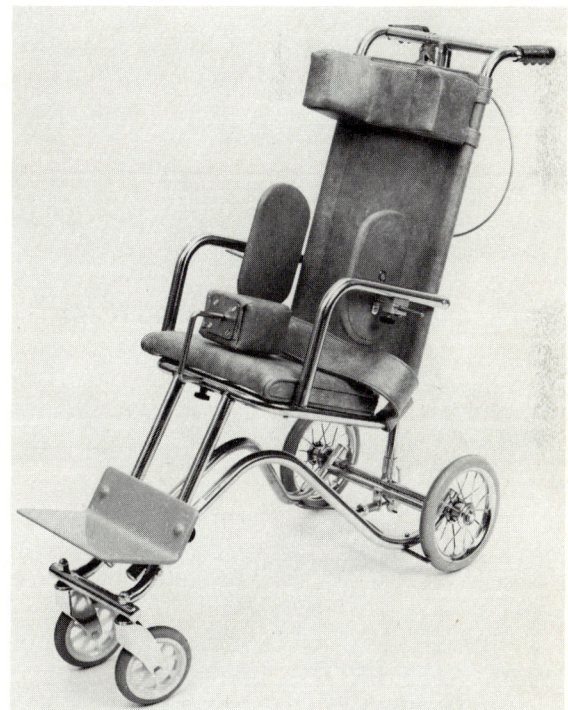

### 6.137 WHEELCHAIR

Easy Rider Mark II has innerspring and foam upholstery on seat, back, and arms. The extendable, adjustable footrest is upholstered the same way. Back adjusts to semi-reclining. Arms swing up on either side. Cut-out tray table and self-storing leg rest are options at additional cost.

**PRICE E** From EDCO/Pasco

### 6.138 RECLINING BACK, RETRACTABLE ARM WHEELCHAIR

Back adjusts to infinite positions from vertical to horizontal. Automatic wheelbase extension assures balance when back is lowered. Accessibility to hand rims when back is upright. Three-position retractable arms give support to user. Aide-operated brakes give added safety on sloping ground.

**PRICE E** From Invacare (similar, Preston)

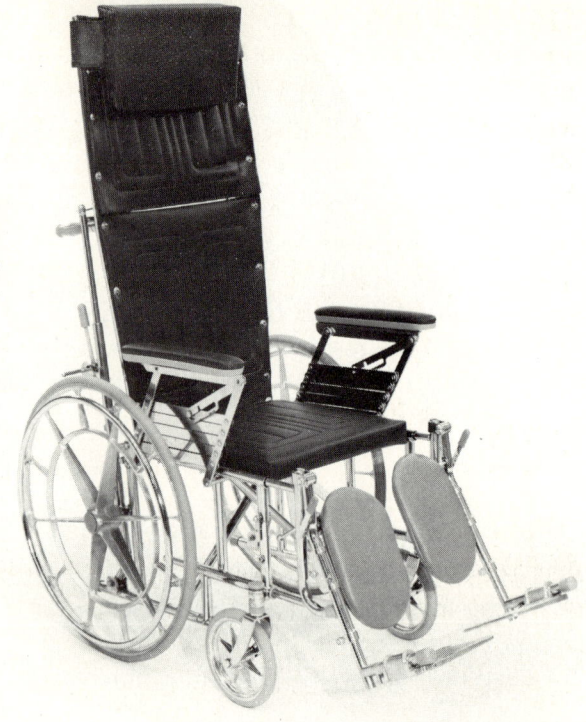

### 6.139 WHEELCHAIR, LIGHTWEIGHT

Folding, adult, lightweight wheelchair, with removable legs, nondetachable arms. Weight 27½ lb.

**PRICE E** From Everest & Jennings

### 6.140 SELF-PROPELLING WHEELCHAIR, PORTABLE

Freedomchair® folds to 20" in height. Ideal for traveling. Carrying case available. Various sizes available. Weight 36 lb. Armrests reverse so as to enable them to be used for support of tray or writing board. Fits into trunk of smallest car. Footrests adjust, fold and detach.

**PRICE D** From Freedomchair

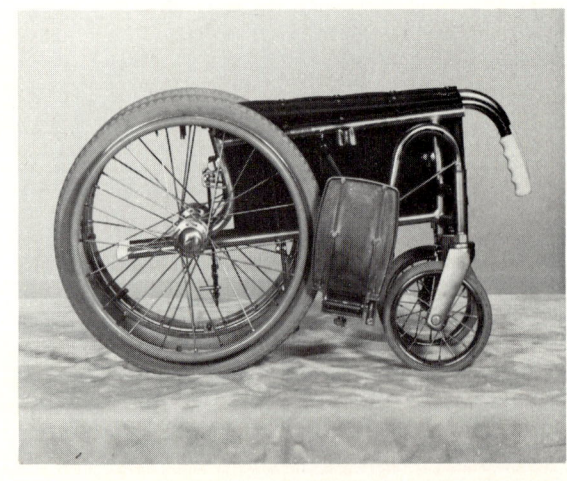

## 6.141 SYMBOL OF ACCESS

International symbol of access. Lets disabled know area displaying symbol is barrier-free. Available 4" by 4", 6" by 6", 9" by 9", 12" by 12", 24" by 24"—other types of symbols available (ramp, telephone, etc.).

**PRICE A** (for all but 24" by 24"), **B** (24" by 24") From Processed Signs & Display Company (Pict-O-Signs)

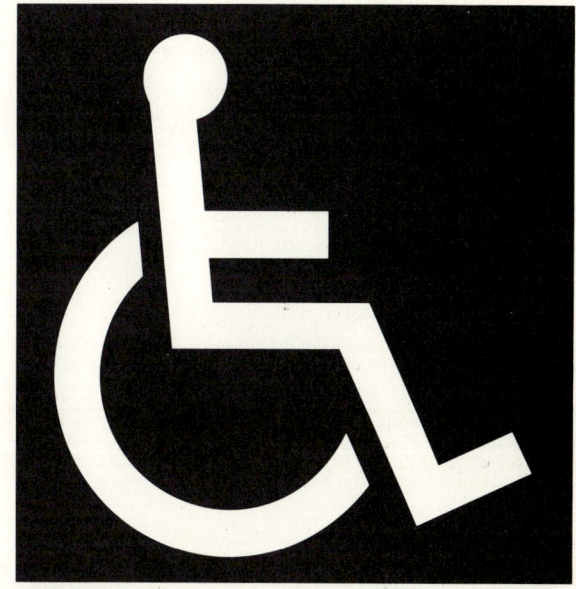

## 6.142 PARKING SYMBOL

Symbol of parking facility for physically disabled. Available in various sizes. Other types of symbol-identifying signs available (elevator, telephone, etc.).

**PRICE A** (all sizes but 24" by 24"), **B** (24" by 24") From Processed Signs & Display Co. (Pict-O-Signs)

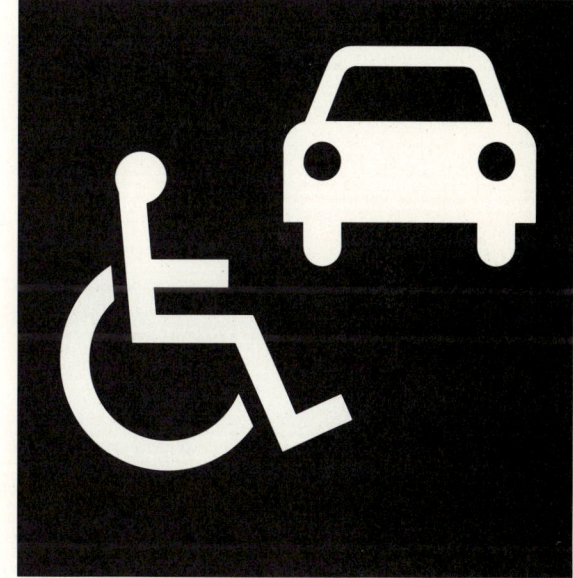

## 6.143 ACCESS CLEARANCE SIGN

For disabled driver to display in his car when parked. Various other graphic signs, for use to help disabled, are available. Embossed steel up to 18" by 24". Larger signs available.

**PRICE A** From Seton Name Plate Corp. (Graphic Symbol Signs for Disabled)

### 6.144 BUILDING SYMBOL SIGNS

Building signs with each message presented in three forms—International pictorial symbol, raised large print, and Braille. Available in plastic or aluminum. Various other signs available similar to the three shown.

**PRICE A** *(each)* From Arts Associates

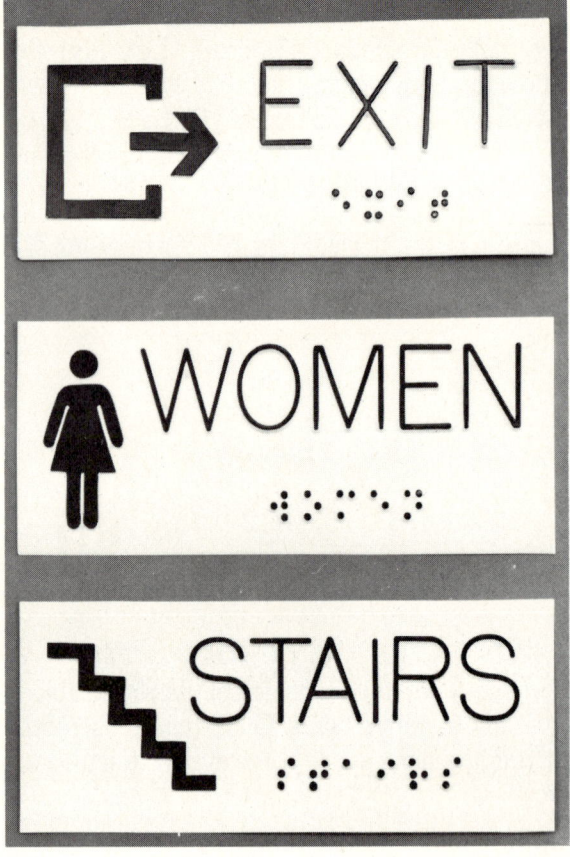

### 6.145 ELEVATOR TAGS

Braille and raised large-print tags that attach to elevator control panels and landing-door frames to allow visually impaired to select a floor and determine which floor they are on. Heat-sensitive glue forms molecular bond to resist vandalism.

**PRICE A** From Arts Associates

# Household Activities ⑦

### 7.1 MINI BUCKET
Has pour-spout, recessed handgrips and 6¾-quart capacity. Calibrations in U.S. and metric. Convenient to use because of small size.

**PRICE A** From Rubbermaid (also at hardware stores)

### 7.2 BROOM AND MOP HOLDER
Offers storage center for floor cleaning items. Vinyl-coated retainer hooks hold brooms and mops. Dustpan fits into specially designed holds. 13½" wide, 2¾" deep by 10" high.

**PRICE A** From Rubbermaid (also at hardware stores)

## 7.3 BAG AND WRAP ORGANIZER

Stores plastic wrap, foil, and bags. Attaches with screws to walls or inside cabinet doors. 11" wide by 5" deep by 14" high. Keeps necessary kitchen items in one convenient area.

**PRICE A** From Rubbermaid (also at hardware stores)

## 7.4 BAG HOLDER

Bag holder stores grocery bags. Size 11" wide by 13" high. Keeps bags conveniently in one area.

**PRICE A** From Rubbermaid (also at hardware stores)

## 7.5 STORAGE TURNTABLE

Helps keep items within easy reach inside cabinet interiors. 19" by 21". Made of durable plastic.

**PRICE A** From Rubbermaid

## 7.6 BROOM—ADJUSTABLE

Hoky Broom® weighs just over 1 lb. Handle adjusts from 30" to 49" long. All parts replaceable. Brush is 10% to 30% wider than old-type brooms. Broom head swivels 180°. Bristles won't scratch finish.

**PRICE A** From Hukuba-Cowdery (also at hardware stores)

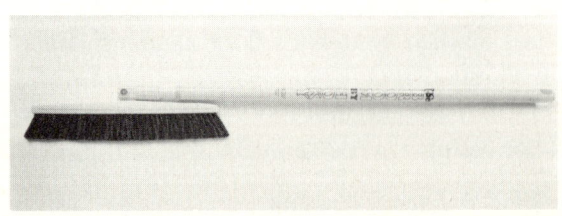

## 7.7 CLEAN-UP CADDY

Mounts inside standard-size cabinet doors. Holds cleaning supplies out of sight, but within easy reach. Attaches with screws. 11" wide by 5 1/2" deep by 14 3/4" high.

**PRICE A** From Rubbermaid (also at hardware stores)

## 7.8 CLIPIT/PAPERCUTTER

Clips coupons, articles, recipes, etc. Faster, safer, neater than scissors.

**PRICE A** From Ozburn-Janesville

### 7.9 CARPET SWEEPER, LIGHTWEIGHT
Weighs just 2½ lb. Three-section telescoping handle. No downward pressure needed. Low profile makes for easy cleaning under furniture. Simple to empty. Use on carpet or floor.

**PRICE B** From Hukuba-Cowdery (also at hardware stores)

### 7.10 CARRY CADDY
A handy carry-all for garden tools and supplies or household items. Has three compartments and easy-grip carrying handle. 15½" long by 10" wide by 5¼" high.

**PRICE A** From Rubbermaid (also at hardware stores)

### 7.11 CARPET SWEEPER, LIGHTWEIGHT
Weighs under 3 lb., is 9" wide and works on carpet or floor. Has natural hog-bristle brush. Can be hung up to stand no more than 2" away from a wall.

**PRICE B** From Dorsay (Carpet Cat)

### 7.12 ULTRASONIC CLEANER
It ultrasonically cleans-in-seconds—jewelry, silver, cutlery, eyeglasses, dentures, combs, golf balls, etc. Simple and safe. Removes tarnish, corrosion, oil, grease, rust, paint, soap, wax, dirt, etc., from any object that can be immersed in a liquid. Comes with beaker, 5⅝" scoop, chemicals.

**PRICE C** From Chris-Craft (Clean n' Brite)

### 7.13 SAFETY FAN
Rubber blades. 6" high palm size. Has two speeds. Safe for children. Safety flex blades won't cut fingers. Quiet and cool.

**PRICE B** From Camping World

### 7.14 HEATER AND FAN
Compact. Delivers heat and air flow greater than that of heaters twice its size. Size 10½" by 8½". Safety shut-off guards against accidental overheating. Push-button control. Hot, warm, and fan settings. Shock- and fire-resistant case.

**PRICE B** From Camping World

HOUSEHOLD ACTIVITIES   **147**

### 7.15 EXPANDING DRAWER DIVIDERS
Subdivides any drawer to organize cutlery, gadgets, cosmetics, medicines, jewelry, clothing, etc. Dividers expand from 12 3/8" to 23 1/2" in length. They fit into end tracks secured by self-adhering tape. Easily removed for cleaning or rearranging.

*PRICE A (each)* From Rubbermaid (2 1/2" high and 4 1/2" high) (or at hardware stores)

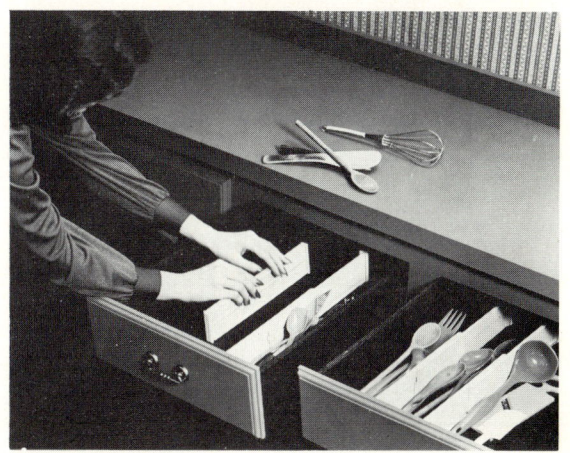

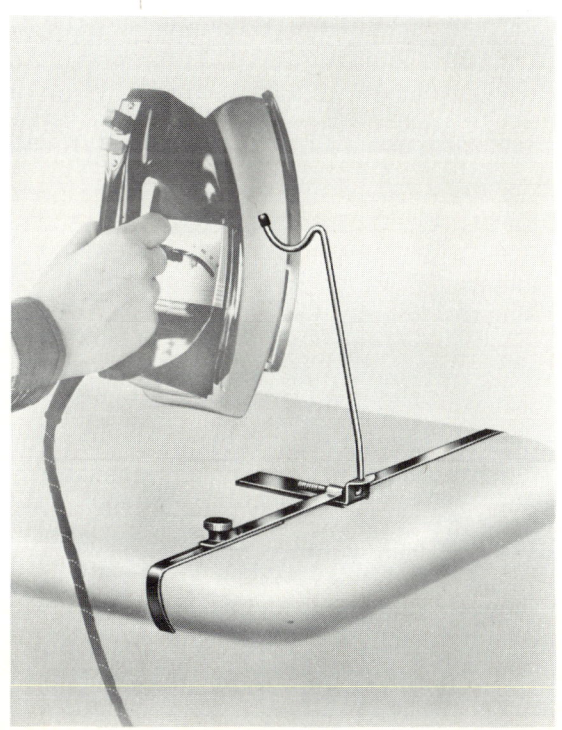

### 7.16 IRON HOLDER
Can't-Fall Iron Holder minimizes ironing board accidents; prevents fires, injuries, breakages and burns. Can't fall on your board. Permanently attaches to any conventional ironing board. No screws necessary. Adjustable, folds for storage. Latches securely into upright position.

*PRICE A* From Zim Manufacturing

### 7.17 SPACEMAKER DRAWERS

Create additional storage space under cabinets. Attach to base of wall cabinet with two fasteners. Complete with necessary hardware. Size 15" wide by 12" deep. Utility drawer is 4" high. Bread drawer is 5½" high.

**PRICE A** From Rubbermaid

### 7.18 INSTANT DRAWER ORGANIZERS

Makes it easy to find odds and ends in various-size compartments. Comes with interlocking edges in four sizes, 9" by 3", 9" by 6", 15" by 3", 15" by 6".

**PRICE A** From Rubbermaid (also at hardware stores)

### 7.19 PLASTIC IRON, LIGHTWEIGHT

Steamstress II weighs less than 1 lb. It requires no pressure to press garment. Simple to use, has no temperature selection or long waiting period to heat up or cool down. Works on any fabric with no special care. Uses one-half energy of conventional iron. Shuts off automatically when water is used up. Uses tap water.

**PRICE B** From Osrow Products

## 7.20 NO-STOOP DUSTPAN AND BROOM

Ends bending. Easy, one-hand use. Folds up to trap dust on way to waste can. Dustpan, black enamel on metal. 26" handle. Broom 30".

**PRICE A (both)** From FashionAble (also at hardware stores)

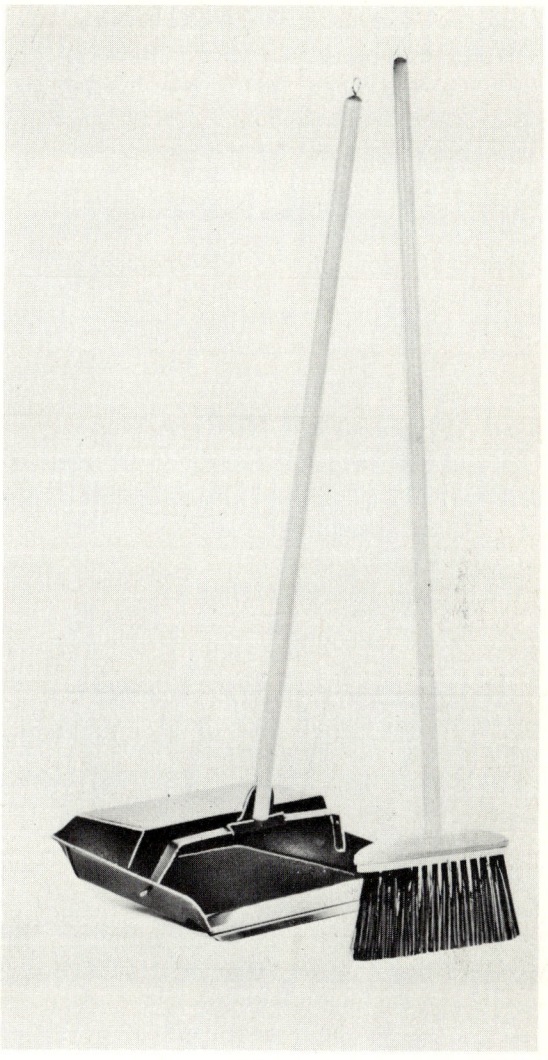

## 7.21 FOLDING DUSTPAN

Folds in center. Prevents spilling dirt when carrying to waste basket. Can fold at right angles to get into tight places. One-piece polypropylene. Will not break.

**PRICE A** From Foley (also at hardware stores)

## 7.22 SPECIAL LAUNDRY KNOBS

Specially designed knobs for washers and dryers by Maytag Company have raised dots at various settings. For visually impaired.

**PRICE FREE** From Maytag Company (Laundry Knob—Special)

### 7.23 LARGE-LETTER LABLER

For visually impaired. Makes letters 1/2" high on 3/4"-wide tape. Can be read by feel also. Has carrying case and two rolls of vinyl tape and two of magnetic tape.

**PRICE D** From American Foundation for Blind

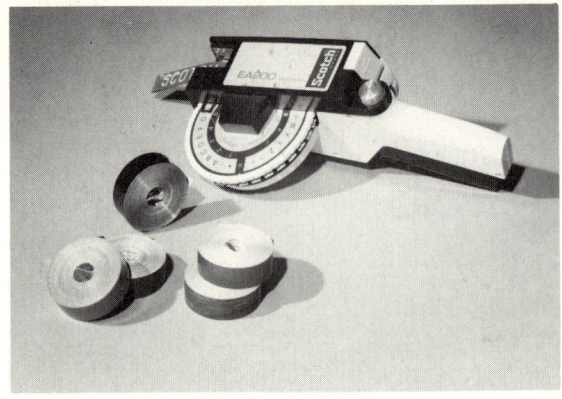

### 7.24 SPECIAL LAUNDRY KNOB

Made of durable rubber, large 4-pronged knob fits over standard control dial on most Maytag Automatic Washers and Dryers manufactured since early 1970's. Makes dial turning easy for those with limited hand use.

**PRICE A** From Maytag Company (Special Laundry Knob)

### 7.25 SPECIAL LAUNDRY CONTROLS

Braille control panels for laundry equipment available on some models.

**PRICE FREE** From General Electric Local Service Centers (give model and serial number of appliance)

### 7.26 BENDING MOP

Long-handled dust mop bends at the flip of a trigger. Cleans under almost anything. Eliminates need for user to bend. Can also be used rigid like regular mop.

**PRICE A** From Handibend Manufacturing (Handibend Mop)

### 7.27 EXTENSION MOP

Old fashioned ostrich-plume feather duster. Extends from $4^{1}/_{2}'$ to over 7'. Aids in reaching high areas.

**PRICE B** From Hammacher Schlemmer; (similar, Brookstone)

## 7.28 EASY-WRING MOP

Mop without bending. Easy-to-pull control lever is 20" above floor. Rollers do wringing. Hand never touches mop or water. 47" length. Head of sponge rubber 8½" wide.

**PRICE B**  From FashionAble

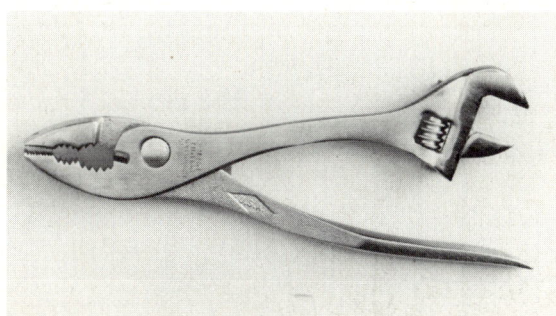

## 7.29 FOUR-IN-ONE TOOL

Versatile plier, adjustable wrench, screwdriver, and slotted wire cutter. Handyboy® plier of special alloy steel is 7¾" long, weighs 9 oz. Eliminates need for several tools.

**PRICE A**  From L. L. Bean

## 7.30 DINNERWARE RACK

Space-saving rack makes practical use of cabinet space. Organizes complete service for eight. Cup rack slides out for easy access.

**PRICE A**  From Rubbermaid (also at hardware stores)

### 7.31 TURNTABLE RACK
Fits into kitchen cabinets to swing items into easy reach. Stores cups and plates compactly. Size $9^{1}/_{2}''$ diameter by $6^{1}/_{4}''$ high.

**PRICE A** From Rubbermaid (also at hardware stores)

### 7.32 STAPLER
Attaches paper together without staples. No chance of injury from metal staples. Welds up to six sheets of bond paper or up to ten sheets of onionskin. Weld easily removed with stroke of thumbnail. Free repair.

**PRICE B** From Paper Welder (also at office supply stores)

### 7.33 STACKING BINS
Storage is simplified with these bins which make access to contents easy. Size 16'' by 8'' by $7^{1}/_{4}''$.

**PRICE A** From Rubbermaid (also at hardware stores)

### 7.34 ELECTRIC SCISSORS
Can't cut fingers. Two speeds.

**PRICE A** From Hamilton Beach

## 7.35 PISTOL-GRIP TOOL KIT

Pistol-grip ratchet device with interchangeable tools which can be operated with one hand. Tools can be tightened in chuck with one finger. Three settings—forward, center, reverse. Includes four metric socket wrenches, two flat screwdrivers, two Phillips-type screwdrivers, four hex wrenches. Comes with vinyl pouch.

**PRICE B** From Maddak (also at hardware stores)

## 7.36 SINGLE TURNTABLE

Easy way to bring spices, small jars, and other items into quick reach. Size $10^{1}/_{2}''$ diameter. Also comes in twin turntable model. Same diameter.

**PRICE A** From Rubbermaid

## 7.37 TELEPHONE CENTER

Bill collector, telephone center, and household file (left to right). Help keep letters, notes and reminders at finger-tip reach. Telephone center gathers telephone, directory, and note pad into one location with four wells for pencils and pens and recessed area for paper clips, etc. Size $12^{1}/_{2}''$ by $10^{1}/_{2}''$ by $5''$ high.

**PRICE A (each)** From Rubbermaid

### 7.38  PORTABLE VACUUM
Dyna Clean Multi-Vac™. Three vacuums in one. Upright vac for floors and carpets; tank vac for upholstery, drapes, and car; hand vac for stairs, workshop, camper or use from wheelchair.

**PRICE B**  From Bissell

### 7.39  PORTABLE VACUUM
Hoover Portapower™ cleaner. Compact yet powerful cleaner that does many different cleaning jobs well. Comes with complete set of attachments. Has re-usable, easy-to-empty dust bag. Weight 9 lb. Size 12" long, 11" high, 5" wide. Carrying handle. Can also be towed across floor by the hose.

**PRICE C**  From The Hoover Company / Camping World

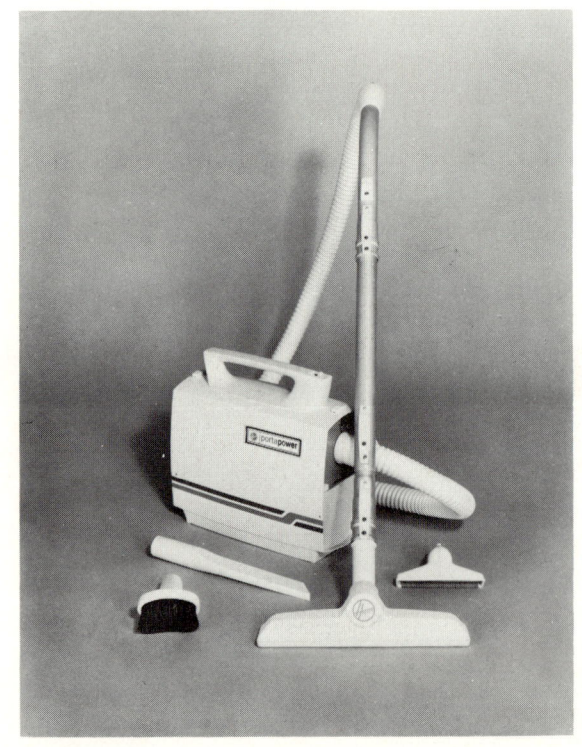

### 7.40  YARDSTICK, LEFT-HAND
Numbers begin at right to make measuring an easy task for left-handers. Reinforced metal ends.

**PRICE A**  From The Left Hand

### 7.41  ADDRESS BOOK, LEFT-HAND
An index collated in a looseleaf binder especially for left-handed users.

**PRICE A**  From The Left Hand

HOUSEHOLD ACTIVITIES 155

### 7.42 MICROMETER, LEFT-HAND
This instrument has been designed in reverse for left-handed use. Precise measuring can be done accurately.

**PRICE C** From The Left Hand

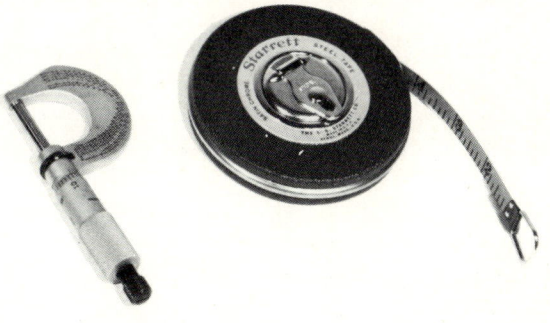

### 7.43 MEASURING TAPE, LEFT-HAND
50′ tape of tempered steel pulls out to the right so numbers read from right to left. Winds with ease, counterclockwise. Vinyl-covered case.

**PRICE B** From The Left Hand

# 8
# Access at Home and Elsewhere

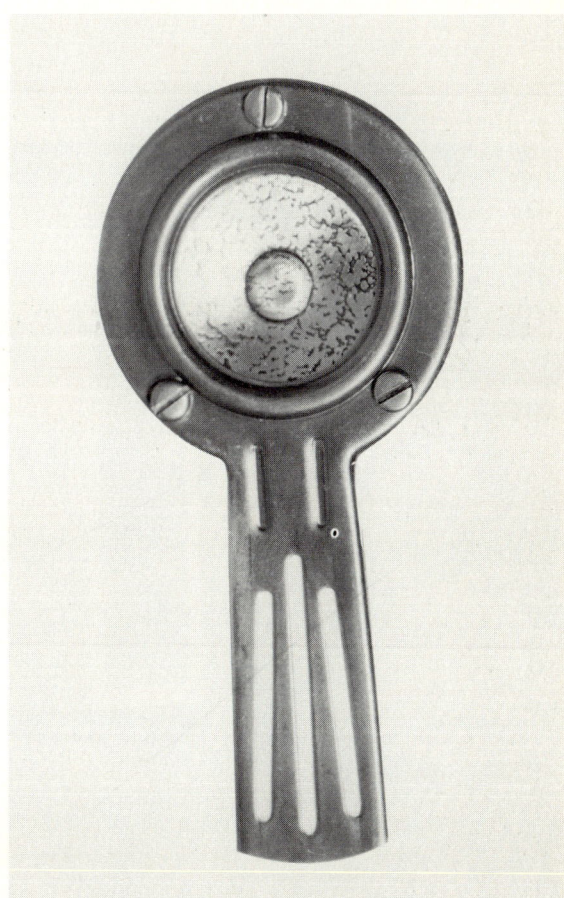

## 8.1 DOOR-KNOB AID
A handle attachment for round door knobs helps open doors with a light touch of the hand. Ideal for disabled with limited motion. Also attaches to barrel or pear-shaped knobs. Fits knobs up to 2¾" in diameter.

**PRICE A** From Dow Knob (Dow Knob®)

## 8.2 DOOR-KNOB HELPER

Rubber lever with round end that fits over door knob. Can be pushed down with arm, elbow, etc., to open door. Cut-out in center allows keyhole to be accessible.

**PRICE A** From FashionAble

## 8.3 DOOR OPENER, AUTOMATIC

Converts existing doors to powered operation. Can be used in homes, schools, nursing homes—virtually anywhere that door automation is required. Operates by a variety of sensors such as wall-mounted switches, floor mat switches, and radio control. Installation requires no special equipment or service personnel.

**PRICE E** From Power Access

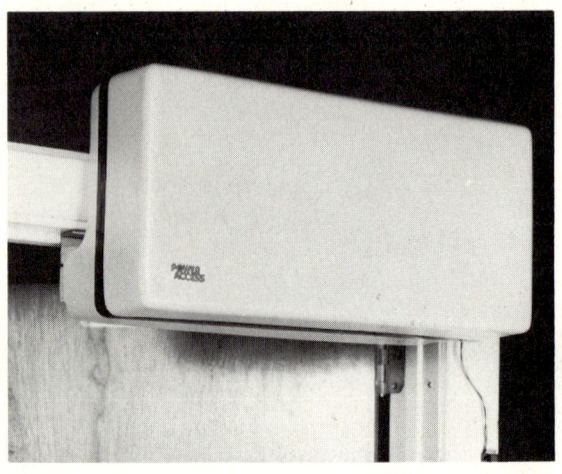

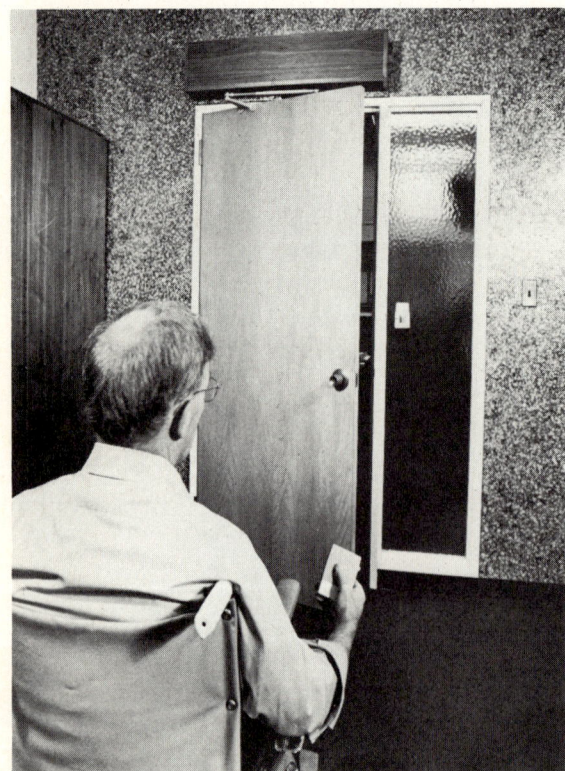

## 8.4 DOOR OPERATOR, AUTOMATIC

For bedroom and other interior doors. A variety of controls can be used. Push plates activated by foot, hand, elbow, or head. Portable wireless radio controls. Used on doors up to 42" wide and 150 lb. weight. Can be mounted on either side of door.

**PRICE E** From The Stanley Works (Silent Swing™)

## 8.5 DOOR OPENER, SLIDING

For internal sliding doors. Specially designed for installation in homes of disabled.

**PRICE E** From Besam (EUPJ)

## 8.6 ELEVATOR, REMOTE-CONTROL

Person holding control can keep elevator door open until he is inside elevator cab. Control also is able to bring elevator to pre-selected floor. Elevator also always stops at ground floor.

**PRICE D** From Elevator Safety Products (Elevator Door Remote Control)

## 8.7 KEY HOLDER

For four keys. Made of three bars of stiff plastic and brass screws. Holder gives extra leverage in turning key in lock. Size 3" by 1" by ⅝".

**PRICE A** From Maddak

## 8.8 DOOR LOCK, PUSH-BUTTON COMBINATION

No key necessary. Burglar-proof (no key hole to pick). Combination can be changed by user. Easy to install above any existing lock or knob on wood or metal doors. To open, press appropriate buttons.

**PRICE C** From Simplex Security Systems (200 series—1¾" to 2⅛" thick door)

## 8.9 SWING-CLEAR HINGES

Gives up to 2" more clear opening in doorways. Allows doors to swing flat against walls. Available in residential, commercial, and institutional sizes and types.

**PRICE B** From Stanley Works / MED

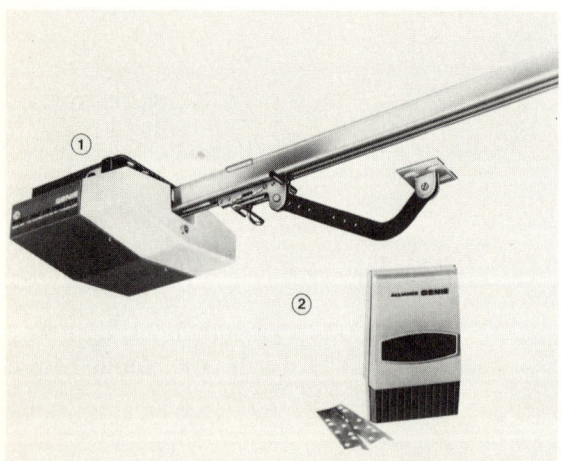

## 8.10 GARAGE DOOR OPENER, AUTOMATIC

Figure 1—Deluxe Automatic Garage Door Opener and Figure 2—Digital Control. For single and double, sectional, or one-piece residential garage doors up to 7'6" high. Has instant reverse system and emergency quick-release chain. Has radio control plus wall-mounted push button to open door from inside house or garage.

**PRICE E** From Alliance Manufacturing Company

## 8.11 SECURITY LOCK, KEYLESS

Fits most standard door jambs. Comes in surface-mount model. Can also be installed on door and wall surfaces. When correct button combination is punched, latch opens for three seconds then automatically relocks. Exit button makes opening door from inside easy and quick. Locks automatically as door closes.

**PRICE D** From ESP Systems Development, Inc. (Comp-U-Lock)

## 8.12 PLUG OUTLET

Four grounded outlets. Use TV, toaster, iron, and coffee maker at the same time. Use any four electrical appliances, lights, etc., at same time.

**PRICE B** From Girard (also at hardware stores)

## 8.13 REACHING TONGS

Scissors-action, nonslip ends, 27″ long. Extends user's reach to shelves, tables, floors. Magnetic tip picks up pins, clips, etc. Made of 5-ply birch. Eliminates bending or reaching for light items.

**PRICE A** From Better Sleep (E-Z Reach) / FashionAble

## 8.14 REACHER

Grab-All extension arm gets items from floor without stooping or from shelf that is too high for you to reach. Has magnet on tip. Double-tong foolproof grip balanced to lift 5 lb. easily. 30″ long.

**PRICE A** From Cleo

### 8.15 REACHER
Extends reach of physically disabled, including the bedridden or those in wheelchairs. Also for elderly. Weighs 9 oz., is 2½' long. Can pick up paper cup without crushing it. Pistol grip, soft rubber grippers on the end.

**PRICE A** From Physical Aids Marketing (E-Z Reacher™)

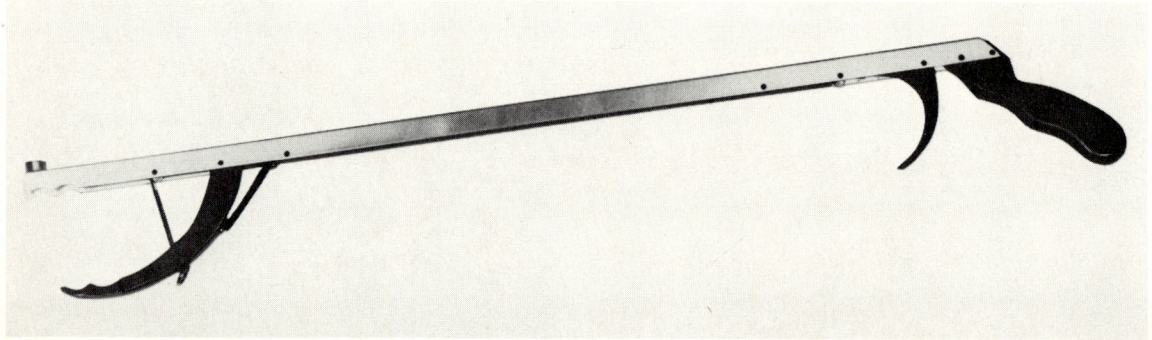

### 8.16 REACHER
26½" long. Weight 6 oz. Made of aluminum with trigger and jaw made of plastic. Light spring keeps jaw open. Squeeze trigger and jaws close with tight grip on even smallest items. Pressure must be maintained to continue grip. Magnet on end to pick up small steel items. Extends user's reach, eliminates bending for light items.

**PRICE B** From Maddak / Cleo / Everest & Jennings

### 8.17 REACHER
Top shelf Reacher™. 21" long. Has super gripping fingers. It fits and holds any size object. Extends reach, eliminates bending for light items.

**PRICE A** From G. T. Water Products, Inc.

### 8.18 REACHER, FOLDING
22" long. Weight 6 oz. Folds to a length of 12½" to be carried in pocket or bag. Made of aluminum with trigger and jaw made of plastic. Light spring keeps jaw open. Squeeze trigger and jaws close. Must maintain pressure to hold jaws closed. Can pick up even smallest objects. Magnet on end to pick up small steel items.

**PRICE B** From Maddak

## 8.19 RAIL STOOL

Offers rail to hold on to for steadying oneself. Top of stool covered in nonslip rubber. Size 10" by 14" by 8" high. Handrail is 30" above step.

**PRICE B** From Hausman Industries / Winfield Company

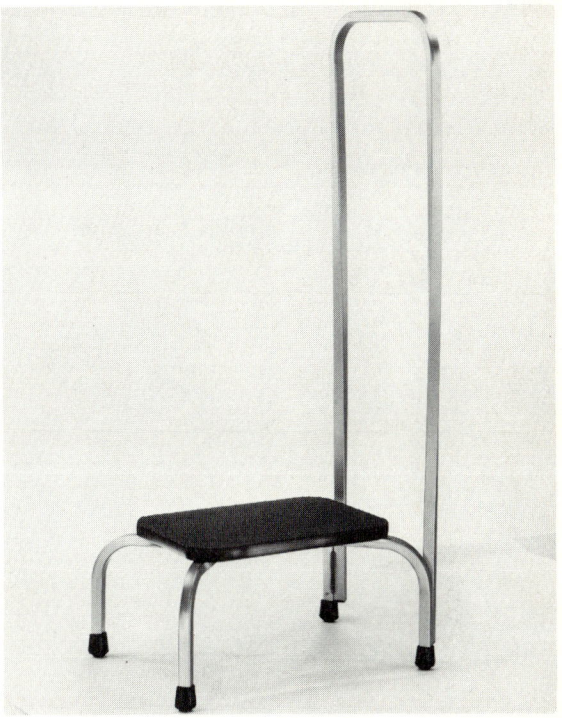

## 8.20 SAFETY STOOL

Kick it where you want it, step up, base grabs floor. Won't slide. No need to stoop and lift stool.

**PRICE C** From Cramer Industries (Kik Step) (also office supply stores)

## 8.21 LIGHT SWITCH EXTENSION

A plastic strip 22" long by 2" wide attaches to standard light switch by screws supplied. Handle at bottom of strip permits seated person to operate light switch.

**PRICE A** From Maddak

# Communication ⑨

### 9.1 BOOKHOLDER, FOLDING
Plastic bookholder which keeps books, magazines, paperbacks, and papers at comfortable reading angle without use of hands. Saw-toothed strips at base prevent pages from turning of their own accord. Size open 10" by 8" by 6 1/2", closed 8 1/2" by 1 3/4" by 3/4". Weight 2 oz.

**PRICE A** From Maddak

### 9.2 BOOKHOLDER—FOR BED
Extended support with angle adjustments for overhead use from headboard or traction frames. With aluminum C-clamp and 1/2" diameter by 27" extension with tilt and swivel adjustment. Allows reading while flat in bed.

**PRICE C** From C. Beil Designs

### 9.3 BOOKHOLDER—FOR BED
Bed Reader enables person to read in bed while lying completely flat. Pages turn effortlessly. Holds large books and paperbacks. Adjusts as to tilt and nearness to reader. Folds when raised.

**PRICE C** From Aparco (Bed Reader)

### 9.4 BOOKHOLDER, ADJUSTABLE

Book Maid can be used on wheelchair, armchair, bed, or table. The width adjusts. Page tilt adjusts. Pages are held flat. No finger coordination needed to turn pages. Folds for storage.

**PRICE B** From Aparco (Book Maid)

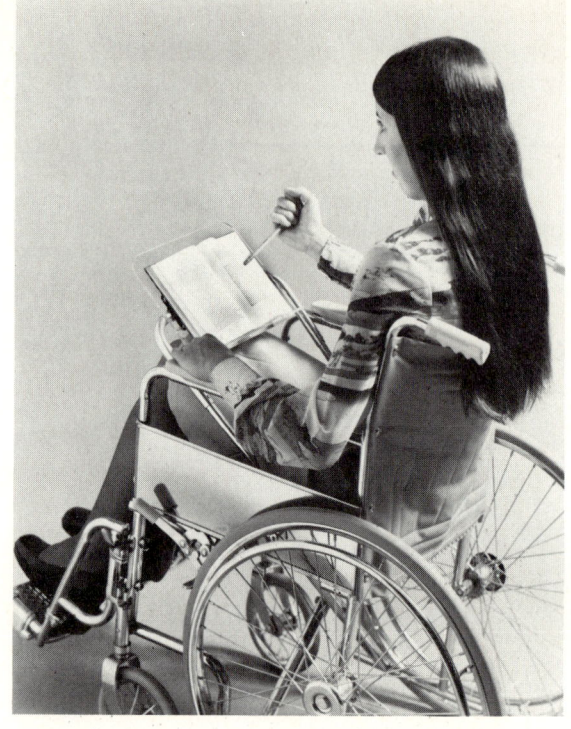

### 9.5 BOOKHOLDER

Fixed at 60° angle to base. Suction cup mounting for table use. Stand is plastic.

**PRICE B** From C. Beil Designs

### 9.6 BOOKHOLDER

Adjusts to any angle, upright or inverted. Cushioned C-clamp for bed, table or armchair use.

**PRICE B** From C. Beil Designs

## 9.7 BOOKHOLDER
Holder with vacu-base stand and tilt adjustment. Hardcover books, paperbacks, or magazines can be attached to high-impact molded plastic panel support. Nylon plastic fingers hold pages. Holder can also be used as easel, copyholder, or mirror holder.

**PRICE B** From C. Beil Designs

## 9.8 BOOKHOLDER/LAP DESK
This bookholder has other uses, as well. With top level, use for eating, writing, hobbies. With top at a tilt, use for reading. Holds heaviest books firmly in place. Can also be used as lectern. Raises to 17" height. Size 11 5/8" by 20" top. Has legs, clips, and book rest. Folds flat for carrying or storage.

**PRICE B** From Replogle

## 9.9 LARGE-PRINT BOOK
There are over 1,300 titles in large print available from this publisher. All Ulverscroft books are sewn, hardbound, light in weight, printed in dark type, designed to be useful to disabled and elderly. Catalog for list of books available from Stiskin.

**PRICE A** (each book) From Oscar B. Stiskin (Write for free catalog)

## 9.10 LARGE-PRINT-BOOKS DIRECTORY
*Large Type Books in Print*—Directory has 3380 entries. They include books or periodicals published in large print (14-point type or larger). This large reference book is available at most major public libraries, but cannot be borrowed for home use.

**PRICE B** From R. R. Bowker Company (*Large Type Books in Print*)

## 9.11 LARGE-PRINT DICTIONARY
1117-page *Webster's Dictionary* for large-print users. This publisher also puts out a great many fiction and nonfiction books of general interest in large-type editions. Write for a catalog.

**PRICE B** From G. K. Hall (*Merriam-Webster Dictionary for Large-Print Users*)

### 9.12  NEW YORK TIMES, LARGE-PRINT
Large-type (18–34 pt.) weekly newpaper. Size: 11 1/2" by 14 1/2".

**PRICE** (13 issues) **A** (20 issues) **B** (52 issues) **B** From New York Times (Large Print Weekly Newspaper)

### 9.13  READER'S DIGEST—LARGE-PRINT
Large-type edition (monthly) 20 pt. 6" by 9". **Twelve-issue subscription**

**PRICE A** From Reader's Digest (Large-Type Edition)

### 9.14  AUDIO BOOK
New Testament, King James Version, on 12 cassettes, **with album.** Playing time 20 hours, 19 minutes. Narrated by Marvin Miller.

**PRICE C** From Audio Book Company

### 9.15  RECORD ADAPTOR
Adaptor converts speed of a 33 1/3" RPM. turntable into 16 2/3 RPM. talking speed for 16 2/3 RPM. records.

**PRICE B** From Audio Book Company

### 9.16  TALKING RECORD OR CASSETTES
A library of outstanding talking records or cassettes of childhood favorites, poetic treasures, classics, contemporary fiction and nonfiction.

**PRICE**—See list of titles  From Audio Book Company (order list of titles)

### 9.17  VERSA BRAILLE
This paperless Braille system is a silent Braille note-taking device, an indexable filing system, an economical way of storing and reading Braille text, and an audio recorder. Connected to electric typewriters and computers, it can be used for word processing or data processing and retrieval.

**PRICE E** From Telesensory Systems

## 9.18 COPYHOLDER
Makes copying much easier. Saves eyestrain, promotes accuracy, adjustable to vision, takes any width copy from tape to 20". Holds notebook; completely portable. Comes with magnifier for small additional cost. A touch of finger on space bar moves copy up 1, 2, or 3 spaces.

**PRICE A** From Rite-Line Corp. (also at office supply stores)

## 9.19 DIGITAL CLOCK—LARGE NUMBERS
Electronic digital clock with .6" readout and snooz-alarm. Has top mounted dual function alarm control, 24-hour alarm set and AM indicator, fast or slow time set.

**PRICE B** From General Electric (also from appliance stores)

## 9.20 TAPE COMPUTER
A printing calculator that fits in your hand. Eleven-digit display. Prints on $2^{1}/_{4}$" roll of standard plain paper tape. Has 4-key independent memory and full-calculator functions.

**PRICE C** From Toshiba (also from department stores)

## 9.21 VOICE COMMUNICATOR
Phonic Mirror® Handivoice™ is an electronic device that actually talks for nonoral individuals. It has a numeric keyboard and liquid crystal display with vocabulary selections entered via three-digit numeric codes. Can be equipped with optional auxiliary switches such as blow or paddle switches, for individuals who need them.

**PRICE F** From H. C. Electronics / Votrax

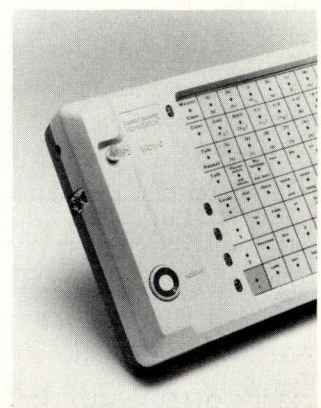

## 9.22 VOICE COMMUNICATOR
Phonic Mirror® Handivoice™ is the world's first hand-held, battery-operated electronic voice system. It is unique for the vocally impaired because it can simulate the human voice, produce complete sentences, and articulate virtually every word in the English language. Features touch-sensitive display board with 128 stations which can be represented as words, pictures, or symbols.

**PRICE E** From H. C. Electronics / Votrax

170  CATALOG OF AIDS FOR THE DISABLED

## 9.23  CODE-COM SET

Connected to conventional telephone, allows a hearing-impaired person to "see" phone messages in coded flashes of light or "feel" them in vibrations of a finger pad. A sending key can be used by hearing-impaired without speech. It is used like a telegraph key. If the person can talk he uses the telephone handset normally. To converse with hearing-impaired with code-com set, caller hums or whistles dots and dashes.

*PRICE*—Check local Telephone Company office—From American Telephone & Telegraph

## 9.24  TELLATOUCH

A simple device for communicating with a deaf-blind person who knows Braille. Keys are arranged like those on standard typewriter keyboard and there are also six keys like those on a Braille typewriter. Depressing a key on keyboard activates a Braille cell on other side of Tellatouch. Person with finger on Braille cell feels the letter (or contractions) activated by keyboard.

*PRICE D*  From American Foundation for the Blind

## 9.25  PORTA-TEL

The Porta-Tel™ enables hearing- or speech-impaired individuals to communicate by telephone via typed messages that are transmitted over standard telephone lines.

*PRICE E*  From Specialized Systems

## 9.26  TVphone™

Attached to antenna of any household TV, the TV phone converts user's home TV into a keyboard-controlled alphanumeric display screen, similar to TV displays used in airline terminals. To communicate over telephone, each user places phone handset on TV phone. Characters typed on either TV phone keyboard apppear on screens at both ends. When eight lines of display are filled, top line rolls off to make room for another line at bottom. Various options are available.

*PRICE E*  From Phonics Corp.

## 9.27 COMMUNICATOR AID

"Help Me to Help Myself Handbook" is useful to persons with speaking, seeing, hearing, learning, and language difficulties. An index card-size ring-bound booklet has 50 color-coded pages showing six major areas of basic needs with self-explanatory illustrations accompanied by words in bold black print and script. A "spell it" alphabet allows user to spell out other messages. A picture of the body with words "pain/where?" translated into 20 languages is included. A chart for people unable to hold a book is available.

**PRICE A**  From C. Green (Help Me Help Myself Communication Aids)

## 9.28 LIGHTWRITER–COMMUNICATOR

Clear and easy communication for those unable to speak. A portable unit consisting of keyboard and luminous display. As keys are depressed, characters enter right-hand end of display, moving those previously entered to the left, in the manner of a moving news strip. Corrections are made by using backspace or erase keys. There is a bleeper for summoning attention. Various options available.

**PRICE D**  From Toby Churchill Ltd. (Lightwriter)

## 9.29 SCANNING STRIP PRINTER COMMUNICATOR

For those unable to communicate verbally with others. This aid can be used to spell words one letter at a time. The letters are seen by looking at the aid as it lights up and also are printed on a $1/4''$-wide tape that is part of the aid.

**PRICE E**  From Prentke Romich

## 9.30 COMMUNICATION AID

For those unable to communicate verbally with others. Lights up each letter and prints it on strip as each letter is chosen by user. Has symbols and pictures for nonspellers. A wide range of user capabilities can be assessed and utilized with this aid. Also can have programs easily changed. Can simulate other, more specialized aids.

**PRICE F**  From Prentke Romich (Express 1)

## 9.31 COMMUNICATOR

This is a portable communication aid for nonoral, motor-impaired persons. As entries are made on keyboard, letters and symbols are produced on paper tape display, facilitating communication.

**PRICE E** From Telesensory Systems (Canon Communicator)

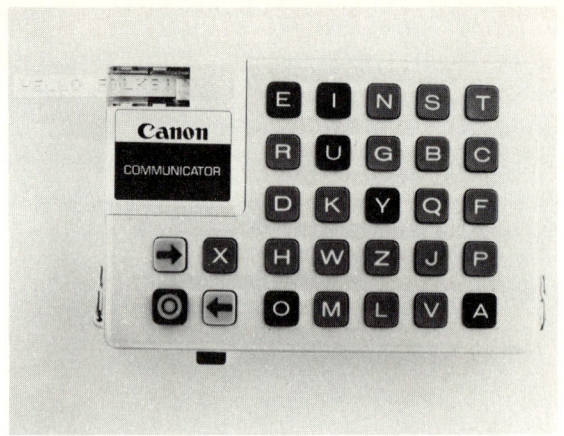

## 9.32 TALKING CALCULATOR

This calculator talks to the user. Its 24-word vocabulary announces every entry and result, offering visually impaired a new way to make math personally useful. This is totally new. Not a modified calculator. Weighs under 1 lb. Size $7^{1}/_{2}''$ by $4^{1}/_{2}''$ by $1^{1}/_{2}''$. Does six basic functions (including square root and percent). Has accumulating memory, automatic constant, and a change of sign key.

**PRICE E** From Telesensory Systems (Speech Plus) / American Foundation for the Blind

## 9.33 TV MEMORY COMMUNICATOR

Permits display of 16 lines of 64 characters each on any standard black and white TV set. Can be used with the strip printers by Prentke Romich. Text can be assembled, changed, erased, and corrected. Connected to TV set at antenna terminals. Uses standard AC house current, or can be equipped with connections for a 12-volt battery.

**PRICE E** From Prentke Romich

## 9.34 MESSAGE SELECTOR COMMUNICATOR

A small unit capable of presenting messages, letters, words, pictures, symbols, written on white plastic panel or clip-on cards. A lamp or tone indicates which position is "on." From two to nine panels can be scanned.

**PRICE D** From Prentke Romich

## 9.35 LARGE-PRINT VIDEO TERMINAL COMMUNICATOR

An interactive input-output device that displays messages in three optional sizes (up to $1\frac{1}{2}''$) and eight interchangable foreground and background colors. Lets visually impaired and normally sighted use same device and adjusts it to their own visual needs.

*PRICE E* From Arts Associates (Large Print Video Terminal)

## 9.36 FORM-A-PHRASE COMMUNICATOR

A new portable electronic voice allows verbally disabled to communicate through spoken words. User selects desired word or phrase by using control unit. The main unit then speaks the selected utterance in a clear, natural-sounding voice.

*PRICE E* From SciTronics (Form-A-Phrase—Main Unit)

## 9.37 COMMUNICATOR

This visual aid uses picture or word messages on interchangable panels. Included are word panels, alphabet and numbers panels, and blank panels for foreign language or Bliss symbol use. The unit is portable.

*PRICE E* From Preston

## 9.38 SYMBOL SCANNER COMMUNICATOR

For some persons the use of symbols or pictures can provide the best means of communication. This aid uses a standard 200-symbol vocabulary. The unit is portable.

*PRICE E* From Prentke Romich

## 9.39 EYEGLASS REPAIR KIT

Has jeweler's screwdriver, assortment of eyeglass screws and nuts, and magnifying glass.

*PRICE A* From Bernell (also available from other opticians)

### 9.40 EYEGLASS CADDY
Flexible plastic with self-adhesive backing strip for mounting on wall, desk, auto dashboard, etc.

**PRICE A** From Bernell

### 9.41 EYEGLASS FRAME PROTECTORS
Keep eyeglasses from digging into the ears. Soft, nontoxic plastic tubes. Slip easily over tips of eyeglass frames.

**PRICE A** From Dorsay

### 9.42 EYEGLASS EAR-LOKS
Soft elastic rubber (nontoxic) tabs permanently keep glasses from slipping. Stretch easily on eyeglass frames.

**PRICE A** From Dorsay

### 9.43 ILLUMINATED ENLARGER
Optiscope™ enables visually limited to read books, newspapers, magazines, and personal letters, and view photographs. It projects images on 9" by 14" polarized screen. Illumination can be regulated. Unit is compact, portable, and simple to use. Weight 14 lb.

**PRICE E** From Stimulation Aids

### 9.44 ILLUMINATED ENLARGER
For visually limited. Magnification up to 15 times with adjustments. So small and light it travels as a briefcase. Place book, letter, or any other reading matter under unit.

**PRICE E** From Visualtek (The Commuter)

## 9.45 BABY-COM
Enables one to hear sounds from nursery, playroom, or sickroom, or can be used as security protection anywhere in home. Just plug in—no wiring or installation. Portable. Any AM table radio, battery or car, can receive from Baby-Com, up to 300 feet from it.

**PRICE B** From Fanon Courier

## 9.46 WIRELESS INTERCOM
Each intercom is plugged into house outlet and uses house wiring as a message path. Has "press to talk" panel with lock switch for monitoring or babysitting. No installation required.

**PRICE C** From Fanon Courier

## 9.47 LAP DESK–CUSHION
Wedge-shaped cushion. Sturdy surface sloped at 20° angle. Promotes good vision, posture, and improved writing skills.

**PRICE B** From Bernell Corp. (Posture-Rite Lap Desk)

## 9.48 POCKET MAGNIFIER
Double lens in plastic case. 5- and 10-power, weight, 2 oz. Other models: 4-power single lens; 4x and 8x double lens.

**PRICE A** From Swift Instruments

### 9.49 WATCHMAKER'S LOUPE
Lightweight, plastic mounting. Easily retained in eye without using hands. 5x, 12x, focal length 1". Lens diameter 9/16".

**PRICE A** From Swift Instruments

### 9.50 CHEST-SECURED MAGNIFYING GLASS
Held on chest by two rubber-encased feet and secured by neck strap, allowing user to work with both hands free.

**PRICE A** From Swift Instruments (similar, ATCO)

### 9.51 READING MAGNIFIER
Designed to cover a full page-width of print. Lies flat on page. Made of optical-grade plastic. 5¼" long by 1" wide. Has vinyl case.

**PRICE A** From Swift Instruments (similar, ATCO; Bernell)

### 9.52 ILLUMINATED MAGNIFIER
Masterlens System is a visual aid that magnifies twice. Makes regular print into super-large print. Not telescopic, this system is for use with both eyes open. Hands are left free for needlework or crafts, if desired.

**PRICE D** From The Ednalite Corp.

### 9.53 ILLUMINATED MAGNIFIER
Optiscope® has two lenses in one with swivel mount. Convex side permits easy reading with wider field. Flat side is for closer work. Good for enlarging printed material.

**PRICE D** From Stimulation Aids

COMMUNICATION    177

### 9.54  MAGNIFYING GLASS, BIFOCAL
Bifocal Rectangular Reader. 2″ by 4″ plastic lens. 4 oz.

**PRICE A**  From Swift Instruments

### 9.55  MAGNIFYING GLASS
For reading. 2″ by 4″ lens, weight 6 oz.

**PRICE A**  From Swift Instruments (Bernell; similar, ATCO)

### 9.56  EYEGLASS MAGNIFIER AID
Opticaid® clips onto any eyeglass frame. It magnifies as much as $3^{1}/_{2}$ times even with bifocals. Swings up out of line of vision when not needed. Plastic lens.

**PRICE A**  From Edroy Company (Clip-on Plastic Lens)

### 9.57  READING AID WITH SCROLL
The Saltus Reader holds books printed on scrolls—places them in a convenient position to read, and rolls them forward and back, one page at a time. 600 most-read books are on scrolls. Saltus Reader can be adapted to use magazine and pocketbook pages in scroll setup. Also, blank scroll can be used for teaching. Has various accessories, including magnifying attachment to enlarge print for visually impaired.

**PRICE E**  From The Ealing Corp. (Saltus Reading System)

### 9.58  PAGE-TURNER
Page-turner batons with patterns to make support straps or mouthpiece. Lightweight aluminum and molded plastic with rubber tips. Standard size adjusts 11″ to 16″. Extra-length adjusts 20″ to 25″. Pattern for headband support strap included.

**PRICE A (each)**  From C. Beil Designs (Standard Baton and Extra-Length Baton)

### 9.59 NIGHT PEN
A ballpoint pen with a lighted tip for easy use in the dark or light. Goes on automatically when cap is placed on top. Extra nib and batteries included.

**PRICE A** From Hammacher Schlemmer

### 9.60 PENCIL HOLDER
A help for persons who have lost muscular control of fingers. Pencil length can be adjusted easily. Strong plastic 1" wide by 4½" long with loop to hold pencil firmly.

**PRICE A** From Maddak

### 9.61 PAGE TURNER
Turns paperback books in forward direction. Weight 8 lb. Base 8" deep by 12" wide. Height 12". Eight "C" flashlight batteries required. Capable of turning pages of 100 books without battery change.

**PRICE D** From Touchturner

### 9.62 PAGE TURNER
Reversible, allowing reader to turn pages either forward or backward. Weight 14 lb. Base 9" by 18" wide. Height 15". Turns pages of 100 hardbound books on 8 "D" batteries.

**PRICE D** From Touchturner

### 9.63 PAGE TURNER
Accepts largest and smallest magazines, hardback books and pocket-size books. Easy to set up—ready to operate in one minute. Operates by foot, elbow, head or flexing muscle. Weight 10½ lb. Size 14" by 24". Conveniently portable.

**PRICE D** From Lakeland Products—Automatic Page Turner (similar, Preston)

### 9.64 PAGE TURNER
Turns pages of book or magazine both forward and backward. It is a podium designed to sit on a table. Can be operated by two sensitive switch "wands" or by breath.

**PRICE D** From Technical Aids to Independence

COMMUNICATION 179

### 9.65 PAGE TURNER
Holds any size book or magazine. Plugs into wall outlet. Can be adjusted for horizontal to vertical. Can be placed over bed table, wheelchair tray, or work table. Four suction-cup feet. Size 23" by 8" by 18" high. Weight 11 lb.

**PRICE D** From Maddak

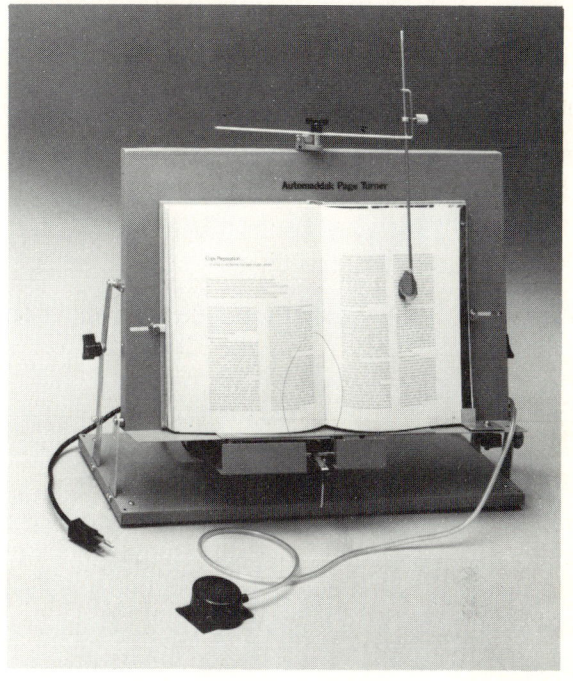

### 9.66 REMOTE SWITCH
Touch 'N Puff™ switch is a safe, convenient control mechanism to aid the disabled, elderly and infirm in controlling electrical appliances from bed, chair, or even bathtub. Control plugs into outlet. Appliance to be controlled plugs into control. Switch operates by pressing bellows with finger, elbow, foot, etc.

**PRICE C** From Maddak

### 9.67 WHISTLE SWITCH
Ultrasonic on/off control to any TV, stereo, lamp or other electrical appliance up to 400 watts. Plug whistle switch into 110 outlet and plug appliance into whistle switch. Control by squeezing the "Whistler," size about 4" by 2" by 1". No cords, wires, batteries. Effective up to 50' in any direction.

**PRICE B** From Universal Controls Corp. (also at appliance stores)

### 9.68 EASY SWITCH
A remote control operated by the slightest touch of any part of the body. Controls any electric appliance, etc., up to 300 watts. Requires no installation.

**PRICE B** From Rayl Distributing Company

### 9.69 ENVIRONMENTAL CONTROL

Has ten channels which allow user to operate various electrical devices at home, on the job or in the hospital. Control can do automatic telephone dialing and user can answer incoming calls. It can turn off and on appliances like stereo, lamps, TV. It can control battery-operated devices, intercom, etc.

**PRICE D** From Prentke Romich Company (ECU-2)

### 9.70 ENVIRONMENTAL CONTROL

Genie Electronic Control System designed to provide some freedom, independence, and security for seriously disabled persons. By use of a simple switch (pneumatic, touch, finger-operated) a disabled person can control such items as call bell, radio, TV, electric blanket, lamps, hospital bed, etc. The telephone, including full dialing for making calls, is an integral part of the Genie system. The system has twelve independent control circuits.

**PRICE E** From Western Technical Prod.

### 9.71 ENVIRONMENTAL CONTROL

Switch-O-Matic is an inexpensive system of electronic devices which control items in home or office for the disabled. No wiring or complex installation required. Controlled by sensitive switches, items can be orally or visually selected and turned off and on by a switch. Unit transmits an ultrasonic signal to command console from distances of up to 30'. Permits operation of up to sixteen separate locations for appliances.

**PRICE D** From Down East Electronics Manufacturing

### 9.72 PORTABLE COMPUTER

"Tim" is a completely portable system providing a range of communication for the severely disabled. The video screen presents nine verbal programs. Options include printer, call system, page turner, telephone equipment and remote control of nearly any electrical household function.

**PRICE E** From Computers for the Physically Handicapped

## 9.73 READING MACHINE

Reading machine for visually disabled. It works by converting inkprint into a readable, vibrating, tactile form. User moves Optacon™ across line of print with one hand. Index finger of other hand is placed on Optacon™ screen. Finger feels enlarged letter (vibrating) on screen. Machine is portable. Weight 4 lb. Size 2" by 6" by 8".

**PRICE F** From Telesensory Systems (Optacon™)

## 9.74 ROLLING RULER

12" rolling ruler for drawing horizontal, vertical, and angled lines any distance apart at will. Brings fingers, hands, wrists into play when used. An aid to those with hand- or finger-control problems.

**PRICE A** From Rol-Ruler Company

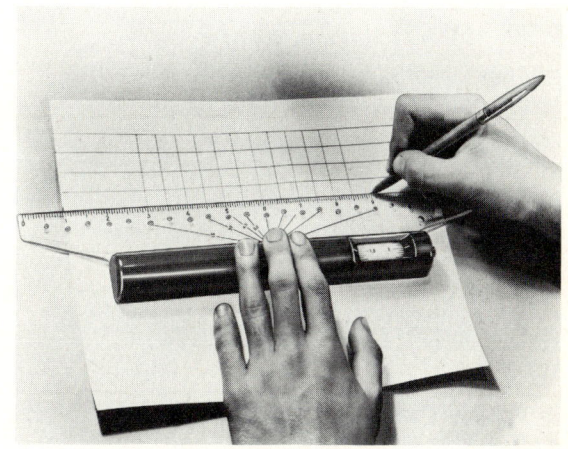

## 9.75 MAGAZINE RECORDINGS

Current issues of *Reader's Digest* and *Newsweek* available on records.

**PRICE B** From American Printing House for the Blind

## 9.76 TIME COMPRESSION SYSTEM

Cassette Recorder allows you to listen to taped speech played twice as fast as normal with no sound distortion. Anything recorded at normal rate can be played back faster than recorded. Useful for class lectures, business meetings, talking books, etc.

**PRICE D** From Science for the Blind Products

## 9.77 VARIABLE SPEECH CONTROL

For hearing- or sight-impaired. Variable Speech Controller allows voice recordings to be played back faster or slower (from 60% to $2^{1/2}$ times normal) with no change in pitch. Users who cannot comprehend normal speech benefit by listening more slowly. Users with hearing disorders in higher frequencies can bring pitch of speech to range where they can hear.

**PRICE D** From The Variable Speech Control Company (similar, American Foundation for the Blind)

### 9.78 COMMUNICAID–VOICE AMPLIFIER

This aid is designed specifically to increase substantially the voice volume of laryngectomees with less effort. It is also valuable to others with weak voices. It comes with hand mike and other accessories.

**PRICE C** (each) From Communicaid (Communicaid and Hands Free Mike)

### 9.79 TV CHANNEL SELECTOR

Attaches to any standard black-and-white or color TV set. Permits user to select VHF or UHF station and to turn set on and off from a distance. Has dual control switch. Requires only connection to TV antenna terminals.

**PRICE D** From Pentke Romich

### 9.80 A TOLL FREE DIGEST™

Directory of the "800" toll-free telephone numbers that can be called free for information and service across the nation. 150 pages and over 17,000 listings in 490 categories from airlines to wallpaper. Aid to those who want to "shop" by phone at no cost for telephone calls.

**PRICE A** From Toll Free Digest

### 9.81 TYPING WITH ONE HAND, INSTRUCTIONS

Provides a keyboard approach which aids rapid learning. Complete details and diagrams show hand positions and precise fingering for each key. Separate sections for left and right hands.

**PRICE A** From FashionAble

### 9.82 TYPEWRITER—SIMPLIFIED KEYBOARD

American Simplified Keyboard has a scientific key arrangement designed for two-handed persons. It can be beneficial to the disabled because it reduces fatigue. Finger travel at the end of a day's work is 16 times less with A.S.K than conventional keyboard. This keyboard is available on Smith-Corona office typewriters, models 7000 and 8000, and on portable models 2200, 1200, and Classic 12. There is no extra charge added to cost for these models. A.S.K is also available for right- or left-hand operation, for an additional charge.

**PRICE**—same as cost for Standard Keyboard Models—From Smith-Corona

## 9.83 TYPEWRITER WITH LARGE-SIZE TYPE
Large, bold printed characters for ease of reading by persons with poor vision. Size of letters is about twice regular type size. Large print (6-pitch) is available on models listed below.

**PRICE A** (Price above cost of standard model) From Smith-Corona (On 7000, 8000, 2200, 1200, Classic 12 models) / also Typewriting Institute for the Handicapped

## 9.84 TYPEWRITER MASK
Mask aid sits slightly above keyboard. It prevents users with poor hand guidance control from hitting more than one key at a time. It also supports hands so a finger can locate desired holes in mask to depress desired key. Cover plate over space bar prevents accidental spacing. Bar has opening for finger to operate.

**PRICE B** From Smith-Corona / Platt Luggage Company

## 9.85 ONE-HAND TYPEWRITER
Dvorak one-hand typewriter has new shift-easy bar for one-hand typist with no function of opposite typing hand. Typewriter comes with Dvorak one-hand keyboard.

**PRICE E** From Typewriting Institute (Dvorak One-Hand Typewriter)

## 9.86 TYPEWRITER AIDS FOR DISABLED
1. Keyboard rest and finger guide.
2. Armrest, mounted on typewriter frame.
3. Paddlewheel-shaped platen knob.
4. Electric Braille typewriter—Grade I and II Braille

**PRICE** (Contact IBM) From IBM

## 9.87 TYPING STICK
Allows those with weak hands to operate typewriters, push-button or dial telephones, computers, etc. Touch-N-Type™ stick is a 12" rod covered with plastic and a no-slip tip. Has adjustable hand loop that can be raised, lowered or shortened. Can be used as a mouth stick. Weight 1 oz. Diameter 3/8".

**PRICE A** From Therafin

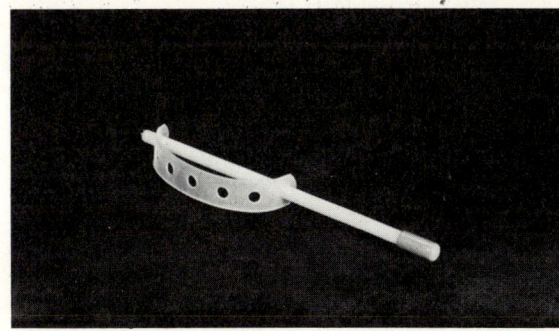

### 9.88 TELEPHONE SILENCER
Keeps phone from ringing with a flip of a switch. Clips easily onto any phone.

**PRICE A** From Zoom Telephonics

### 9.89 TELEPHONE STAND, CLAMP, AND INTERRUPTER
Stand is steel base on four rubber feet. Level-operated line interrupter can be operated by hand, elbow, or foot. Handset clamp is mounted on end of adjustable rod which can be positioned in any direction through swivel and ball-and-socket joint. Handset can be left permanently in clamp ready for talking and listening. Base 9½" by 11½".

**PRICE C** From Maddak

### 9.90 TELEPHONE EXTENSION ARM
Allows use of phone with hands free. In use, phone is always in position for user. Set can be left attached to extension arm at all times. When device is not in use, a flat steel bar is placed on cradle to cut off phone signal. Arm is 29" long. Other length arms available.

**PRICE B** From FashionAble / Maddak / Sparr Telephone Arm

### 9.91 TELEPHONE EXTENSION ARM
Allows phone receiver to be extended and held for those who need aid and still permits nondisabled to hold receiver in usual fashion. Has on/off switch which closes circuit with little effort.

**PRICE B** From Jal Company

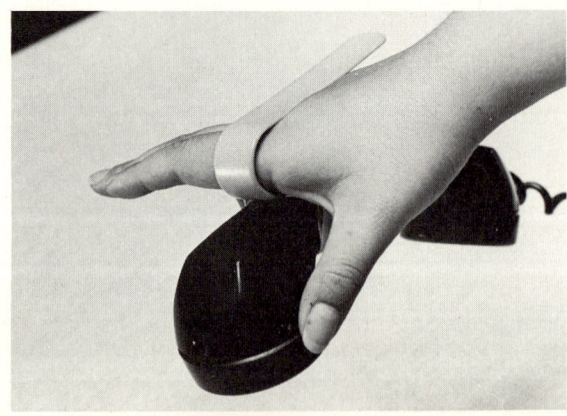

### 9.92 PHONE-HOLDING AID
Puts a handle on phone receiver. Plastic-covered metal frame can be bent to hand size. Fastens to receiver with Velcro closure.

**PRICE A** From Cleo

### 9.93 SPEAKERPHONE AND TOUCH-A-MATIC®
Allows hand-free telephoning. Touch-a-matic® with its ability to dial prerecorded telephone numbers is a great aid to users who have difficulty remembering or reading telephone numbers. Speakerphone is useful for disabled not able to hold phone.

*PRICE*—check with local telephone company office—From AT&T

### 9.94 JACK-EQUIPPED TELEPHONE AND HEADSET
Telephone with built-in jack arrangements for standard headsets type 52 or 53. This aid is for persons unable to hold handset. They can hear and talk with headset. The telephone itself can also be used as standard phone by others.

*PRICE*—check with local telephone company office—From AT&T

### 9.95 TELEPHONE TONE RINGER
SIA Tone Ringer concentrates all of the sound energy in a frequency which the majority of persons with impaired hearing can hear.

*PRICE*—check with local telephone company office—From AT&T

### 9.96 SIGNALMAN
For persons who can't hear telephone ring. Any lamp when plugged into the unit will flash on and off each time phone rings. If lamp is on, it flashes off; if lamp is off, it flashes on at each ring. Unit has pilot light to indicate if it is in working order.

*PRICE*—check with local telephone company office—From AT&T

### 9.97 ADAPTER, TELEPHONE HEARING AID
The 100A coupler is designed to enable persons with hearing aids to use telephone apparatus equipped with L-type receiver units. Just attach to earpiece of telephone. Small enough to carry in pocket or purse. This aid is not an amplifier.

*PRICE*—check with local telephone company office—From AT&T (Telephone Adapter)

### 9.98 AMPLIFYING PHONE
A handset with two buttons that allows hearing-disabled to increase phone's amplification by ten decibels when one button is depressed, or by twenty decibels when both are used.

*PRICE*—check with local telephone company office—From AT&T

### 9.99 LARGE TELEPHONE DIAL NUMBERS
Made of durable white plastic. Has large raised black numerals and smaller letters also raised. Has self-stick tape on back. Fits standard dial telephones.

*PRICE A* From American Foundation for the Blind (similar, numbers not raised, AT&T)

### 9.100 LO-VISION PUSHBUTTON PHONE ATTACHMENT
Larger numbers and letters are easier to see. Larger buttons, with wider spaces between, eliminate errors. Plastic module fits over standard pushbuttons.

*PRICE A* From FashionAble / American Foundation for the Blind

### 9.101 INDOOR TELEPHONE GONG
8" gong for hearing disabled. A very loud bell in the bass frequency range for people with severe hearing problems. Can be heard over high-level background noise at considerable distance.

*PRICE*—check with local telephone company office—From AT&T (Eight Inch Gong)

### 9.102 LOUD BELL
Ringing signal for people with impaired hearing. Much louder than normal telephone bell.

*PRICE*—check with local telephone company office—From AT&T

### 9.103 CORDLESS TELEPHONE
Works like a regular phone, within 300' of base unit. Can be carried anywhere since it has no cord to plug in or attach.

*PRICE E* From Eton (Eton Phone) / Also from Teletronics (Portacall Rotary)

COMMUNICATION    187

### 9.104  CORDLESS TOUCH-DIAL MEMORY TELEPHONE
Touch desired digits lightly. Will accommodate up to 21 digits. Re-dial feature can store emergency number. This will be retained until another number is called. Is good for emergency during night—just push re-dial button.

**PRICE E**  From Teletronics (Portcall Touch/Dial)

### 9.105  TWO-WAY TELEPHONE VOICE AMPLIFIER
Portable, leaves hands free, allows others to participate in phone conversation. Telephone headset is placed in cradle of amplifier unit. Volume adjustment controls sound.

**PRICE B**  From Fanon Courier

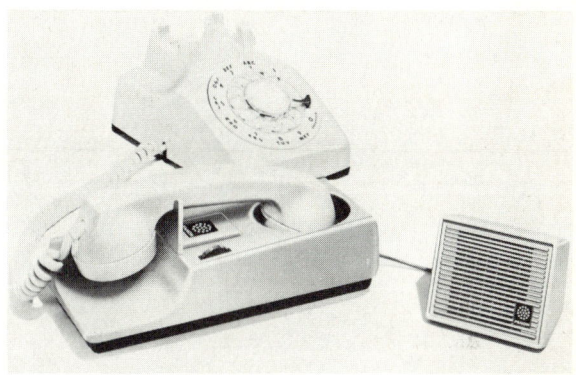

### 9.106  AUTOMATIC PHONE DIALER
Rapidial™ lets you dial any twenty frequently called numbers by pressing one button for each. There is digit display of number you are calling. Easily attaches to any 4-prong or new modular phone. Portable. Size $6^{1}/_{2}''$ by $3^{1}/_{2}''$ by $1^{3}/_{4}''$.

**PRICE C**  From Technology Applications (Rapidial™)

### 9.107  AUTOMATIC PHONE DIALER
Code-A-Phone Dialer® III allows one-button dialing of sixteen phone numbers. Has battery back-up if power is lost. Has digital display of number dialed. Accommodates 15 digits. Other models hold up to 32 phone numbers.

**PRICE D**  From Ford Industries

### 9.108 ARTIFICIAL LARYNX

Artificial Larynx is a special device used to produce audible speech by persons who have lost the use of their vocal cords.

**PRICE**—check with local telephone company office— From AT&T

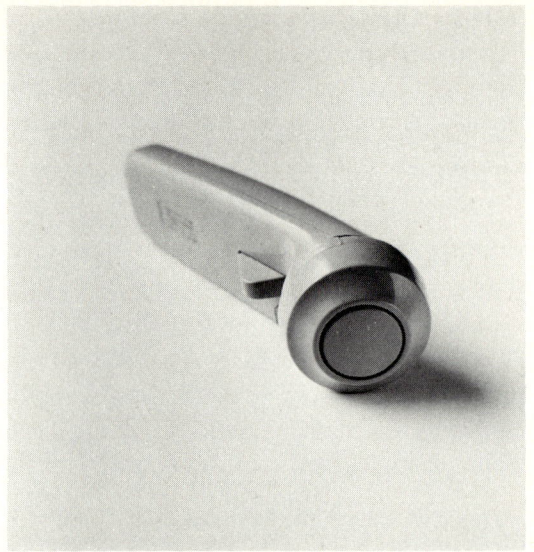

### 9.109 ALERT SIGNAL

Vibralite™ changes sound to light or vibrations. It alerts hearing impaired when doorbell or telephone rings, when smoke detector signals or any type of sound is made. Even when baby cries. No special installation needed. Can be left on continuously.

**PRICE C** From Vibralite Products (Vibralite)

### 9.110 WRITING AND READING AID

Makes reading, writing, sketching, and playing magnetic board games possible from a flat-on-the-back position. A vertical bar is clamped to headboard and has a gooseneck fixture which rotates to any desired horizontal position. Easel suspends from it and adjusts to suit user. Easel size 14$^{5}/_{8}$" by 10", with 2"-wide pencil trough.

**PRICE D** From Maddak

### 9.111 LEFT-HAND NOTEBOOK

Opens from left to right.

**PRICE A** From The Left Hand

### 9.112 SCRIPT GUIDE FOR VISUALLY IMPAIRED

This aid forms the basis for a course in longhand writing that is enabling many who have never learned to write script to master this skill. It has special clipboard, carriage, and instructions.

**PRICE B** From The American Foundation for the Blind

### 9.113 LEFT-HAND NURSE'S WATCH

The first left-handed watch to have a second hand. Available in 1″ or 1¼″ diameter dial. Gold or silver case. Black or brown strap. Winding stem on left.

**PRICE B** From The Left Hand

### 9.114 LEFT-HAND MEN'S WATCH

17-jewel with stem on left side. Automatic winding. Swiss-made.

**PRICE C** From The Left Hand

### 9.115 LEFT-HAND CHARACTER WATCH

Swiss made. Stem on left. Choose from 81 characters. Good for children. 1 or 1¼″ diameter dial. Gold or silver case.

**PRICE B** From The Left Hand

# Recreation

### 10.1 BOWLING BALL GRIP
Unique handle permits bowler to grasp ball without usual finger-hold grip. Simply grasp handle and roll ball. Handle retracts completely flush into ball when released. Comes in 10-, 12-, 14-, and 16-lb. ball weights.

**PRICE C** From Maddak / North American Recreation Convertibles

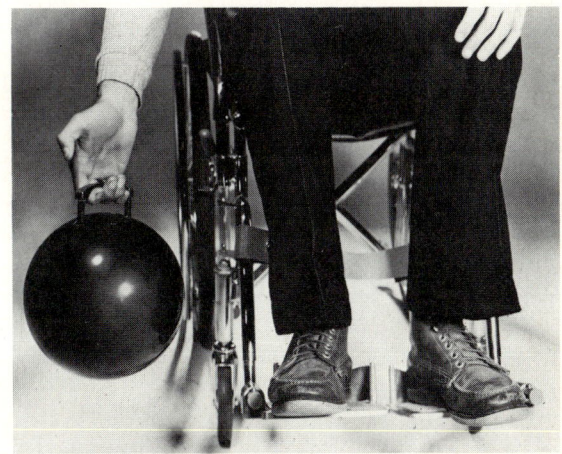

## 10.2 BOWLING BALL HOLDER

A third hand for the wheelchair bowler. Safely holds bowling ball while bowler pushes up to foul line. Easily attached to most wheelchairs.

**PRICE A** From George H. Snyder / Maddak

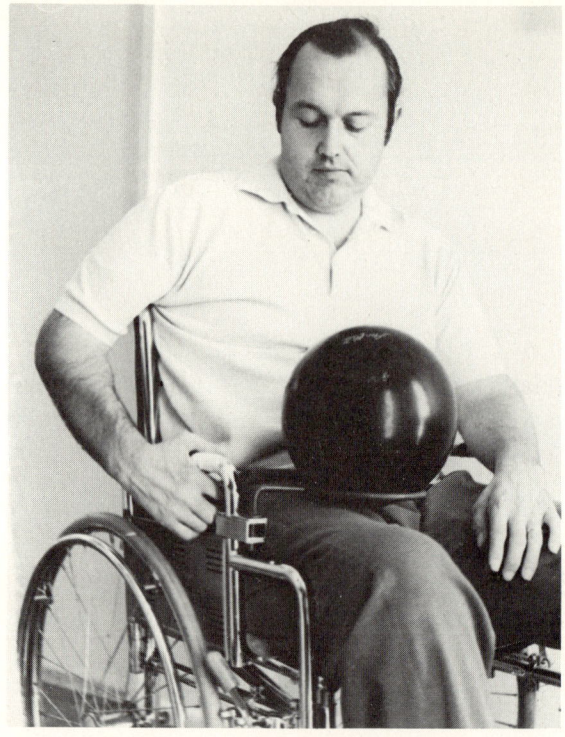

## 10.3 BOWLING BALL HOLDER-DESK

Bowling ball holder fits into slot of table. Turns ball holder into table or lap-desk.

**PRICE A** From George H. Snyder

## 10.4 BOWLING RAMP

Ideal for users with limited use of arms. Ramp is placed near front of lane, assistant puts ball on frame. User gives ball slight push to roll it toward bowling pins. May be used from standing or sitting position. Tubular construction allows storage in car trunk. Can be set up in a few minutes.

**PRICE C** From North American Recreation Convertibles / J. A. Preston Corp. / Maddak

## 10.5 STICK BOWLING
Instead of throwing a bowling ball, the disabled can aim and push the ball with the Alleycat Bowling Stick after a helper has positioned the ball in front of the stick. Size 39" to 51" (adjustable). Weight 3¼ lb. Nylon tips slide without damage to alley surfaces.

**PRICE B** From Therafin Corp. (Alleycat) / George H. Snyder / North American Recreation Convertibles

## 10.6 BICYCLE CONNECTOR
Pedal-Partner™ kit fits almost any two bicycles having same wheel size. Connecting tubes snap on to make two bicycles into a safe and sturdy people-powered vehicle. Tubes snap off in seconds for individual bicycle use.

**PRICE C** From Gandy Company (Pedal-Partner™ Kit)

## 10.7 BICYCLE POWER KIT
Series-3 attachable power kit converts bicycles into electrically powered vehicles. Top speed 17 mph. Install with one nut and clamp. Requires no pedaling to start and requires no readjustment. Can be mounted on front or rear wheel to provide assist or full power. Uses 12-volt rechargeable battery. Recharger plugs into household outlet. Travel range on one charge is 15 miles on level ground.

**PRICE D** From Palmer Ind. (Series 3)

## 10.8 SPORTSMAN 4-IN-1 CHAIR
Chair has fishing-rod holder, drink holder, built-in tackle box. Converts to regular chair or camp stool.

**PRICE B** From Camping World / Sleepy Hollow Gifts

## 10.9 MAGNETIC PLAYING CARDS
Thin steel magnetic playing cards are wind-proof and slide-proof on a light metal playing board. Folding playing board opens to 20" by 20".

**PRICE B** From Maddak / Hammacher Schlemmer

### 10.10  VARIOUS-SIZE PLAYING CARDS
52-card decks in various sizes to assist persons having sight, manipulation, or confinement problems. Extra small $1^{3}/_{4}''$ by $2^{5}/_{8}''$; standard poker size $2^{1}/_{2}''$ by $3^{1}/_{2}''$ with large numerals, letters and suit indexes. Extra large $4^{9}/_{16}''$ by $7''$ with large numerals, letters, and suit indexes.

**PRICE A** From Maddak (Extra Small, Standard Poker, Extra Large) / Help Yourself Aids™

### 10.11  CARD HOLDER
Easily used by those with poor sight or reduced finger control. The $1/2''$-wide slot opening narrows down to $1/8''$ creating easy entry and good holding area. Made of plastic. Cleans easily. Light and stable. $2''$ wide by $1^{3}/_{8}''$ high. Either $10''$ or $15''$ long.

**PRICE A** From Maddak

### 10.12  CARD HOLDER DISCS
Round, spring-loaded plastic discs help hold cards for persons with weak hands. For one-handed person, clamp secures disc to table. For one-handed person, stand that is weighted holds disc.

**PRICE A (each)** From Help Yourself Aids™

### 10.13  WOODEN CARD HOLDER RACK
Holds four rows of cards in tiers. For those with weak hands.

**PRICE A** From Help Yourself Aids™ (4 Row Wood Card Holder)

### 10.14  CARD SHUFFLER
Manual shuffler. Place half the cards on each shelf, turn knob. Cards drop from each side to bottom—ready to deal. Holds up to three decks. Heavy-gauge-steel construction.

**PRICE B** From FashionAble / J. A. Preston / Cleo Living Aids

### 10.15  AUTOMATIC CARD SHUFFLER
Place cards on either side, flip switch, they mix into a single deck ready to be dealt. Battery operated.

**PRICE B** From Hammacher Schlemmer

## 10.16 HOLDER FOR KNITTING, CROCHETING

Enables person with use of only one hand to knit, crochet, embroider, and darn socks. Holder can be raised and lowered, turned and placed in any position. Flexible post clamps to table.

**PRICE B** From Maddak / Cleo Living Aids / FashionAble

## 10.17 DRAWING KIT

For visually disabled. Allows user to draw or write and feel lines on the top surface as they are made. Rubber-covered board $8^1/_2''$ by $11''$ with hold-down clips. Ballpoint pen with special fluid. A package of polyester sheets to use as paper. By using these items lines can be felt on one side of a page. They can also be seen quite easily.

**PRICE C** From American Foundation for the Blind

## 10.18 ONE HAND FISHING BELT

"Spare Hand" fishing belt enables person with one hand to use fishing rod. User casts, then attaches rod handle to belt. Rod automatically locks securely to belt until handle is gripped for next cast. Ratchet device holds rod at any desired angle to land fish.

**PRICE B** From Roy Dodgen Shop (Fishing Belt)

## 10.19 PEG GAMES

Peg games were designed for use by physically disabled and visually impaired. Use of pegs as playing pieces makes them easier to pick up and hold. They are less easy to knock out of position than marbles or flat pieces. They are good for travel games. Pegs come in colors and are shaped to make them identifiable by touch. Each color a different shape. Some games have lines made in board so user can locate pegs on the board. Games available are peg Chinese checkers; nine-man Morris; peg tic-tac-toe; peg shuttle puzzle; peg French solitaire puzzle; peg triangle puzzle.

**PRICE A (each)** From World Wide Games (see above) / Gantts Wood Things (Tic-Tac-Toe)

## 10.20 PEG SATELLITE

For physically disabled and visually impaired, different colors, different shapes, lines in wood, and pieces that are difficult to knock out of position. This all adds to making it easier to play the game.

**PRICE A** From Gantts Wood Things

### 10.21 THERA-PEG™ CHESS AND CHECKERS

Unique design of the board and playing pieces accomplishes five goals: (1) pieces cannot be knocked off board; (2) each player uses different shape (round or triangle) for easy differentiation—even for the blind; (3) holes face in different directions to encourage hand movements; (4) round dowels slip easily into holes; (5) Velcro on pieces gives added resistive exercise.

**PRICE D** From North American Recreation Convertibles

### 10.22 MONOPOLY® FOR VISUALLY IMPAIRED

Played by two to eight players. Specially modified with a transparent, molded plastic mat laminated over the standard Monopoly® board. Aids such as property boundaries that can be felt; property names, selling prices and other designations overlaid in Braille. All cards are in both Braille and ink print, as is currency, so game can be played by the sighted also. Other aids to identify have been incorporated in the game also.

**PRICE B** From American Foundation for the Blind

### 10.23 BINGO FOR VISUALLY IMPAIRED

Bingo board for individual players is 7" by 10" and lightweight. It is royal blue with recessed white squares that contain large black print numbers and Braille symbols. Each board has a different number pattern and a package of thirty blank plastic markers. Weight 6 oz. Larger board is master Bingo board 9" by 16". Similar in construction to Bingo board. It has five columns numbered consecutively from 1 to 75. Comes with package of blank marker pieces. Weight 1 lb.

**PRICE A (each)** From American Foundation for the Blind

### 10.24 COMPUTER BRIDGE

Computerized game that challenges player. Can be partner (plays one hand) or opponents (plays two hands). Or it's you against the computer (plays all three hands). Plugs into electric outlet.

**PRICE D** From Fidelity Electronics, Ltd. (Bridge Challenger)

### 10.25 COMPUTER CHESS

Computerized game that challenges player. From beginner through intermediate, experienced, advanced, superior, postal chess. Excellent tournament practice. Plugs into electric outlet.

**PRICE D** From Fidelity Electronics, Ltd. (Chess Challenger)

## 10.26  COMPUTER CHECKERS
Has four levels of playing difficulty. The computer challenger invites player to sharpen skills, improve game, and play when he wants. Plugs into electric outlet.

**PRICE D**  From Fidelity Electronics, Ltd. (Checker Challenger)

## 10.27  COMPUTER BLACKJACK
Blackjack can be played on this 10-digit, full-featured calculator. Both dealer and player hands are visible in split display. (Player sees dealer's first card, then plays complete hand. Dealer's hand then becomes visible.) They can split, hit, stay or bet double. It shuffles deck, shows the face card, accumulates winnings and losses. Calculator can also be used as regulation calculator.

**PRICE B**  From Toshiba / Some Department Stores

## 10.28  COMPUTER BACKGAMMON
Challenges player to beat the computer. Allows him to handle the dice. Uses all the strategies of the game. Plays offense or defense. Responses vary every game. Does not permit illegal moves. Has position verification by computer memory recall. Plugs into standard electric outlet.

**PRICE D**  From Fidelity Electronics, Ltd. (Backgammon Challenger)

## 10.29  GAME CENTER
Both blind and sighted people can compete in eight electronic games relying exclusively upon sound cues. Games include: Audio-Paddleball, Skeet Shoot, Chain Game, Tug-O-War, Blackjack, Craps, Tic-Tac-Toe, and Number Run. Uses standard house current.

**PRICE D**  From Telesensory Systems

## 10.30  VIDEO COMPUTER GAMES
Thirty-two games are possible on separate cartridges. System has microprocessor console, two "Joystick" controls, two paddle controls, player difficulty options, game select/reset control; on-screen scoring; action sounds.

**PRICE D**  (Includes 1 cartridge only) From Atari® (Video Computer System™) (also department stores)

### 10.31 POTTER'S WHEEL FOR DISABLED
Designed specifically for the disabled. Height is adjustable and allows the potter to work from wheelchair. Wheel is electric. Height adjusts from 26" to 32". Wheel can also be used by anyone who prefers hand-operated potter's wheel.

**PRICE E** From Soldner

### 10.32 HEADPHONE RADIO
Cordless AM radio. Adjustable to any head size. High-impact plastic. Listen without disturbing others. Use when walking on crutches, in wheelchair, etc.

**PRICE B** From Hammacher Schlemmer

### 10.33 WRIST RADIO
A mini AM radio, 2" diameter. Mounted on a removable wrist band. Operates on penlite battery. Weight 1 lb. Useful for those not able to carry radio.

**PRICE A** From Hammacher Schlemmer

### 10.34 BUOYANT CHAIR
Buoyant arms and strap seat support user in pool. Back is 20" by 30". Separate valves for each arm and back.

**PRICE A** From Better Sleep

### 10.35 ROUND SCOOTER BOARD
Children with muscular dysfunction can use hand, arm, or legs to propel board. Wood platform 16" diameter. Ball-bearing casters.

**PRICE C** From Preston (similar, G. E. Miller, Inc.)

## 10.36 FLIP SKI OUTRIGGER

For disabled skiers. Utmost control in both skiing and walking. Built-in adjustable braking action. Converts instantly to walking crutch with ice-gripping points.

**PRICE D** From PSI

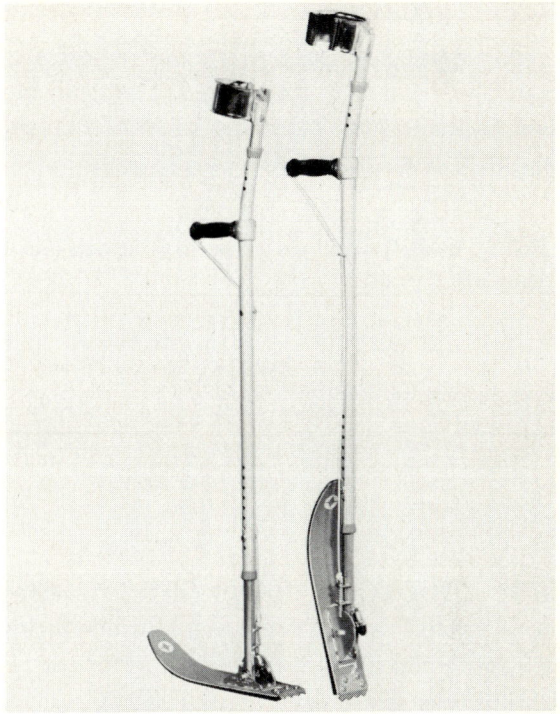

## 10.37 REVOLVING GAME TABLE

Table heights adjust from 27" to 36". Top of 24" square plywood revolves on ball-bearing turntable in either direction. Designed to play from a wheelchair such games as Bumper Puck, Fore Par, and Maze, plus many more games.

**PRICE O** From World Wide Games, Inc.

## 10.38 FM/AM PORTABLE TV SOUND

Listen to TV programs without set. Channels 2–13. Battery power or plug-in cord. Portable. Also AM/FM stations.

**PRICE B** From American Foundation for the Blind / Some Appliance Stores

## 10.39 TRICYCLE—CHILD AND ADULTS

Saf-T-Trike™ is the safest and most stable tricycle available for disabled children. Safe travel at twice the incline possible with conventional trikes. Extra-wide rear wheel base will not allow it to tip or roll over. Comes in two sizes: Saf-T-Trike™ (38 lb.) and Super Saf-T-Trike™ (48 lb.).

**PRICE C** From Playlearn Products

### 10.40 HANCYCLE

Janssen Hancycles operate by hand. There are eight models in sizes for all ages. They can be used for transportation, touring, or sport. Length 86", width 39", height 37", height of seat 24", weight 59 lb.

**PRICE E** From Tri-World Industries (Centauri Freewheeler)

### 10.41 TRICYCLE—HAND DRIVEN—CHILD'S

Maddacycle™ is a seat tricycle with chain drive and steering mechanism. Rear wheel swivels independently. Very suitable for indoor use. For children two to seven years old. Seat adjusts $4^{1}/_{2}$" front to back. Adjustable heel support. 36" long by $19^{1}/_{2}$" wide by 17" high.

**PRICE D** From Maddak

### 10.42 ROW-CAR

Designed for children four to ten years old. Helps child with limited use of lower extremities or spine to overcome disability. Is therapeutic as well as fun. An easy way to get around without crutches or wheelchair. Weight 22 lb. 37" long by 17" wide. Foot rests adjust from 22" to 31".

**PRICE D** From Lossing Company / Preston

### 10.43 ROLLING CART

Hand-propelled, nontippable rolling cart. Two swivel casters in back and one in front make Kiddie Maddavan™ very maneuverable. Rubber bumpers protect furniture. Place in front for attaching rope to pull cart. Fiberglass body, backrest, rubber tires.

**PRICE D** From Maddak (similar PCA)

## 10.44 SCOOTER, CHILDREN'S
Low-level, padded floor scooter is covered with foam-backed tweed carpet. Has nonmarring ball-bearing casters for multi-directional guidance by hand and foot. Available in 12" square, weight 5½ lb.; or 16" square, weight 9 lb. Supports up to 200 lb.

**PRICE B** From PCA

## 10.45 ELECTRIC THREE-WHEELER
Happy Wanderer provides transportation and recreation for those who desire support and pedal-free cycling. Vehicle travels on dirt and paved roads, wet or dry grass. Two speeds forward, reverse. Steering and dual braking are controlled by single-hand operation. Range 15 to 20 miles—speed 3 to 7 mph. Batteries can be recharged by plugging into house-current outlet.

**PRICE E** From Palmer Industries

## 10.46 WATERING STICK
The Yard Arm eliminates need to crawl in bushes to get to outdoor faucet. No stooping or bending, or muddy feet. Just leave hose attached to faucet, and Yard Arm on faucet handle. Just turn Yard Arm and faucet goes on.

**PRICE A** From Shur-Lock

## 10.47 CRAWLER
Encourages movement by disabled child. Platform supports child on stomach and chest for freedom of arm and leg motion. Height and angle of platform adjustable.

**PRICE B** From Invacare

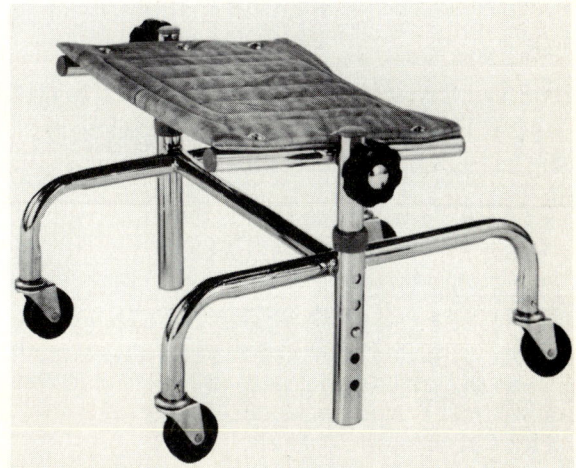

### 10.48 ROLLING "SLED," CHILDREN'S

Roll-A-Mat is a rider-directed rolling sled of molded washable plastic, mounted on four non-marring ball-bearing casters. Children lie on 1"-thick vinyl-covered foam mattress. Roll-A-Mat can be moved by using hands or feet. Size 19" by 34" by 6". Weight 12 lb.

**PRICE C** From PCA

### 10.49 GUITAR INSTRUCTIONS—LEFT HAND

Chords especially for left-hand players. Fifteen popular folk songs. Group or individual instruction.

**PRICE A** From The Left Hand

### 10.50 LEFT-HAND CAMERA

Shutter button on left side assures steady positive control. 35mm picture. Four-time magnifier, waist-level viewfinder. Shutter speeds $1/25$th to $1/150$th sec. focuses down to 3'.

**PRICE D** From The Left Hand

### 10.51 NEEDLEPOINT FOR LEFT-HANDERS

*New York Times Book of Needlepoint for Left-Handers.* 256 pages. By Elaine Slater. Hardcover edition.

**PRICE A** From The Left Hand

### 10.52 LEFT-HANDED EMBROIDERY

Primer of left-handed embroidery by Carole Robbins Myers. Directions for 55 stitches. 158 pages.

**PRICE A** From The Left Hand

### 10.53 LEFT-HAND LIGHTWEIGHT SHEARS

Reversed steel blades, sculptured yellow molded handles with left-hand thumb grip. 8" full length. Superior lightweight shears.

**PRICE A** From The Left Hand

### 10.54 LEFT-HAND SEWING SCISSORS

Has nickel-plated reversed blades, glazed inside, bowed shanks. Left-hand finger grips. 6" full length. Made in West Germany.

**PRICE B** From The Left Hand

## 10.55   LEFT-HAND STRAIGHT TRIMMERS
Nickel-plated reversed blades, glazed inside, left-hand finger grips, bowed shanks. 7 1/2" full length. Made in West Germany.

**PRICE B**   From The Left Hand


## 10.56   LEFT-HAND PINKING SHEARS
Hand-forged tested special steel. Fully chromed reversed blades. Sculptured handles with left-hand thumb grip. Precision set teeth assure smooth cutting. 7 1/2" full length.

**PRICE A**   From The Left Hand


## 10.57   LEFT-HAND BENT TRIMMERS
These scissors will cut through quadruple thickness polyesters with ease. Nickel-plated reverse blades, glazed inside, left-hand thumb grip. 8" full length.

**PRICE B**   From The Left Hand

# Travel ⑪

## 11.1 CAR ASSIST BAR
Enables user to pull himself up and slide to either side of vehicle. Adjustable for length and head room. Mounts on interior of car roof.

**PRICE B** From Wright Way (Assist Bar)

## 11.2 CAR TRANSFER AID
A hand-hold to aid in transferring from wheelchair to car. Plastic-coated feet rest in rain gutter of car. As person using aid pulls down, it grips and provides enough support to bear weight of transferring person. Hand-hold is hard rubber.

**PRICE B** From Medical Equipment Distributers

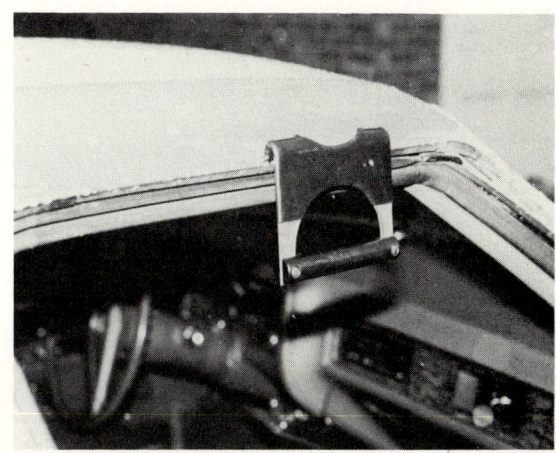

## 11.3 LEFT-FOOT ACCELERATOR
Does not interfere with operation of standard gas pedal or replace it.

**PRICE B** From Wright-Way / Cleo Living Aids / Kroepke Kontrols, Inc. (some automobile hand-control companies)

## 11.4 BAGGAGE TOTER
Compact luggage carrier. Holds one large and one small suitcase. Fits in tote bag or attaché case. Carries 80–90 lb., weighs 15 oz. Pull handle to open; push to close. Loaded unit won't tip.

**PRICE A** From Aparco (also luggage stores and department stores)

## 11.5 BAG TOTER
Carries heavy or bulky loads. Shut, 25" long by 6" wide. Smaller model carries over 150 lb. and weighs 4 lb. Large model carries 250 lb. and weighs 6 lb.

**PRICE B** From Grip Toter (also luggage stores and department stores)

## 11.6 ROLLING LUGGAGE
Retracto® Luggage has a concealed stainless-steel pull cord that automatically rewinds inside the case. Lets user pull luggage on small rollers.

**PRICE C or D *(depends on size)*** From United States Luggage Corp. (various brands of Retracto® Luggage) (also luggage stores and department stores)

### 11.7 HAND PARKING BRAKE
Mounts directly to parking brake pedal. Adjustable for leverage and mounting position. Made of chrome-plated steel.

**PRICE B** From Wright Way / Wells-Engberg Company / Drive-Master Corp. / Automobile Hand Control Companies

### 11.8 CAR DOOR OPENER
A simple device to open push-button car doors. Operates every type handle on car door in lever fashion, inside and out. Good for handles recessed down inside door armrests. Vinyl coated to avoid scratching surfaces. Vinyl bicycle-type handles.

**PRICE B** From ComfortAble-Aids / Maddak / Cleo Living Aids

### 11.9 CAR DOOR OPENER
Designed to assist in manipulation of push-button type car door handle. Translucent plastic base with special fingers that withstand severe stress and temperature change. Nonslip covering on thumb.

**PRICE B** From Camp International, Inc.

### 11.10 TWO-INCH FOLDING CHAIR
Folds or unfolds in one second. Folds to 2″ thick. Acrilan back and seat are removable for washing.

**PRICE B** From CareFree of Colorado (Colorado Camp Chair) / Camping World / Zip Dee, Inc.

### 11.11 COIN DISPENSER
Organizes coins for quick, convenient use for parking meters, tolls, vending machines, telephones. Coinholder for car, home, office. Easy-mount adhesive backing. Coinholder is removable for security. Holds $10 in nickels, dimes and quarters.

**PRICE A** From Ozburn-Janesville (Dash Cash) (also some stationery stores)

### 11.12 MINIATURE CLOCK RADIO
Cordless travel clock radio for home, car, travel. Set alarm and wake to radio or bell. Size 4″ by 7″. Weighs less than 1 lb.

**PRICE B** From Hammacher Schlemmer

### 11.13 PORTABLE COFFEE MAKER
Can be used with house current or 12-volt car lighter receptacle or battery pack. Has floor bracket to prevent spills. 6-cup size. Comes with 12-volt adapter.

**PRICE B** From Girard

### 11.14 SUPPORTING CUSHION
Self-conforming back pal supports small of back in car, office, home. When driving, counter balance weight and strap hold it in position. Inflates for desired firmness. Folds flat.

**PRICE A** From Better Sleep

### 11.15 CONVERTER TRAVEL KIT
Contains all converters and adapters necessary for world travel. One for electronic equipment; another for heating and portable motor appliances; four wall adapters for different outlets throughout the world. Weight 2 lb.

**PRICE B** From Hammacher Schlemmer / Brookstone Company

### 11.16 HAND CONTROL BRAKE AND CLUTCH
Right- or left-hand operation. Adjustable leverage for standard or power brakes and for the travel distance of the clutch.

**PRICE D** From Wright-Way, Inc. (Brake and Clutch Control) / Wells-Engberg / Drive-Master Corp. / Automobile hand control companies

### 11.17 HAND DRIVING CONTROLS
Has rotation gas feed, dimmer switch, brake control. Car can also be operated in normal way, by another driver.

**PRICE D** From Wells-Engberg (Hand Controls) (similar, Kroepke Kontrols, Inc. / Wright-Way, Inc. / Smiths Hand Control Service / Hughes Hand Driving Controls, Inc.)

## 11.18 MOTOR HOME

Designed to accommodate disabled person. Large side door used by wheelchair user to exit and enter on electric-powered lift. Shower has fold-away seat and grab bars, also low-level water controls. Kitchen sink has open area underneath for wheelchair.

**PRICE F** From Xplorer Motor Home (Explorer 307)

## 11.19 FLYING CONTROLS, HAND

Controls for disabled for flying own plane.

**PRICE—custom-made** From Bill Blackwood

## 11.20 PANORAMIC REAR-VIEW MIRROR

Hind Sight™ mirror lets you see rear and both sides of car at same time. No blind spots. Gives total panoramic sight. No-glare shatter-proof mirror. Clips over present mirror. Fits all sizes.

**PRICE A** From FashionAble / The Braun Corp.

## 11.21 VEHICLE WHEELCHAIR LIFT

For vans. Powered from vehicle battery. Hydraulically operated. Installed in side or rear door, folds inside door in upright position. Operates by one control switch on coil cord. No modification to vehicle needed.

**PRICE F** From Time Savers

### 11.22 VEHICLE WHEELCHAIR LIFT

Swing-in action. Only 3' side clearance needed. Electric drive. Lifts 700 lb. Fully automatic door openers, lift grab bars. Chair lock prevents rolling while on lift. Can be manually operated if power fails.

**PRICE F** From Electro Van Lift

### 11.23 VEHICLE WHEELCHAIR LIFT

Can be installed on any sliding door of $1/2$- or $3/4$-ton van. Rotary lift design allows one to use normal vehicle parking space. Lift is completely electric. Requires no major modification to vehicle. Can be stopped at any position. Takes up minimum amount of space.

**PRICE F** From ABC Enterprises (ABC Lift)

### 11.24 VEHICLE WHEELCHAIR LIFT

Nonhydraulic, fold-in-half platform can be mounted right, left, or rear. Other models for buses and motor homes. Custom designs available.

**PRICE F** From Crow River Industries

### 11.25 VEHICLE WHEELCHAIR LIFT

Electric-screw drive power. Large expanded metal platform with automatic wheelchair lock. Stops at any level. Self-storing (10" width) lifts up to 400 lb. Models to fit all vans.

**PRICE F** From Fred Scott & Sons (Translift TLA)

### 11.26 PORTA-POTTI

Completely portable. Easily emptied, leakproof, odor-tight holding tank unsnaps, self seals and carries like suitcase. Contains own fresh water supply. Up to fifty flushes. $18 1/2"$ deep, $18 1/2"$ wide, $14 1/2"$ high. Weight 18 lb.

**PRICE D** From L. L. Bean / Camping World

## 11.27 FOLDING POCKET SCISSORS
Precision stainless-steel blades and chrome handles. Folds to small size. Blade tips are covered for carrying.

**PRICE A** From Camping World

## 11.28 DUAL PURPOSE STROLLER
Rear-facing baby safety seat is secured in car's safety belt system. Safety "LOVE" seat can be transferred to stroller. Love Mobile™ is rugged, lightweight and folds easily. Has snap-in seat to convert to regular stroller for larger child.

**PRICE B (each)** From AC-Delco (Love Mobile™; stroller)

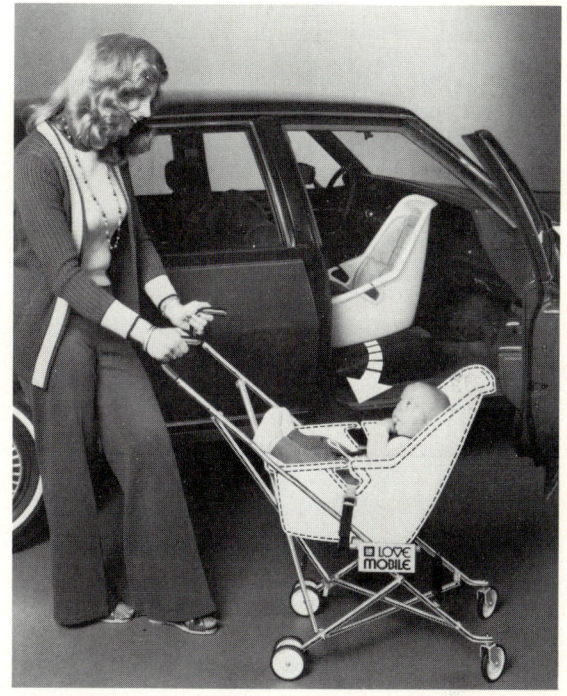

## 11.29 PORTABLE SPOTLIGHT
Portable, emergency spotlight. Plugs into 12-volt car cigarette lighter. Fits in glove compartment. 35,000 candlepower.

**PRICE B** From On-Guard Corp. of America (also, some hardware and automobile-supply stores)

## 11.30 UMBRELLA HAT
100% nylon hat protects you from rain or sun. Adjustable head band. No need to use hands. One size fits all.

**PRICE A** From Camping World (also available from various mail-order firms)

### 11.31 ALL TERRAIN VEHICLE
Two passenger. Six wheels. Travels over rivers, deserts, swamps, snow, mud. Four-wheel drive. Goes up 45° grades. Size 87" length, 54" width, weight 440 lb.

**PRICE F** From Scrambler, Inc. (Scrambler)

### 11.32 ALL TERRAIN VEHICLE
Four passenger. Six-wheel drive goes over sand, mud, snow, water. Goes up 60° slope. Size 94" length, 54" width, 39" height, weight 790 lb.

**PRICE F** From Hustler Corp.

### 11.33 WHEELCHAIR WINCH
Miniwinch is a small hand-operated hoist which facilitates the job of lifting a folded wheelchair into a car. Use only with two-door hard top models. Winch cord attaches to wheelchair. Turn crank handle of winch to pull chair into space behind front seat.

**PRICE C** From Owen-Pacific Assoc. (Miniwinch)

### 11.34 WHEELCHAIR TOP LOADER
Electromatic top loader allows wheelchair user to load and unload wheelchair without assistance, into container on top of car. Power from car battery. Fits on any car or pick-up.

**PRICE F** From The Wheelchair Carrier Corp. (Mark VII)

## 11.35 WHEELCHAIR TOP LOADER
Hoyer Kartop™ lift is hydraulically operated. Suction cups and hooks hold lift securely on car roof (not for use on vinyl tops). Models for small and regular cars and vans.

**PRICE E** From Everest & Jennings / Ted Hoyer & Company

## 11.36 WHEELCHAIR TRUNK LOADER
Lady-Lift provides strain-free method of lifting folded wheelchair into and out of car trunk or station wagon luggage area. Electric hoist does all the work. Lift then folds out of the way.

**PRICE D** From Loyal LaPlante Supply Company (Lady-Lift)

## 11.37 WHEELCHAIR TRUNK LOADER
Manual trunk loading aid. E-Z™ tilt loader requires no installation. To load, fold wheelchair, fasten E-Z™ security strap and ease wheelchair into trunk. Size, 25″ wide, 38″ high.

**PRICE C** From Physical Aids

## 11.38 WHEELCHAIR CAR RACK
Easily adjustable to most auto bumpers. Holds most wheelchairs. Nonrusting finish. Complete with three nylon straps and special cover.

**PRICE C** From Cleo Living Aids

## 11.39 WHEELCHAIR TIE DOWN
Tie-down and seat belt set provide safe restraint of passenger and chair during travel. Prevent wheelchair from rolling and tipping on curves, during acceleration, and braking.

**PRICE C** From Fred Scott & Sons (Translock)

### 11.40 WHEELCHAIR CAR RACK

Allows quick, easy placement of wheelchair into rack. Automatic lock-in device instantly fastens it into rack. Total access to trunk whether rack is in use or folded away. When Pak-A-Rak® is not in use, folds flat against rear of automobile.

**PRICE D** From Summit Corp. (Pak-A-Rak®)

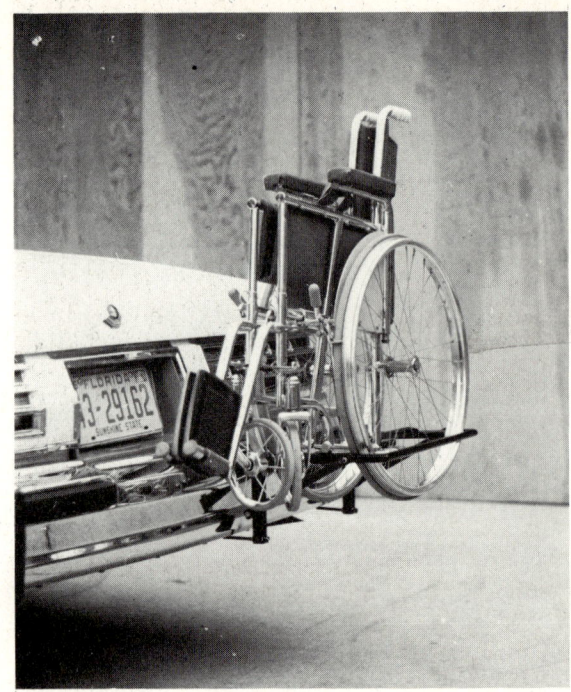

# ⑫ Accident Prevention at Home

## 12.1  POWER FAILURE LIGHT
Goes on automatically when power fails. Fits any wall socket. Use also as night light or flashlight. Self-charging.

**PRICE B**  From FashionAble / Nicoll Brothers, Inc. / Chris Craft Industries, Inc. / hardware stores

## 12.2  RESPIRATOR ALARM
Will sound alarm at loss of pressure, loss of breath cycling, loss of power, if standby battery gets low. It is completely solid state. No mechanical switches. Has test button to test condition of internal battery. Uses 12-volt DC battery or house current.

**PRICE D**  From Technical Aids to Independence

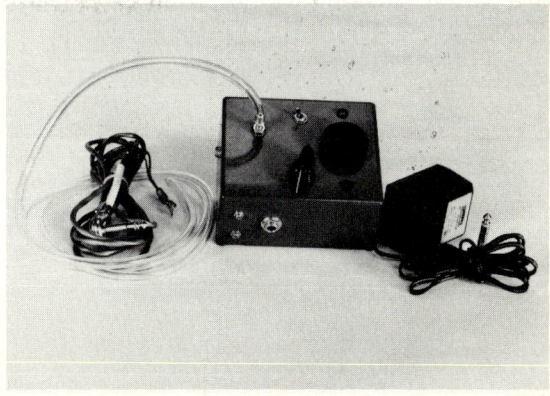

## 12.3  BLANKET CLIPS

Have no metal, no pins, no sharp edges, are nontoxic. Flexible plastic clips loop around crib spokes to hold covers in place.

**PRICE A** From Glenco (some department stores)

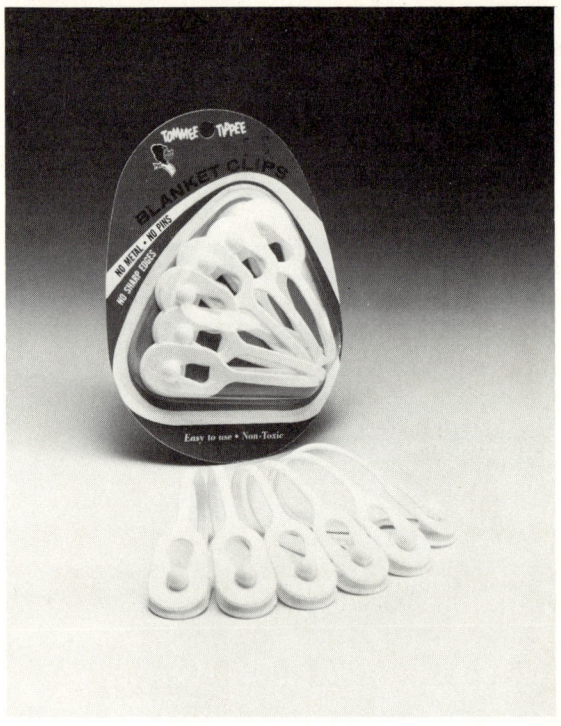

## 12.4  REMOTE CIGARETTE HOLDER

Clip-on ash tray with built-in cigarette holder. Has 6' vinyl tube and hard plastic mouthpiece. Smoking through tube avoids fire from falling ashes, or if user falls asleep while smoking. Clips attach to wheelchair leg or any vertical leg of appropriate size.

**PRICE A** From Maddak (similar, no clip—Preston; similar, no clip—Cleo Living Aids)

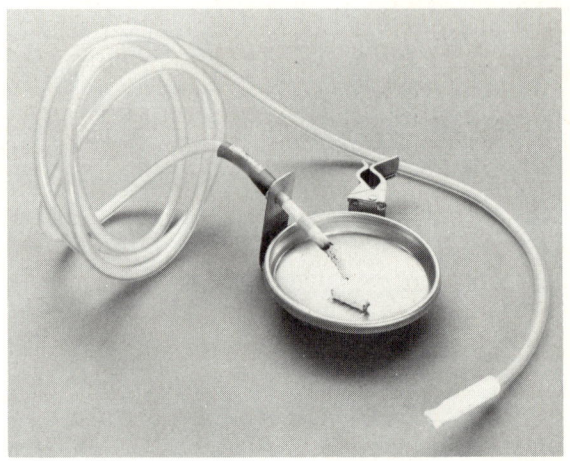

## 12.5  DOORTOP LOCK

For child protection. Can be fixed to either side of door. Is out of child's reach. Fits all standard doors. Easily installed.

**PRICE A** From Glenco (similar, Shur-Lok Manufacturing Company; some hardware stores)

## 12.6 CABINET LOCK

Helps keep cabinets closed to children. Easily installed—no tools, no screws, no marred woodwork. Made of unbreakable nylon. Just slide on and it's locked.

**PRICE A** From Glenco (some hardware stores)

## 12.7 SAFETY DOOR KNOB

Prevents young child from turning door knob to open door. Turns harmlessly in child's grasp. Adults squeeze to turn.

**PRICE A** From Glenco (some hardware stores)

### 12.8 DRAWER STOPPER
For child protection. Prevents drawers from being pulled out all the way, spilling, or falling on children. Easily installed.

**PRICE A** From Glenco (some hardware stores)

### 12.9 CABINET DOOR LOCK
Prevents little children from opening cabinet doors and also drawers. Adults easily open drawers or cabinets with the touch of a finger. Each time door or cabinet is shut it relocks automatically. Easy to install.

**PRICE A** From Shur-Lok Manufacturing Company; (some hardware stores)

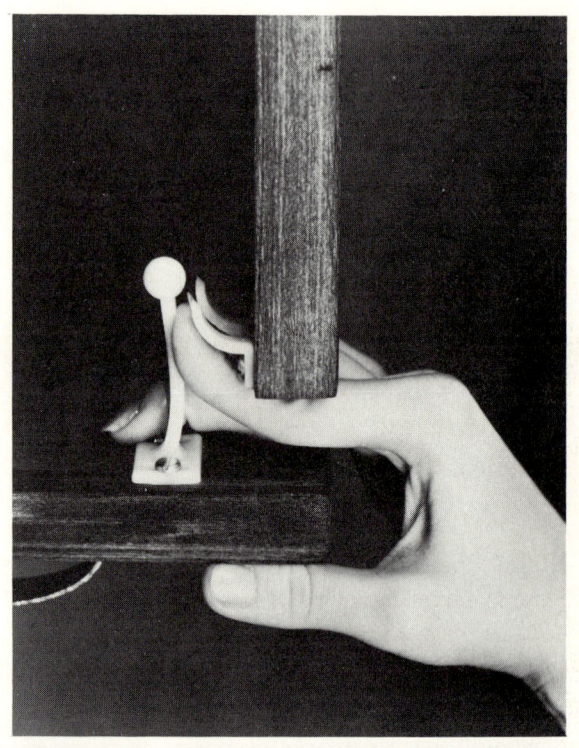

### 12.10 SAFETY OUTLET CAP
Protects children against electric shocks. Fits in wall outlet. Prevents children from inserting metal objects into electrical outlets.

**PRICE A** From Shur-Lok Manufacturing Company / Glenco Infants Items, Inc.; (some hardware stores)

### 12.11 SAFETY TREADS
For bath or shower use. Ends danger of slips or falls in tub or shower. 18" pressure-sensitive treads.

**PRICE A** From Wal-Jan Surgical Products, Inc. / Cleo Living Aids; hardware stores

# ⑬ Safety from Crime

## 13.1 PERSONAL WIRELESS ALARM
For people who live alone. Protects in case of crime and illness. Panic button can be carried on belt, in pocket or on neck pendant. In emergency when pushed, it triggers communicator up to 300' away. This in turn automatically dials telephone for help by prerecorded tape. This is part of Home Alarm System.

    *PRICE E* From Delta Medical Ind. (Delta Sentry™) (Many home alarm systems companies can supply "Panic Button.")

## 13.2 PERSONAL ALARM
Small hand size, can be heard for blocks. Push thumb lightly on alarm to make it work.

    *PRICE A* From Walking Stick Emporium (Shriek Alarm) (Many mail-order firms carry this type of alarm.)

## 13.3 PERSONAL ALARM
Can be heard for one mile. Just press top of can. Hand size.

    *PRICE A* From Hammacher Schlemmer (Invento Hand Alarm) (Many marine stores carry this type of alarm)

### 13.4 PORTABLE DOOR ALARM

Just hang it on inside door knob and adjust sensitivity control. Powered by 9-volt battery. Portable. Works on wood and nonmetallic doors. A touch on outside door knob sets off the Startler™ alarm.

>**PRICE B** From Regal Ware Inc. (Many hardware stores carry this type of alarm)

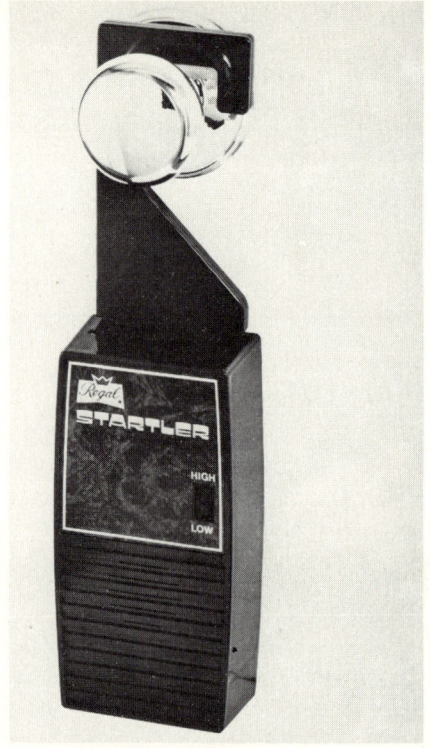

### 13.5 PERSONAL PROTECTION ALARM

Cordless electric Escort™ touch button, emits loud, high-pitched sound similar to siren. Can be heard 1/4 mile away and cannot be shut off. Shuts itself off after three minutes and automatically resets for instant reuse. Made of high impact plastic. Can be carried in palm of hand. Weighs less than 6 oz. Size 3 3/4" by 2 1/2" by 1". For pocket, purse or glove compartment. Battery included.

>**PRICE A** From Hammacher Schlemmer

### 13.6 DOOR ALARM

Attaches to door—no tools necessary for installation. Tamper-proof.

>**PRICE A** From S. Parker Hardware (Perma-Guard) (many hardware stores and locksmiths carry this item)

### 13.7 SELF-SET COMBINATION LOCK

User can reset combination when desired. Can't be picked, won't rust or jam. Combination padlock. Over 10,000 different combinations. Solid brass body.

>**PRICE A** From The Orvis Company, Inc. (Many locksmiths have this item)

## 13.8  200° DOOR VIEWER

Provides full 200° field of vision. User can see anyone hiding alongside door against wall. Solid brass with ground glass. Fits all standard doors 1³/₈" to 2" thick.

>**PRICE B**  From VSI Hardware Ind. (Many hardware stores carry this item.)

## 13.9  LEVER PADLOCK

Combination lock with levers instead of dial. Can be opened by feeling or hearing clicks. Case is 2³/₄" long. Braille copies of combination are available on request.

>**PRICE A**  From American Foundation for Blind / Klick Lock

## 13.10  LOCK ALERT

Red-alert indicator warns when bolt isn't locked, disappears when bolt locks. Single cylinder dead lock. Jimmy-proof.

>**PRICE B**  From S. Parker Hardware

### 13.11 PORTABLE TRAVEL LOCK

A portable lock requiring no permanent attachment to doors or drawers. A hook on end of locking bar fits into latch hole in the strike. Door is closed and locking unit is moved down, locking bar against surface of door.

**PRICE A** From Scovill Security Products (Yale Travel Lock) (locksmiths and hardware stores sometimes carry this item)

### 13.12 DISGUISED SAFE

Cache hanger has shape of coat hanger and can be hidden by coat or sweater. It is locked to closet pole. Steel and cast-aluminum construction. When touched, sounds alarm. Works on one 9-volt battery. Hides valuables. Keeps dangerous medications away from children. Weight 5 lb.

**PRICE C** From Hammacher Schlemmer

### 13.13 PROGRAM TIMER SWITCH

Turns lights on and off automatically once, twice, or oftener daily. Has two sets of on/off trippers; push-button on/off switch. Maximum "on": $23\frac{1}{2}$ hours—minimum "on": $\frac{1}{2}$ hour.

**PRICE B** From Intermatic, Inc. (Hardware stores sometimes carry this item)

### 13.14 MASTER CONTROL TIME SWITCH

Has twenty-four separate tabs. Slide out one tab for each hour of "on" time desired. Controls lamps, radio, TV when you are away from home. Has manual on/off switch to permit use without disturbing automatic operation. Maximum "on" time: 23 hours—minimum "on" time: 1 hour.

**PRICE B** From Intermatic, Inc. (hardware stores sometimes carry this item.)

## 13.15 AUTOMATIC VARIABLE TIMER

Automatically turns lamps, radio, TV on and off at slightly different times daily. Variable pattern confuses potential intruders. Has manual on/off switch to prevent interference with automatic operation. Maximum "on": $20^{1}/_{2}$ hours—minimum "on": $3^{1}/_{2}$ hours.

**PRICE B** From Intermatic, Inc. (some hardware stores carry this item.)

## 13.16 AUTOMATIC TIMER

Basic fully automatic timer. Turns lights on and off at preselected times once a day while you are at home or away. Has manual on/off switch. Maximum "on": $21^{1}/_{2}$ hours—minimum "on": 2 1/2 hours.

**PRICE B** From Intermatic, Inc.—Time All (some hardware stores carry this item.)

## 13.17 LIGHT-SENSITIVE CONTROL TIMER

Automatically turns light on at dusk, turns off at dawn. Screw control into standard medium-base socket. Bulb then screws into control.

**PRICE B** From Intermatic, Inc. (some hardware stores carry this item.)

# Appendix
## Useful Names and Addresses

### Organizations, Agencies, and Other Sources of Help for the Disabled and Elderly

Administration on Aging
U.S. Department of Health and Human Services
Washington, D.C. 20201

Advocates for the Handicapped
77 West Washington Street
Room 402
Chicago, Illinois 60602

Alexander Graham Bell Assoc. for the Deaf, Inc.
The Volta Bureau
3714 Volta Place, N.W.
Washington, D.C. 20007

American Alliance for Health, PE, and Recreation
1201 16th Street, N.W.
Washington, D.C. 20036

American Association for the Education of the Severely Handicapped
1600 West Armory Way
Seattle, Washington 98119

American Association of Retired Persons
National Headquarters
1909 K Street, N.W.
Washington, D.C. 20049

American Association of Workers for the Blind, Inc.
1511 K Street, N.W.
Washington, D.C. 20005

American Blind Bowlers Association
150 North Bellair Avenue
Louisville, Kentucky 40206

American Cancer Society, Inc.
National Office
777 Third Avenue
New York, New York 10017

American Coalition of Citizens with Disabilities
Room 817
1346 Connecticut Avenue, N.W.
Washington, D.C. 20036

American Diabetes Association, Inc.
600 Fifth Avenue
New York, New York 10020

The American Dietetic Association
430 North Michigan Avenue
Chicago, Illinois 60611

American Foundation for the Blind
15 West 16th Street
New York, New York 10011

American Heart Association
National Center
7320 Greenville Avenue
Dallas, Texas 75231

American Home Economics Association
2010 Massachusetts Avenue, N.W.
Washington, D.C. 20036

American Lung Association
1740 Broadway
New York, New York 10019

American Medical Association
535 North Dearborn Street
Chicago, Illinois 60610

American Occupational Therapy Association, Inc.
6000 Executive Boulevard
Rockville, Maryland 20852

American Physical Therapy Association
1156 15th Street, N.W.
Washington, D.C. 20005

American Speech & Hearing Association
1081 Rockville Pike
Rockville, Maryland 20852

American Wheelchair Bowling Association, Inc.
2424 N. Federal Highway #109
Boynton Beach, Florida 33435

Amputees' Service Association
P.O. Box A-3819
Chicago, Illinois 60690

Amyotrophic Lateral Sclerosis Society of America
12011 San Vicente Boulevard
Los Angeles, California 90049

Architectural & Transportation Barriers Compliance Board
Washington, D.C. 20201

The Arthritis Foundation
3400 Peachtree Road, N.E.
Atlanta, Georgia 30326

Association for Children with Learning Disabilities
4156 Library Road
Pittsburgh, Pennsylvania 15234

Association of Handicapped Artists, Inc.
503 Brisbane Boulevard
Buffalo, New York 14203

Blind Outdoor Leisure Development
National Office
533 East Main
Aspen, Colorado 81611

Bureau of Education for the Handicapped
U.S. Office of Education
Washington, D.C. 20202

Canadian Arthritis & Rheumatism Society
45 Charles Street East
Toronto, Ontario M4Y 1S3
Canada

Canadian Paraplegic Association
153 Lyndhurst Avenue
Toronto, Ontario M4G 3V9
Canada

Canadian Rehabilitation Council for the Disabled
Suite 2110
1 Yonge Street
Toronto, Ontario M5E 1E8
Canada

"The College Guide for Students with Disabilities"
ABT Publications
55 Wheeler Street
Cambridge, Massachusetts 02138

Commission on Accreditation of Rehabilitation Facilities
4001 West Devon Avenue
Chicago, Illinois 60646

Congress of Organizations of the Physically Handicapped
7611 Oakland Avenue
Minneapolis, Minnesota 55423

Consumer Product Information Service
Public Documents Distribution Center
Pueblo, Colorado 81009

Disabled American Veterans
3725 Alexandria Pike
Cold Spring, Kentucky 41076

Disabled Living Foundation
346 Kensington High Street
London W14 8NS, England
   (Publications for persons with disabilities)

Easter Seal Home Service
2 Park Avenue
New York, New York 10016

"Employment Assistance for the Handicapped" (publication) and "Careers for the Homebound" (publication)
President's Committee on Employment of the Handicapped
Washington, D.C. 20210

Federal Office for Handicapped Individuals
U.S. Department of Health and Human Services
200 Independence Avenue, S.W.
Washington, D.C. 20201

Federation of the Handicapped
211 West 14th Street
New York, New York 10011

Goodwill Industries of America
9200 Wisconsin Avenue
Washington, D.C. 20014

Guiding Eyes for the Blind
Yorktown Heights, New York 10598
   (*See also* The Seeing Eye, Inc.)

Handicapped Artists of America, Inc.
8 Sandy Lane
Salisbury, Massachusetts 01950

Hearing Dogs
Administrator of Special Programs
American Humane Association
P.O. Box 1266
Denver, Colorado 80201

Homebound Book Service
359 McLean Boulevard
Paterson, New Jersey 07509

Independence Factory
P.O. Box 597
Middletown, Ohio 45042

Indoor Sports Club
1145 Highland Street
Napoleon, Ohio 43545

Institute of Rehabilitation Medicine
New York University Medical Center
400 East 34th Street
New York, New York 10016

International Association of Laryngectomees
777 Third Avenue
New York, New York 10017

International Association of Rehabilitation Facilities
5530 Wisconsin Avenue
Suite 955
Washington, D.C. 20015

International Federation on Aging
1909 K Street, N.W.
Washington, D.C. 20049

International Senior Citizens Association, Inc.
17753 Wilshire Boulevard
Los Angeles, California 90025

Just One Break
373 Park Avenue South
New York, New York 10016

Library of Congress
Division for the Blind and Physically Handicapped
Washington, D.C. 20542

Little People of America
P.O. Box 126
Owatonna, Minnesota 55060

Medic Alert Foundation International
P.O. Box 1009
Turlock, California 95380
  (Comprehensive emergency medical identification system for individuals)

Muscular Dystrophy Associations of America, Inc.
810 Seventh Avenue
New York, New York 10019

National Amputation Foundation
12–45 150th Street
Whitestone, New York 11357

National Association of the Deaf
814 Thayer Avenue
Silver Spring, Maryland 20910

National Association of the
  Physically Handicapped
2 Meetinghouse Road
Merrimack, New Hampshire 03054

National Association of Social Workers
1425 H Street, N.W.
Suite 600
Washington, D.C. 20005

National Center for a Barrier-Free Environment
8401 Connecticut Avenue, N.W.
Washington, D.C. 20015

National Center for Law and the Handicapped, Inc.
1235 North Eddy Street
South Bend, Indiana 46617

National Center for Voluntary Action
1214 16th Street, N.W.
Washington, D.C. 20036

National Commission on Architectural Barriers for
  Rehabilitation of the Handicapped
Social & Rehabilitation Services
Washington, D.C. 20210

National Congress of Organizations of the Physically
  Handicapped
1627 Deborah Avenue
Rockford, Illinois 61103

National Council on the Aging
1828 L Street, N.W.
Washington, D.C. 20036

National Council for Homemaker–Home Health Aide
  Services, Inc.
67 Irving Place
New York, New York 10003

National Council of Senior Citizens
1511 K Street, N.W.
Washington, D.C. 20005

National Easter Seal Society for Crippled Children & Adults
2023 West Ogden Avenue
Chicago, Illinois 60612

National Federation of the Blind
1346 Connecticut Avenue, N.W.
Washington, D.C. 20036

National Foundation of Dentistry for the Handicapped
1121 Broadway, Suite 5
Boulder, Colorado 80302

National Foundation—March of Dimes
Box 2000
White Plains, New York 10602

National Heart & Lung Institute
9600 Rockville Pike, Bldg. 31
Bethesda, Maryland 20014

National Institute of Arthritis and Metabolic Diseases
Bethesda, Maryland 20014

National Multiple Sclerosis Society
205 East 42nd Street
New York, New York 10017

National Paraplegia Foundation
333 North Michigan Avenue
Chicago, Illinois 60601

National Rehabilitation Association
1522 K Street, N.W.
Washington, D.C. 20005

National Safety Council
444 North Michigan Avenue
Chicago, Illinois 60611

National Society for the Prevention of Blindness
79 Madison Avenue
New York, New York 10016

National Wheelchair Athletic Association
40–24 62nd Street
Woodside, New York 11377

National Wheelchair Basketball Association
Office of the Commissioner
110 Seaton Building
University of Kentucky
Lexington, Kentucky 40506

New England Spinal Cord Injury Foundation, Inc.
369 Elliot Street
Newton Upper Falls, Massachusetts 02164

North American Riding for the Handicapped
   Association
c/o Leonard Warner
P.O. Box 100
Ashburn, Virginia 22011

Nutrition Foundation
489 Fifth Avenue
New York, New York 10017

Office of Consumer Services
U.S. Department of Health & Human Services
Washington, D.C. 20201

Office for Handicapped Individuals
U.S. Department of Health & Human Services
Office of the Secretary
Washington, D.C. 20201

Paralyzed Veterans of America, Inc.
4330 East West Highway, Suite 300
Washington, D.C. 20014

President's Committee on Employment of the Handicapped
Washington, D.C. 20210

Public Affairs Pamphlets
381 Park Avenue
New York, New York 10016
   (Catalog of publications)

Registry of Interpreters for the Deaf, Inc.
P.O. Box 1339
Washington, D.C. 20013

Rehabilitation International
432 Park Avenue South
New York, New York 10016

Rehabilitation Services Administration
U.S. Department of Health & Human Services
Washington, D.C. 20402

Scouting for Handicapped
Education Relationships Service
Boy Scouts of America
North Brunswick, New Jersey 08902

The Seeing Eye, Inc.
Morristown, New Jersey 07960
   (*See also* Guiding Eyes for the Blind)

Senior Citizen Service Organizations
   (Check local telephone directory)

Sister Kenny Institute
A/V Publications Office
Chicago Avenue at 27th Street
Minneapolis, Minnesota 55407

Society for the Advancement of Travel for the Handicapped
26 Court Street
Brooklyn, New York 11242

Superintendent of Documents
U.S. Government Printing Office
Washington, D.C. 20402

Telephone Pioneers of America
Frank B. Jewett Chapter
Bell Tel Lab.
600 Mt. Avenue
Murray Hill, New Jersey 07974

Travel Information Center
Moss Rehabilitation Hospital
12th Street & Tabor Road
Philadelphia, Pennsylvania 19141

United Cerebral Palsy Associations, Inc.
66 East 34th Street
New York, New York 10016

United States Library of Congress Division for the Blind
   & Physically Handicapped
Washington, D.C. 20542

United States Ski Association
Central Division
Handicapped Skiers Committee
Wm. E. Stieler, Chairman
6832 Marlette Road
Marlette, Michigan 48453

United States Social Security Administration
Division of Disability Operations
6401 Security Boulevard
Baltimore, Maryland 21235

Urban Mass Transit Transportation Administration
Office of Public Affairs
400 7th Street, S.W.
Washington, D.C. 20590

Visiting Nurse Association
   (Check local telephone directory)

"Vocational and Educational Opportunities for the
   Disabled" (publication)
Insurance Co. of North America
Human Resources Center
Willets Road
Albertson, New York 11507

Vocational Guidance and Rehabilitation Services
2239 East 55th Street
Cleveland, Ohio 44103

## Periodicals Useful to the Disabled and Elderly

*Accent on Living*, P.O. Box 700, Bloomington, Illinois 61701. Quarterly.

*Achievement*, 925 N.E. 122nd Street, North Miami, Florida 33161. Monthly.

*Amicus*, National Center for Law and the Handicapped, 135 North Eddy Street, South Bend, Indiana 46226.

*Caliper*, The Canadian Paraplegic Association, 520 Sutherland Drive, Toronto, Ontario, M4G 3V9 Canada.

*COPH Bulletin*, National Congress of Organizations of the Physically Handicapped, 7611 Oakland Avenue, Minneapolis, Minnesota 55423. Quarterly.

*The Deaf American*, National Association of the Deaf, 5125 Radner Road, Indianapolis, Indiana 46226.

*Encore*, Division for the Blind and Physically Handicapped, Library of Congress, Washington, D.C. 20540. Bimonthly recordings for Talking Book readers of selections from publications for the disabled. Available on free loan from your regional library.

*Green Pages: A Directory of Products and Services for the Handicapped*, 641 West Fairbanks, Winter Park, Florida 32789. Quarterly.

*Handi-Cap Horizons*, 3250 East Loretta Drive, Indianapolis, Indiana 46227.

*Mainstream*, 861 Sixth Avenue, San Diego, California 92101.

*NAPH (National Association of Physically Handicapped) Newsletter*, 2 Meetinghouse Road, Reeds Ferry, New Hampshire 03078. Quarterly.

*National Hookup*, 536 Mason Street, Riverside, California 92503. Monthly.

*National Star Newsletter*, 6219 Naper Avenue, Chicago, Illinois 60631. Bimonthly.

*Newsletter*, Committee for the Handicapped, People-to-People Program, 1146 16th Street, N.W., Washington, D.C. 20036. Free. Write to be added to mailing list.

*On Your Own*, Newsletter, The University of Alabama, Continuing Education in Home Economics, P.O. Box 2967, University, Alabama 35486. Free. Write to be added to mailing list.

*Open Window*, National Shut-In Society, Inc., 225 West 99th Street, New York, New York 10025. Monthly.

*Ostomy Quarterly*, United Ostomy Association, Inc., 1111 Wilshire Boulevard, Los Angeles, California 90017.

*Paraplegia Life*, National Paraplegia Foundation, 333 North Michigan Avenue, Chicago, Illinois 60601. Bimonthly.

*Paraplegia News*, Paralyzed Veterans of America and National Paraplegia Foundation, 935 Coastline Drive, Seal Beach, California 90740. Monthly.

*Performance*, President's Committee on Employment of the Handicapped, Washington, D.C. 20210. Monthly. Free. Write to be added to mailing list.

*Rehabilitation Gazette*, International Journal and Information Service for the Disabled, 4502 Maryland Avenue, St. Louis, Missouri 63108.

*Sports 'N Spokes*, 6043 North Ninth Avenue, Phoenix, Arizona 85013.

*Talking Book Topics*, United States Library of Congress, Division for the Blind and Physically Handicapped, Washington, D.C. 20542.

## SUPPLIERS

ABC Enterprises
8905 Mentor Avenue
Mentor, Ohio 44060

AC-Delco
400 Renaissance Center
Suite 1200
Detroit, Michigan 48243

Alimed, Inc.
138 Prince Street
Boston, Massachusetts 02113

Alliance Manufacturing Company, Inc.
22790 Lake Park Boulevard
Alliance, Ohio 44601

Alsons Corporation
42 Union Street
Hillsdale, Michigan 49242

Aluminum Housewares Company, Inc.
11700 Fairgrove Industrial Blvd.
P.O. Box 1599
Maryland Heights, Missouri 63043

American Bidet Company
P.O. Box 1500
Hollywood, Florida 33022

American Coil Company
P.O. Box 9
Algonquin, Illinois 60102

American Family Scale Company, Inc.
3718 South Ashland Avenue
Chicago, Illinois 60609

American Foundation for the Blind, Inc.
15 West 16th Street
New York, New York 10011

American Printing House for the Blind
1839 Frankfort Avenue
P.O. Box 6085
Louisville, Kentucky 40206

American Stair-Glide Corporation
4001 East 138th Street
Grandview, Missouri 64030

American Telephone & Telegraph Company
1776 On the Green
Morristown, New Jersey 07960

American Thermo-Ware Company (ATCO)
16 Warren Street
New York, New York 10007

Amigo Sales, Inc.
6693 Dixie Highway
Bridgeport, Michigan 48722

Amsco
2425 West 23rd Street
Erie, Pennsylvania 16512

Anik, Inc.
P.O. Box 3232
San Rafael, California 94901

Aparco, Inc.
215 A Street
Boston, Massachusetts 02210

Apor Industries, Inc.
251 West Garfield Road
Aurora, Ohio 44202

Aquatherm Corporation
P.O. Box 266
1582 Hart Street
Rahway, New Jersey 07065

ARTS Associates, Inc.
80 Boylston Street
Boston, Massachusetts 02116

Atari, Inc.
1265 Borregas Avenue
Sunnyvale, California 94086

Audio Book Company
14937 Ventura Boulevard
Sherman Oaks, California 91403

Bathing Aids to the Handicapped
P.O. Box 1956
Greeley, Colorado 80632

Battle Creek Equipment Company
307 West Jackson Street
Battle Creek, Michigan 49016

L. L. Bean, Inc.
Freeport, Maine 04033

C. Beil Designs
5435 N. Artesian Avenue
Chicago, Illinois 60625

Bernell Corporation
422 East Monroe Street
South Bend, Indiana 46601

Besam, Inc.
P.O. Box 2197
Bridgeport, Connecticut 06608

Beth Shalom Braille Committee
8831 Ensley Lane
Leawood, Kansas 66206

Better Sleep, Inc.
New Providence, New Jersey 07974

Betty Crocker Kitchens
P.O. Box 1113
Minneapolis, Minnesota 55440

Bissell, Inc.
Grand Rapids, Michigan 49501

The Black Cottle
  (*See* Single Hander Company)

B. Blackwood
1117 Rising Hill
Escondido, California 92025

Bollen Products Company
P.O. Box 17043
Cleveland, Ohio 44117

R. R. Bowker Company
1180 Avenue of the Americas
New York, New York 10036

The Braun Corporation
1014 South Monticello
Winamac, Indiana 46996

E. F. Brewer Company
P.O. Box 159
Menomonee Falls, Wisconsin 53051

Brookstone Company
Vose Farm Road
Peterborough, New Hampshire 03458

Burke, Inc.
P.O. Box 1064
Mission, Kansas 66202

Camp International, Inc.
109–113 West Washington Avenue
P.O. Box 89
Jackson, Michigan 49204

Camping World
Beech Bend Road
Bowling Green, Kentucky 42101

Carefree of Colorado
2760 Industrial Lane
Broomfield, Colorado 80020

CHEC Medical Products
P.O. Box 1112R
166 Ridgedale Avenue
Morristown, New Jersey 07960

The Cheney Company, Inc.
3015 South 163rd Street
New Berlin, Wisconsin 53151

Chris-Craft Industries, Inc.
600 Madison Avenue
New York, New York 10022

Toby Churchill Ltd.
20 Panton Street
Cambridge CB2 1HP, England

Cleo Living Aids
3957 Mayfield Road
Cleveland, Ohio 44121

Clos-O-Mat, Inc.
244 Bayberry Lane
Franklin Lakes, New Jersey 07417

Collins Industries, Inc.
P.O. Box 58
Hutchinson, Kansas 67501

Comfort-Able-Aids
P.O. Box 275
Somerset Street
Raritan, New Jersey 08869

Communicaid®
1560 West William Street
Decatur, Illinois 62522

Computers for the Physically Handicapped
7602 Talbert Avenue
Huntington Beach, California 92647

Contourpedic Corporation
280 Midland Avenue
Saddle Brook, New Jersey 07662

Convaid Product Development
P.O. Box 2731
Palos Verdes, California 90274

Cramer Industries
625 Adams Street
Kansas City, Kansas 66105

Crow River Industries, Inc.
1415 East Wayzata Boulevard
Wayzata, Minnesota 55391

Dakon Corporation
1836 Gilford Avenue
New Hyde Park, New York 11040

Dazy Products Company
1 Dazy Circle
Johnson County Industrial Airport
Industrial Airport, Kansas 66031

Delta Medical Industries
1378 Logan Avenue
Costa Mesa, California 92626

Roy Dodgen Shop
Blue Eye, Missouri 65611

Dorsay
240 Kinderkamack Road
Oradell, New Jersey 07649

Dow Knob, Inc.
P.O. Box 721
515 North Lee Street
Bloomington, Illinois 61701

Down East Electronics Manufacturing Company
44 Bucknam Road
Falmouth, Maine 04105

Drive-Master Corporation
16 Andrews Drive
West Paterson, New Jersey 07424

The Ealing Corporation
22 Pleasant Street
South Natick, Massachusetts 01760

Earl's Stairway Lift Corporation
2513 Center Street
Cedar Falls, Iowa 50613

Easy Bath Manufacturers, Inc.
1374 North Killian Drive
Lake Park, Florida 33403

Easy Riser, Inc.
87 Millstone Road
Wilton, Connecticut 06897

Eaton E-Z Bath Company
P.O. Box 172
Garden City, Kansas 67846

Eco-Filters, Inc.
1451 East Gunhill Road
New York, New York 10469

EDCO/Pasco, Inc.
P.O. Box 328
125 South Street
Passaic, New Jersey 07055

The Ednalite Corporation
200 North Water Street
Peekskill, New York 10566

Edroy Products Company, Inc.
130 West 29th Street
New York, New York 10001

Electro Van
744 North Concord Street
South St. Paul, Minnesota 55075

Electropedic Products
907 Hollywood Way
Burbank, California 91505

Elevator Safety Products
Thompson Avenue
Highway 22
Bound Brook, New Jersey 08805

Escalera, Inc.
P.O. Box 1359
Yuba City, California 95991

ESP Systems Development, Inc.
28189 Kehrig Drive
Mt. Clemens, Michigan 48045

Eton Phone Company
555 Greenbrier Drive #29
Oceanside, California 92054

Evenflow Company
771 North Freedom Street
Ravenna, Ohio 44266

Everest and Jennings, Inc.
1803 Pontius Avenue
Los Angeles, California 90025

Evlo Plastics, Inc.
1432 Tiffin Avenue
Sandusky, Ohio 44870

Falcon Research & Development
1225 South Huron
Denver, Colorado 80223

Fanon Courier
990 South Fair Oaks Avenue
Pasadena, California 91105

Farberware®
1500 Bassett Avenue
Bronx, New York 10461

FashionAble
Rocky Hill, New Jersey 08553

Fidelity Electronics Ltd.
5245 Diversey Avenue
Chicago, Illinois 60639

Fimco
35-02 154th Street
Flushing, New York 11354

The Flinchbaugh Company, Inc.
390 Eberts Lane
York, Pennsylvania 17403

Foley Manufacturing Company
3300 Fifth Street Northeast
Minneapolis, Minnesota 55418

Ford Industries, Inc.
5001 S.E. Johnson Creek Boulevard
Portland, Oregon 97206

Freedomchair
P.O. Box 698
Colonial Plaza
Binghamton, New York 13902

Frohock Stewart, Inc.
455 Whitney Avenue
Northboro, Massachusetts 01532

Gandy Company
528 Gandrud Road
Owatonna, Minnesota 55060

Gantts Wood Things
111 South Glenwood Avenue
Orlando, Florida 32803

General Electric Company
Housewares & Audio Business Division
Bridgeport, Connecticut 06602

Girard Engineering Company
211 Industrial Avenue
P.O. Box 1000
Bronson, Michigan 49028

Glenco Infants Items, Inc.
108 Fairway Court
Northvale, New Jersey 07647

Gorman Products
189 Lake Street
Brooklyn, New York 11223

Grant Water Corporation
1010 Washington Boulevard
Stamford, Connecticut 06901

Grayline Housewares
1616 Berkley Street
Elgin, Illinois 60120

Carol Green
324 Acre Avenue
Brownsburg, Indiana 46112

Grip Toter, Inc.
401 Carter Road
Goshen, Indiana 46526

G. K. Hall & Company
70 Lincoln Street
Boston, Massachusetts 02111

Hamilton Beach
Division of Scoville Manufacturing Company
P.O. Box 2027
Washington, North Carolina 27889

Hammacher Schlemmer
147 East 57th Street
New York, New York 10022

Handee For You
7674 Park Avenue
Lowville, New York 13367

Handibend Manufacturing Company
R.R.2, R.D. 161
Accord, New York 12404

Handi-Ramp, Inc.
P.O. Box 745
1414 Armour Boulevard
Mundelein, Illinois 60060

Harper-Lee International, Inc.
308 Prince
St. Paul, Minnesota 55101

Hausman Industries, Inc.
130 Union Street
Northvale, New Jersey 07647

H.C. Electronics, Inc.
250 Camino Alto
Mill Valley, California 94941

Carl Heald, Inc.
P.O. Box 1148
Benton Harbor, Michigan 49022

Help Me Help Myself Communication Aids
(*See* Carol Green)

Help Yourself Aids
P.O. Box 15
Brookfield, Illinois 60513

Hoffman Manufacturing Company
22346 Hesperian Boulevard
Haywood, California 94541

Holo Industries
12920 Haster Street
Garden Grove, California 92640

The Hoover Company
North Canton, Ohio 44720

Ted Hoyer & Company, Inc.
2222 Minnesota Street
Oshkosh, Wisconsin 54901

Hughes Hand Driving Controls, Inc.
P.O. Box 275
Lexington, Missouri 64067

Hukuba-Cowdery Corporation
9905 Hamilton Road
Eden Prairie, Minnesota 55344

Hustler Corporation
P.O. Box 1283
Jonesboro, Arkansas 72401

IBM (International Business Machines)
Office Products Division
400 Parsons Pond Drive
Franklin Lakes, New Jersey 07417

Inclinator Company of America
P.O. Box 1557
2200 Paxton Street
Harrisburg, Pennsylvania 17105

Intermatic, Inc.
Intermatic Plaza
Spring Grove, Illinois 60081

Invacare Corporation
1200 Taylor Street
P.O. Box 550
Elyria, Ohio 44035

Invento
(*See* Hammacher Schlemmer)

The JAL Company
3046 Bamlet Road
Royal Oak, Michigan 48073

Jefferson Industries, Inc.
205 Nassau Street
Princeton, New Jersey 08540

Jobst Institute Inc.
P.O. Box 653
Toledo, Ohio 43694

Jones-Zylon, Inc.
P.O. Box 158
West Lafayette, Ohio 43845

Kady-Kart, Inc.
Mapletree Industrial Park
Palmer, Massachusetts 01069

S. E. Kewer
514 Cathedral Parkway
New York, New York 10025

KGB Research & Development
7025 Duncan Road
Punta Gorda, Florida 33950

Kohler Company
Kohler, Wisconsin 53044

Kroepke Kontrols, Inc.
104 Hawkins Street
Bronx, New York 10464

Lakeland Products
21 Birnamwood Drive
Burnsville, Minnesota 55337

Lamson and Goodnow
P.O. Box 128
Shelburne, Massachusetts 01370

The Left Hand, Inc.
140 West 22nd Street
New York, New York 10011

Lossing Company
2217 Nicollet Avenue South
Minneapolis, Minnesota 55404

Love-Co Products, Inc.
7173 Navajo Road
San Diego, California 92119

Loyal Laplante Supply Company
1519 South Lewis
Tulsa, Oklahoma 74104

Lumex, Inc.
100 Spence Street
Bayshore, New York 11706

Maddak, Inc.
Pequannock, New Jersey 07440

S. Margolis
1557 Selwyn Avenue
Bronx, New York 10457

The Maxim™ Company
164 Delancy Street
Newark, New Jersey 07105

The Maytag Company
Newton, Iowa 50208

Ken McRight Supplies, Inc.
7456 South Oswego
Tulsa, Oklahoma 74136

MED (Medical Equipment Distributors, Inc.)
1701 South First Avenue
Maywood, Illinois 60153

Medic Alert Foundation International
P.O. Box 1009
Turlock, California 95380

Medpro, Inc.
275 Highway 18
East Brunswick, New Jersey 08816

Microlert Systems International
3029 San Fernando Boulevard
Burbank, California 91504

G. E. Miller, Inc.
484 South Broadway
Yonkers, New York 10705

Monadnock Lifetime Products, Inc.
P.O. Box B
Fitzwilliam, New Hampshire 03447

Joseph Muller Corporation
Zurich, Switzerland

Multi Marketing, Inc.
P.O. Box 1125
Littleton, Colorado 80160

National Identification Company
3955 Oneida Street
Denver, Colorado 80207

New York Times
229 West 43rd Street
New York, New York 10036

Newman-Fine, Inc.
P.O. Box 2004
New York, New York 10017

Nicoll Brothers, Inc.
1204 West 27th Street
Kansas City, Missouri 64108

J. E. Nolan & Company, Inc.
P.O. Box 43201
Louisville, Kentucky 40243

Norelco
100 East 42nd Street
New York, New York 10017

North American Recreation Convertables, Inc.
P.O. Box 758
Bridgeport, Connecticut 06601

Northland Aluminum Products, Inc.
Highway 7 at Beltline
Minneapolis, Minnesota 55416

On Guard Corporation of America
350 Gotham Parkway
Carlstadt, New Jersey 07072

Ortho-Kinetics, Inc.
P.O. Box 436
1610 Pearl Street
Waukesha, Wisconsin 53186

The Orvis Company, Inc.
Manchester, Vermont 05254

Osrow Products Corporation
303 Winding Road
Old Bethpage, New York 11804

Oster Corporation
Milwaukee, Wisconsin 53217

Owen-Pacific Associates
412 Woodward Boulevard
Pasadena, California 91107

Ozburn Janesville
133 South Garfield Avenue
Janesville, Wisconsin 53545

Palmer Industries
P.O. Box 707
Union Station
Endicott, New York 13760

Paper Welder, Inc.
Medina, New York 14103

S. Parker Hardware Manufacturing Corporation
27 Ludlow Street
New York, New York 10002

PCA Industries, Inc.
29-24 40th Avenue
Long Island City, New York 11101

P.C.P.
   (See Professional Convalescent Products Company)

Phonics Corporation
814 Thayer Avenue
Silver Spring, Maryland 20910

Physical Aids Marketing Company
144 South Orange Avenue
El Cajon, California 92020

Plakadent International Ltd.
222 East State Street
Westport, Connecticut 06880

The Platt Luggage Company
2301 South Prairie Avenue
Chicago, Illinois 60616

Playlearn
   (See PCA Industries, Inc.)

Porto-Lift Manufacturing Company
Higgins Lake, Michigan 48627

Power Access Corporation
P.O. Box 139
Eatontown, New Jersey 07724

Prentke Romich Company
R.D. 2, Box 191
Shreve, Ohio 44676

J. A. Preston Corporation
71 Fifth Avenue
New York, New York 10003

Processed Signs & Display Company, Inc.
Edison Street
P.O. Box 372
Amsterdam, New York 12010

Professional Convalescent Products Company
Congress Street
Ripley, Ohio 45167

PSI
125 Columbia Court
Chaska, Minnesota 55318


Rayl Distributing Company
P.O. Box 321
Russiaville, Indiana 46979

Raymo Products, Inc.
212 South Blake
Olathe, Kansas 66061

Readers Digest Large-Type Edition
Readers Digest Fund for the Blind, Inc.
Pleasantville, New York 10570

Regal Ware, Inc.
1675 Reigle Drive
Kewaskum, Wisconsin 53040

Replogle Globe, Inc.
1901 North Narragansett Avenue
Chicago, Illinois 60639

R.J. Mobility Systems
715 South 5th Avenue
Maywood, Illinois 60153

Rice Council of America
P.O. Box 22802
3917 Richmond Avenue
Houston, Texas 77027

Rite-Line Corporation
9107A Gaither Road
Gaithersburg, Maryland 20760

Rival Manufacturing Company
36th and Bennington
Kansas City, Missouri 64129

Roho Research & Development, Inc.
3105 Missouri Avenue
East St. Louis, Illinois 62203

Rol-Ruler Company
P.O. Box 164
Riegelsville, Pennsylvania 18077

Rosenthal Manufacturing Company, Inc.
5033 North Kedzie
Chicago, Illinois 60625

Rubbermaid, Inc.
1147 Akron Road
Wooster, Ohio 44691

Rubery Owen Holdings Ltd.
P.O. Box 10
Wednesbury, West Midlands
England WS 10 8 JD

Rush Hampton Industries
3000 Industrial Park
Longwood, Florida 32750

Science for the Blind Products
P.O. Box 385
Wayne, Pennsylvania 19087

Scitronics, Inc.
523 S. Clewell Street
P.O. Box 5344
Bethlehem, Pennsylvania 18015

Fred Scott & Sons
1444 Rand Road
Des Plaines, Illinois 60016

Scovill Security Products
P.O. Box 25288
Charlotte, North Carolina 28212

Scrambler, Inc.
111 Seventeenth Street
Genoa, Ohio 43430

Sears, Roebuck & Company
Sears Tower
Chicago, Illinois 60684

Seaton Name Plate Corporation
592 Boulevard
New Haven, Connecticut 06505

Selby Fifth Avenue
417 Fifth Avenue
New York, New York 10016

Sherry Products, Inc.
1501 Pacific Coast Highway
Hermosa Beach, California 90254

Shur-Lok Manufacturing Company, Inc.
413 North Main Street
Hutchins, Texas 75141

Simplex Security Systems, Inc.
10 Front Street
Collinsville, Connecticut 06022

Single Hander Company
P.O. Box 36
Brantingham, New York 13312

Sleepy Hollow Gifts
6651 Arlington Boulevard
Falls Church, Virginia 22042

Smith-Corona
65 Locust Avenue
New Canaan, Connecticut 06840

Smiths Hand Control Service
1420 Brookhaven Drive
Southaven, Mississippi 38671

George H. Snyder
5809 N.E. 21 Avenue
Fort Lauderdale, Florida 33308

Soldner Pottery Equipment, Inc.
P.O. Box 428
Silt, Colorado 81652

Sparr Telephone Arm Company
P.O. Box 143
Allamuchy, New Jersey 07820

Specialized Systems
11558 Sorrento Valley Road
Building #7
San Diego, California 92121

Springfield Instrument Company
260 Railroad Avenue
Hackensack, New Jersey 07602

Stainless Medical Products
3107 South Kilson Drive
Santa Ana, California 92707

Staircat™, Inc.
1 Pine Street
Nashua, New Hampshire 03060

The Stanley Works
195 Lake Street
New Britain, Connecticut 06050

Steven Motor Chair Company
120 North Gunter Street
Siloam Springs, Arkansas 72761

Stimulation Aids, Ltd.
65 Earle Avenue
Lynbrook, New York 11563

Oscar B. Stiskin
P.O. Box 3055
Stamford, Connecticut 06905

Summit Corporation
P.O. Box 578
Valparaiso, Florida 32580

Sunset House
306 Sunset Building
Beverly Hills, California 90215

Swift Instruments, Inc.
952 Dorchester Avenue
Boston, Massachusetts 02125

Swing Away Manufacturing Company
4100 Beck Avenue
St. Louis, Missouri 63116

Technical Aids to Independence, Inc.
12 Hyde Road
Bloomfield, New Jersey 07003

Technology Applications Corporation
560 San Antonio Road
Palo Alto, California 94306

Telesensory Systems, Inc.
3408 Hillview Avenue
P.O. Box 10099
Palo Alto, California 94304

Teletronics United, Inc.
2910 Rubidoux Boulevard
Riverside, California 92509

Theradyne Corporation
21730 Hanover Avenue
Lakeville, Minnesota 55044

Therafin Corporation
3800 South Union Avenue
Steger, Illinois 60475

Thera-Plast Company, Inc.
132 Nassau Street
New York, New York 10038

Time Savers, Inc.
P.O. Box 7147
Sacramento, California 95826

Toce Brothers Manufacturing
P.O. Box 489
Broussard, Louisiana 70518

Toll Free Digest
P.O. Box 800
Claverack, New York 12513

Toshiba America, Inc.
280 Park Avenue
New York, New York 10017

Touch Turner
443 View Ridge Drive
Everett, Washington 98203

Trans-Aid Corporation
1609 East Del Amo Boulevard at Tajauta
Carlson, California 90746

Tri World Industries
16015 West 5th Avenue
Golden, Colorado 80401

Triaxon, Inc.
3339 West Lake Avenue
Glenview, Illinois 60025

Tubular Specialties Manufacturing, Inc.
8119 Beach Street
Los Angeles, California 90001

Typewriting Institute for the Handicapped
3102 West Augusta Avenue
Phoenix, Arizona 85021

United States Luggage Corporation
951 Broadway
Fall River, Massachusetts 02724

Universal Controls Corporation
10889 Wilshire Boulevard
Los Angeles, California 90024

Universal-Rundle Corporation
217 North Mill Street
New Castle, Pennsylvania 16103

The Variable Speech Control Company
185 Berry Street
San Francisco, California 94107

Ventura—Research & Rehabilitation
    for Handicapped, Inc.
35 Lawton Avenue
Danville, Indiana 46122

Vibralite Products, Inc.
1 Belleview Avenue
Ossining, New York 10562

Visualtek, Inc.
1610 26th Street
Santa Monica, California 90404

Volunteers Service for the Blind, Inc.
919 Walnut Street
Philadelphia, Pennsylvania 19107

Votrax
500 Stephenson Highway
Troy, Michigan 48084

Voyager, Inc.
P.O. Box 1577
South Bend, Indiana 46634

VSI Hardware Industries
12930 Bradley Avenue
P.O. Box 4445
Sylmar, California 91342

Wal-Jan Surgical Products, Inc.
395 Atlantic Avenue
East Rockaway, New York 11518

Walking Stick Emporium
P.O. Box 238
Chateaugay, New York 12920

G. T. Water Products, Inc.
19438 Business Center Drive
Northridge, California 91324

Wells-Engberg Company, Inc.
P.O. Box 6388
Rockford, Illinois 61125

Western Technical Products
923 23rd Avenue East
Seattle, Washington 98112

Westland Plastics, Inc.
800 North Mitchell Road
Newbury, California 91320

The Wheelchair Carrier Corporation
P.O. Box 9328
Phoenix, Arizona 85068

Whirlpool Corporation
Benton Harbor, Michigan 49022

Wieland & Tanner, Inc.
N29 W22930 Marjean Lane
Waukesha, Wisconsin 53186

Wilch Manufacturing, Inc.
P.O. Box 179
Topeka, Kansas 66601

Winfield Company, Inc.
3062 46th Avenue North
St. Petersburg, Florida 33714

World Wide Games, Inc.
P.O. Box 450
3527 West S.R. 37
Delaware, Ohio 43015

Wright Way, Inc.
P.O. Box 907
Garland, Texas 75040

Xplorer Motor Homes
3950 Burnsline Road
Brown City, Michigan 48416

Yad, Inc.
R.R. 2, Box 78
Ladson, South Carolina 29456

Zeus Manufacturing, Inc.
P.O. Box 16397
Irvine, California 92713

Zim Manufacturing Company
2850 West Fulton Street
Chicago, Illinois 60612

Zip Dee Inc.
96 Crossen Avenue
Elk Grove Village, Illinois 60007

Zoom Telephonics, Inc.
65 Franklin Street
Boston, Massachusetts 02110

# Photo Credits

We thank the following suppliers, manufacturers, and photographers for their courtesy in providing photographs used in this book:

Alimed, Inc.; Alliance Manufacturing Co., Inc.; Alsons Corporation; Aluminum Housewares Co., Inc.; American Bidet Co.; American Coil Co.; ULF Studios (for American Family Scale Co., Inc.); American Foundation for the Blind; American Printing House for the Blind; American Stair-Glide Corp.; American Telephone & Telegraph Co.; American Thermo-Ware Co.; Amigo Sales, Inc.; Amsco/American Sterilizer Co.; Aparco, Inc.; Photo-Illustrators (for Apor Industries, Inc.); Aquatherm Products Corp.; Christopher Hasting (for Arts Associates, Inc.); Atari, Inc.; Audio Book Co.; Bathe in Bed; Battle Creek Equipment Co.; L. L. Bean, Inc.; C. Beil Designs; Bernell Corp.; Besam, Inc.; Better Sleep, Inc.; Bissell, Inc.; Bollen Products Co.; R. R. Bowker Co.; Burke, Inc.; Camp International, Inc.; Carefree of Colorado; CHEC Medical Products; Toby Churchill, Ltd.; Chris-Craft; Cleo Living Aids; Collins Industries, Inc.; Communicaid®; Contourpedic Corp.; Convaid Product Development; Cramer Industries, Inc.; Crow River Industries, Inc.; Dakon Corp.; Dazy Products Co.; AC-Delco Division, General Motors Corp.; Delta Medical Industries; Dow Knob, Inc.; The Ealing Corp.; Easy Bath Manufacturers; EDCO/Pasco, Inc.; The Ednalite Corp.; Edroy Products Co., Inc.; Normart Printing (for Escalera, Inc.); Gary & Kilgore, Inc. (for ESP Systems Development, Inc.); Everest and Jennings, Inc.; Evlo Plastics, Inc.; Farberware®, subsidiary of Walter Kidde & Co., Inc.; FashionAble; Fimco; Foley Manufacturing Co.; Ford Industries; Gandy Co.; Lorran Meares (for Gantts Wood Things); General Electric Co.; Glenco Infants Items, Inc.; Drabkin Studios (for Gorman Products); Grant Water Corp.; Grayline Housewares; Carol Green; Hamilton Beach Division, Scoville Mfg. Co.; Hammacher Schlemmer; Handee For You; F. Supnick (for Handibend Manufacturing Co.); Knapp & Sons Advertising (for Handi-Ramp, Inc.); Harper-Lee International, Inc.; Hausman

Industries, Inc.; Carl Heald, Inc.; Holo Industries; Hoover Co.; Ted Hoyer & Co., Inc.; Hukuba-Cowdery Corp.; Inclinator Company of America; Intermatic, Inc.; Geoffrey M. Gear (for Freedomchair); Invacare Corp.; The JAL Co.; Jobst Institute, Inc.; W. H. Woodcock (for KGB Research & Development); Kohler Co.; C. H. Russell (for Lakeland Products); Lamson & Goodnow Mfg. Co.; The Left Hand, Inc.; Lossing Co.; Kathleen Center (for Love-Co Products, Inc.); Loyal Laplante Supply Co.; Lumex, Inc.; Dr. W. P. Lynas; Phil Lowery (for Ken McRight Supplies, Inc.); Maddak, Inc.; The Maytag Co.; The Maxim™ Co.; Medical Equipment Distributors, Inc.; Medic Alert Foundation International; Microlert Systems International; Monadnock Lifetime Products, Inc.; Emerg-Alert® (for National Identification Co.); Newman-Fine, Inc.; Grant Film Productions (for J. E. Nolan & Co., Inc.); Consumer Products Divisions, North American Philips Corp. (Norelco); On Guard Corporation of America; Photographics (for Ortho-Kinetics, Inc.); Orvis Co.; Osrow Products Corp.; Ozburn-Janesville Corp.; Arch Photography (for Palmer Industries); Paper Welder, Inc.; S. Parker Hardware Mfg. Corp.; THERAPLAY Products Division, PCA Industries, Inc.; Physical Aids Marketing Co.; developed by Dr. Robert Pyser (for Plakadent International Ltd.); Power Access Corp.; Prentke Romich Co.; reprinted by permission of J. A. Preston Corp. © 1979; Professional Convalescent Products Co.; PSI; Raymo Products, Inc.; Regal Ware, Inc.; Replogle Globe, Inc.; Rice Council of America; Rite-Line Corp.; Rival Manufacturing Co.; Roho Research & Development, Inc.; Rol-Ruler Co.; Rosenthal Manufacturing Co., Inc.; Rubbermaid, Inc.; Rubery Owen Holdings Ltd.; Rush Hampton Industries; Science for the Blind Products; Scitronics, Inc.; Fred Scott & Sons; Scovill Security Products Division, Yale Locks; Communications Concepts (for Scrambler, Inc.); Sears, Roebuck & Co.; Selby Fifth Avenue Shoe Salon; Tony Kaspar (for Sherry Products, Inc.); Shur-Lok Manufacturing Co., Inc.; Simplex Security Systems, Inc.; Smith-Corona Typewriters; Masako Snyder (for George H. Snyder); design by Paul Soldner for Soldner Pottery Equipment, Inc.; Specialized Systems, Inc.; Springfield Instrument Co.; Stainless Medical Products; Stanley Magic-Door Division, The Stanley Works; Stimulation Aids, Ltd.; Richard Ward (for Oscar B. Stiskin); Swift Instruments, Inc.; Elmer Konradi (for Swing Away Manufacturing Co.); Technical Aids to Independence, Inc.; Telesensory Systems, Inc.; Teletronics United, Inc.; Therafin Corp.; Toll Free Digest; Toshiba America, Inc.; Trans-Aid Corp.; Reames-Hanusin Studio (for Triaxon, Inc.); Typewriting Institute for the Handicapped; United States Luggage Corp.; Ventura—Research & Rehabilitation for the Handicapped, Inc.; Visualtek, Inc.; Votrax; Western Technical Products; Whirlpool Corp.; Wieland & Tanner, Inc.; World Wide Games, Inc.; Wright-Way, Inc.; Xplorer Motor Homes; Zim Manufacturing Co.; Zoom Telephonics.

# Index

*[Italic page numbers are used to denote location of illustrations.]*

Accelerator, left-foot, 206
Access aid(s):
    door knob, *157*, 158
    door openers, 158, *159*
    elevator, remote control, 159
    garage door opener, automatic, *160*
    hinges, swing-clear, *160*
    key holder, 159
    light switch extension, 163
    ramps, 128–*130*, 192
    reachers, 161, *162*
    reaching tongs, 161
    symbols, *141*
    (*See also* Lifts; Transfer aids; Wheelchairs)
Accident prevention aid(s):
    alert signal, *188*
    blanket clips, 216
    cabinet locks, 217, *218*
    cigarette holder, remote, 216
    door knob, safety, 217
    doortop lock, 217
    drawer stopper, 218
    outlet safety cap, electric, 218
    power failure light, electric, 215
    respirator alarm, 215
    safety belts, 131
    shower treads, 218
    stool, safety, *163*
    (*See also* Security)
Address book, left-hand, 154
Air pillows (*see* Pillows)
Air purifier, *15*
Alarm(s):
    alert signal, *188*
    bed-wetting, *1*, 2
    clock winder, 49
    door, 220
    door, portable, *220*
    medical, 34
    personal, 219, 220
    personal, wireless, 219
    power failure light, 215
    respirator, *215*
    wake-up for hearing impaired, 1, *2*
Alert signal, *188*
Apron, hoop, 67
Arm cushion, 7
Art supplies, 195
Ash trays, 91, 99, 114, *216*

Backbrush, long handle, *17*
    with soap, *18*
Backgammon, computer, 197
Backrest, adjustable, 6
Backrest, deluxe folding, *6*
Baggage (*see* Luggage)
Bag(s):
    cane, 102
    crutch, *101*, 102
    holder for, *144*
    rail, *101*
    walker, 99, *100*
    wheelchair, 101–103
    and wrap organizer, *144*
Bar, car assist, 205
Bar, grab, *21*
Bar, safety tub, *37*, 38
Bar, trapeze, *2*, *136*
Barber scissors, left-hand, *41*
Baster, steel, 68
Bathing aids:
    bars, safety tub, *37*, 38
    bath in bed, 19, *20*
    benches, *22*, 23

    caddies, 38, 40
    grab bar, *21*
    guardrail, *21*, *38*, 39
    lift seat, *20*
    lifts, 24–26
    overflow cap, 21
    pillows, 19
    reader, *19*
    scrub cloth, *18*
    seat, tip-up, 40
    seat, transfer, *23*, 24
    shampoo in bed, 42, *43*
    sink, wheelchair, *44*
    sneakers, swim, *39*
    treads, safety, 218
    walk-in bath, *27*
    whirlpools, 50–*52*
    (*See also* Shower aids)
Bathroom, wheelchair, *16*
Bathtub, walk-in, *27*
Bathtub guard, *39*
Bathtub lift seat, *20*
Bathtub rail, *38*
Bathtub reader, *19*
Beater, cordless, 82
Bed(s):
    adjustable electric, 5
    adjustable manual, 6, *7*
    aids for:
        bath in, 19, *20*
        bed-wetting alarm, *1*, 2
        blanket cradle, folding, *4*
        blanket supports, *4*
        block, 3
        board, portable folding, *3*
        bookholder, 165
        eyeglass adapter for bed-ridden, *9*
        lift-hoist, *9*, 10
        lifter, block, 3
        pockets, *7*, *8*
        rails, 6
        raiser, 6
        reader, *4*
        *shampoo in*, 42, *43*
        sleep sound, *13*
        springs, electric, 5
        trays, *13*
        warmers, 3
    ease-o-matic, 5
    long-term-care, *5*
    semi-electric, 5
    (*See also* Mattresses)
Bedspecs, *9*
Belt, safety, 131
Benches, bathtub, *22*, 23
Bible, recorded, 168
Bicycle connector, *193*
Bicycle, hand operated, *200*
Bicycle power kit, 193
Bingo for visually impaired, 196
Bins, stacking, 152
Blackjack, computer, 197
Blanket clips, 216
Blanket cradle, folding, *4*
Blanket supports, *4*
Blender, food, 69
Blind, aids for (*see* Visually impaired)
Block, bed, 3
Blood pressure kits, *27*
Boards, transfer (*see* Transfer aids)
Body exercisers (*see* Exercisers)
Body massage (*see* Massage)
Bookholders, 165–167
Books:
    cookbooks for visually impaired, 69, *70*

    handbook for disabled, 171
    large-print, 167, *168*
    on tape, 168
    toll-free telephone guide, 182
    (*See also* Magazines; Newspapers)
Bottle holder, 68
Bowl with handle, *78*
Bowl, scooper, 87
Bowling aids:
    ball grip, *191*
    ball holder, *192*
    ball holder-desk, *192*
    ramp, 192
    stick, 193
Braille aids:
    building signs, 142
    communicator, 170
    cookbooks, 69, 70
    elevator tags, 142
    laundry knobs, 150
    notation systems, 168
    system, 168
    typewriter, 183
    (*See also* Visually impaired)
Brake, hand parking, 207
Bread slice holder, *68*
Bridge, computer, 196
Broom, adjustable, *144*
Broom and mop holder, *143*
Broom and no-stoop dustpan, *149*
Brushes:
    back, *17*, 18
    denture, suction, 16
    hair, with velcro handle, *18*
    large handle, and comb, *28*
    nail and hand, *18*
    tooth (*see* Toothbrush)
    (*See also* Combs; Toothbrush)
Bucket, measuring, 143
Button hook, large handle, *56*
Buzzer, wake-up, for hearing impaired, *2*

Cabinet door locks, 217, *218*
Caddies:
    bath, stow-away, 38
    clean-up, *145*
    eyeglass, *8*, 174
    shower, 40
    soap, 38
    tool, 146
    walker, *137*
    wheelchair, *113*, 114
Calculator, talking, 172
Camera, left-hand, 202
Can dispenser, 71
Can opener, one-hand, 75
Can rack, rolling, *71*
Cane holder, wheelchair, *105*
Canes:
    adjustable, 105
    bag, 102
    clip, *104*
    cone base for, *107*
    flashlight and whistle, *106*
    folding, 105
    folding, adjustable, *108*
    ice grippers for, *122*
    large base, adjustable, 108
    seat, *106*
    small base, adjustable, 109
    walkane, adjustable, *107*
Cars, aids for:
    accelerator, left-foot, 206
    assist bar, 205
    children's row, 200

241

## 242   INDEX

Cars, aids for: (continued)
  coin dispenser, 207
  door opener, 207
  hand controls, 208
  parking brake, hand, 207
  rear-view mirror, panoramic, 209
  transfer aid, *205*
  wheelchair carriers, *212–214*
  wheelchair lifts, 209, 210
  (*See also* Vehicles)
Cards, playing:
  computer blackjack, 197
  holders, 194
  shufflers, 194
  various-size, 194
Carpet sweeper, lightweight, 146
Carry-alls, wheelchair, 102, 103
Cart, rolling, 200
Carton holder, 69
Cassettes, talking, 168
Chairs:
  buoyant, *198*
  elevating seat, recliner, 113
    swivel rocker, 113
  folding, two-inch, 207
  glider, 121
  leg extenders, *120*
  loading, *115*
  recliner, cushion-lift, 112
  shower, *41, 42*
  sportsman's four-in-one, 193
  traditional, cushion-lift, *112*
  travel, *114*
  wheel (*see* Wheelchairs)
  (*See also* Cushions, Seats, Wheelchairs)
Checkers, 196, 197
Chess, 196
Children's aids:
  bed-wetting alarm, *1*, 2
  blanket clips, *216*
  cabinet locks, *217, 218*
  car, row, *200*
  cart, rolling, 200
  crawler, *201*
  door knob, safety, *217*
  doortop lock, 217
  drawer stopper, 218
  electrical outlet cap, safety, 218
  scooter, 201
  scooter board, 198
  sled, 202
  sleep sound, *13*
  strollers, *133, 211*
  tricycles, 199, 200
Chopper, food, *74*
Cigarette holder, remote, *216*
Cleaner, ultrasonic, 146
Clock(s):
  alarm for hearing impaired, 1, 2
  on ceiling, 8
  digital, large numbers, 169
  -radio, miniature, 207
  winder, 49
Coat hanger aid, *56*
Coffee maker, portable, 208
Coin dispenser, 207
Colander-strainer, 84
Comb, Afro, large handle, *28*
Comb, extension, 29
Comb on handle, *28*
Commode chair, 48
Communicators, 170–173, 180
  Braille, 170
  computer, 180
  form-a-phrase, 173
  large-print video, *173*
  lightwriter, 171
  message selector, 172
  scanning strip, 171
  symbol scanner, 173

  talking calculator, 172
  telephone, *170*
  television memory, 172
  (*See also* Hearing impaired; Speech impaired)
Computer, communicating, 169, 180
Computer games, 196, 197
Container holder, 69
Converter travel kit, electric, 208
Cookbooks, 69, 70
Cooking aids (*see* Kitchen aids)
Copyholder, 169
Corkscrew, left-hand, *73*
Crawler, children's, *201*
Crime prevention (*see* Security)
Crocheting holder, 195
Crock pots, 73, 78
Crutches, aids for:
  bags, *101*, 102
  holder, wheelchair, 105
  ice grippers *122*
Cuff, push, for wheelchairs, *104*
  universal, *94*
Cup(s):
  collapsible, 90
  Manoy, *89*
  plastic handled, *88*
  rack, revolving, *71*
  stacker, *72*
  two-handle, *88*
  wheelchair, 114
  (*See also* Eating aids)
Cushion(s):
  air, twin rest, *110*
  air, wheelchair, 111
  arm, *7*
  back bench, 23
  back, wheelchair, 111
  flotation, dry, *109*
  flotation, water, 110
  foam wedge, *7*
  foam, wheelchair, 110
  gel, wheelchair, *111*
  lap desk, *175*
  lift, chair, 112
  liquid, 110
  seat, wheelchair, *112*
  supporting, *208*
  T-foam, wheelchair, 111
Cutting boards, 72, 73, 83

Deaf, aids for (*see* Hearing impaired)
Dental floss holder, 31
Denture brush, suction, 16
Desk, bowling ball holder, *192*
  lap, *135*, 167
  wheelchair, 114
Dictionary, large-print, *167*
Dinnerware rack, 151
Dialers, telephone, 185, *187*
Disabled, handbook for, 171
  (*See also* individual disabilities)
Disc, non-slip, 92
Dishes (*see* Eating aids)
Dispenser, all-purpose, 29
Dispenser, can, 71
Dividers, expanding drawer, 147
Door(s), aids for:
  alarms, *220*
  hinges, swing-clear, *160*
  knob aid, *157*
  knob, safety, *217*
  lock, pushbutton combination, 159
  lock, top, 216
  opener, automatic, 158
  opener, sliding, *159*
  operator, automatic, 159
  viewer, wide-angle, *221*
Drainer, pan, *79*
Drawer dividers, expanding, *147*

Drawer organizers, instant, *148*
Drawer, spacemaker for, *148*
Drawer stopper, 218
Drawing kit, 195
Dressing aids:
  all-purpose, *55*
  button hook, large handle, *56*
  hanger, coat, *56*
  mittens, heated, *64*
  money belt, *57*
  panty hose aid, *58*
  razor, cordless electric, 53
  shoe heel aid, *59*
  shoe horns, *60, 61*
  shoe-lacing aid, *59, 60*
  shoe removing aid, *58*
  shoelaces, 59
  shoes, *61*
  sock-aid, *62*
  socks, heated, *63*
  sticks, 55–57
  stocking aid, *61, 62*
  trouser aid, *63*
  zipper pull, *65*
Drive, power for wheelchair, 119
Driving aids (*see* Car)
Dryer, hair, portable, *32, 33*
Dustpan, folding, 149
Dustpan, no-stoop and broom, *149*

Earl's stairway lift, *123*
Eating aids:
  bowl with handle, *78*
  bumper, food, *90*
  cuff, universal, *94*
  cup handle, plastic, *88*
  dishes, Manoy, and utensils, *89*
  drinking cup, collapsible, *90*
  egg cup, suction, *90*
  feeding dish, electric, 90
  fork, angle-handle, and spoon, *95*
  fork, side-cutter, *97*
  glass holders, 90, *91*
  knives, left-hand, *77*
  knives, rocker, *91, 92*
  place mat, non-slip, *93*
  scooper-bowl, *87*
  scooper-plate, *88*
  spoons, weighted, *94*
  sporks, *96*
  straw holder, *93*
  straws, large, 93
  suction, rubber, 82
  teaspoon, self-leveling, *95*
  tray, non-slip lined, *92*
  tray, stacking, 93
  two-cupper, *70*
  utensils, 89, *94–97*
  water filter, 97
  (*See also* Household aids; Kitchen aids)
Egg cooker, automatic, 75
Egg cup, suction, 90
Electric beds (*see* Beds)
Electric converter, 208
Electric wheelchairs (*see* Wheelchairs)
Electrical outlet, cap, safety, 218
Electrical outlets, 161
Electricity failure light, 215
Elevating chairs (*see* Chairs; Lifts)
Elevator tags, Braille, 142
Embroidery, left-hand, 202
Enlarger, illuminated, *174*
Environmental control switch, *180*
Exercisers, arm, hand, and leg, *29–31*
Extenders, furniture, 120, *121*
Extenders, mattress, *10*
Extension, light switch, 163
Eyeglasses, aids for:
  adapter for bed-ridden, 9
  caddy, 174

Eyeglasses, aids for: (continued)
   ear-loks, 174
   frame protectors, 174
   holder, 8
   magnifier, 177
   prism for invalid vision, 9
   repair kit, 173
   (See also Magnifiers; Visually impaired)

Fans, *146*
Faucet arm, *201*
Feeding dish, electric, 90
Filter, water, 97
Fingernails (*see* Nails)
Fishing belt, one-hand, 195
Fitness (*see* Recreational aids)
Flashlight and whistle cane, *106*
Flotation mattresses, 10, *11*
Flying controls, hand, 209
Food blender, *69*
Food bumper, *90*
Food chopper, *74*
Food cutting board, 72, 73, 83
Food mill, *83*
Food processor, 80
Food slicer, 84
Food turner, *86*
Foot bath massage, 51
Foot massager, *35*
Foot whirlpool, or hand, *50*
Fork, angle handle, *95*
Fork, side cutter, 97
Furniture leg extenders, *120*, *121*

Game center, 197
Game table, revolving, 199
Games (*see* Recreational aids)
Garage door opener, *160*
Gardening tools, 201
Gas lighter, 86
Glass holders, 90, *91*
Glasses (*see* Eyeglasses)
Glove, rubber half, *75*
Grab bar, *21*
Gripper, 75
Grippers, ice, for canes and crutches, 122
Guardrails (*see* Rails)
Guitar instructions, left-hand, 202

Hair dryer, portable, 32, *33*
Hairbrush, velcro handle, *18*
Hancycle, *200*
Hand controls, driving, 208
Hand controls, flying, 209
Hand exerciser, *30*, *31*
Hand shower, 43
Handbook for the disabled, 171
Hands, aids for (*see* Holders)
Hangers, coat, *56*
Hat, umbrella, 211
Heat pillow (*see* Pillows)
Hearing impaired, aids for:
   alarm, power failure, 215
   alarm, wake-up, 1, *2*
   alert signal, *188*
   communicators, 170–173
   padlock, lever, *221*
   speech control, variable, 181
   telephone aids, *170*, 185–187
Heat mask, 32
Heated mittens, *64*
Heated socks, *63*
Heater, bed, 3
   body, 34
Heater and fan, *146*
Heating muff, *32*
Heating pad, 32
Heel strap, wheelchair, 121
Hinges, swing-clear, *160*
Hobbies (*see* Recreational aids)

Holders:
   bag, *144*
   book, 165–167
   bottle, 68
   bowling ball, *192*
   bread slice, *68*
   broom and mop, *143*
   can and crutch, wheelchair, 105
   carton, 69
   cigarette, remote, 216
   container, 69
   crochet, 195
   eyeglass, *8*, 174
   glass, 90, *91*
   iron, 147
   knitting, 195
   straw, *93*
   telephone, *184*
Hot dog cooker, automatic, 75
Hot water maker, 70
Household aids:
   address book, left-hand, 154
   apron, hoop, 67
   bag holder, *144*
   broom and mop holder, *143*
   brooms, *144*, *149*
   bucket, measuring, 143
   carpet sweeper, lightweight, 146
   carry caddy, 145
   clean-up caddy, *145*
   cleaner, ultrasonic, 146
   dispenser, all-purpose, 29
   dispenser, can, 71
   drawer efficiency aids, *147*, *148*
   dustpans, *149*
   fans, *146*
   faucet arm, 201
   iron holder, 147
   iron, lightweight plastic, *148*
   labeler, large-letter, 150
   laundry knobs, Braille and special, *149*, 150
   measuring tape, left-hand, 155
   micrometer, left-hand, 155
   mops, 150, *151*
   papercutter, 145
   racks, utility kitchen, *71*, *81*, *151*, *152*
   ruler, rolling, *181*
   scissors, 41, *152*, 202, 211
   spice rack, turning, 153
   stacking bins, 152
   stapler, *152*
   stools, *163*
   storage turntable, 144, *153*
   telephone center, *153*
   tools, *151*, *153*
   vacuum, portable, *154*
   yardstick, left-hand, 154
Hygiene aid, *33*

Ice grippers for canes and crutches, *122*
Intercoms, 175
Iron, lightweight plastic, *148*
Iron holder, *147*

Jar lifter, 77
Jar openers, 75, *76*
Jar wrench, *76*
Jogging exerciser, *31*
Juicer, cordlesss, *82*

Key holder, 159
Keyboard communicators, 171, 172
Kitchen aids:
   apron hoops, 67
   baster, steel, *68*
   beater, cordless, 82
   blender, *69*
   bottle holder, 68
   bread slice holder, 68

   can dispenser, 71
   can opener, one-hand, 75
   can rack, 71
   chopper, food, *74*
   coffee maker, portable, 208
   colander-strainer, 84
   corkscrew, left-hand, *73*
   crock pots, 73, 78
   cutting boards, *72*, *73*, 83
   dinnerware rack, *151*
   disc, non-slip, *92*
   drainer, pan, *79*
   gripper, *75*
   hot-dog cooker, automatic, 75
   hot water maker, *70*
   jar aids, 75–77
   juicer, cordless, *82*
   knives, 77, *91*, *92*
   lifter, turkey or roast, *85*
   mill, food, 83
   mitt, oven, 78
   oven, convection, 78, 79
   pan handler, *80*
   pan and pot rack, sliding, *81*
   pans, *81*
   peelers, 74, 79, 80
   racks, utility, *71*, *81*, *151*, *152*
   ranges for disabled, 83, 84
   rubber glove, half, 75
   rubber suction, 82
   sifter, one-hand, 85
   slicing aids, *84*
   spoons, 89, *94*–*96*
   stacker, cup, *72*
   stoves for disabled, 83, 84
   strainer, *83*
   teaspoon, self-leveling, *95*
   timer, big, 64
   tongs, toaster, 85
   tri-pan, *81*
   turner, food, *86*
   (*See also* Eating aids; Household aids)
Knee separator, *123*
Knitting holder, 195
Knives:
   butcher, one-hand, 77
   electric, 77
   left-hand bread, 77
   left-hand wonder, 77
   rocker, *91*
   rocker with fork, *92*

Labeler, large-letter, *150*
Lap desk cushion, *175*
Lapboards, 135
Large-print books, 70, *167*, 168
Large-print magazines, 168
Larynx, artificial, *188*
Laundry knobs, Braille, 150
Laundry knobs, special, 149
Left-handed, aids for:
   camera, 202
   corkscrew, *73*
   embroidery, 202
   guitar instructions, 202
   knives, 77
   measuring tape, *155*
   micrometer, *155*
   needlepoint, 202
   notebooks, 188
   peeler, 74
   scissors, 41, 202
   shears, 202, *203*
   trimmers, 203
   tweezers, 41
   watches, *189*
   yardstick, 154
Leg exerciser, 29
Leg rest, foam wedge, 7
Leg rest, wheelchair, *121*

# 244 INDEX

Lifter, turkey or roast, 85
Lifts:
  bath, *24–26*
  beach, *126*
  bed, *9*, 10
  chair, 112
  portable, multi-purpose, 125–127
  stairway, *123–125*
  stairway for wheelchair, 123, 124, 126, *128*
  toilet, *45*
  vehicle wheelchair, *209*, *210*
  (See also Transfer aids; Travel aids)
Light switch extension, 163
  (See also Switches)
Lighter, gas, 86
Limb warmer, 34
Locks:
  alert, bolt, 221
  cabinet door, *217*, *218*
  combination, self-set, 220
  door, pushbutton combination, 159
  doortop, 216
  keyless, *161*
  padlock, lever, 221
  safe, disguised, 222
  travel, portable, *222*
  (See also Security)
Long-term-care bed, 5
Luggage, rolling, 206
Luggage toters, *206*

Magazines, large-print, 168
  recorded, 181
Magnifiers:
  chest-secured, 176
  eyeglass aid, 177
  glass, 177
  illuminated, 176
  pocket, 175
  reading, 176
  watchmaker's loupe, *176*
Manoy dishes and utensils, 89
Mask, heating, 32
Massage, foot bath, 51
Massager, body, 34
Massager, body pillow, with heat, 34
Massager, foot, *35*
Massager, heat, 35
Mattresses:
  extender, *10*
  flotation, 10, *11*
  raisers, 6, 11, 12
  topper, 10
  (See also Beds)
Measuring tape, left-hand, 155
  (See also Micrometer; Ruler)
Medical aids:
  alarm, 34
  blood pressure kits, 27
  bracelets, condition-identifying, 34
  filter, water, 97
  pill reminder box, *36*
  purifier, air, 15
  respirator alarm, *215*
  warning systems, 34
  whirlpools, *50–52*
Microlert, 34
Micrometer, left-hand, 155
Mill, food, 83
Mirrors:
  extension, 35
  flex-a-mirror, 35
  four-way, *36*
  lock-on, 35
  rear-view, panoramic, 209
Mitt, oven, 78
Mittens, heated, *64*
Mobility aid, *136*
  (See also Canes; Crutches; Walkers; Wheelchairs; Vehicles)

Money belt, 57
Monopoly for visually impaired, 196
Mops:
  bending, 150
  and broom holder, *143*
  easy-wring, *151*
  extension, 150
Motor home, *209*
Muff, heating, *32*
Multi-position tables, *14*
Mute, aids for (see Speech impaired)

Nail care aids:
  clipper on block, *36*
  file, 28
  and hand brush, 18
  machine, 37
  scissors, left-hand, 41
  toenail, 41
Narrower, wheelchair, 128
Needlepoint, left-hand, 202
Newspapers, large-print, 168
Non-slip eating aids, *92*, 93

Opener, can, 75
  car door, 207
  jar, 75, 76
Outdoor wheelchair aids (see Wheelchairs)
Outlet, electrical plug, 161
Outlet cap, electrical plug, 218
Oven, convection, 78, *79*
Oven, crock, 78
Oven mitt, 78
Overflow cap, bath, 21

Padlock, lever, *221*
Page turners, *177–179*
Pan drainer, *79*
Pan handler, *80*
Pan rack, *81*
Pans, 80, *81*
Panty hose aid, *58*
Papercutter, *145*
Parking brake, hand, 207
Parking symbol, handicapped, *141*
Peelers, potato, 74, 79, 80
Peg games, *195*, 196
Pen, lighted, 178
Pencil holder, 178
Pill reminder box, *36*
Pillows:
  air, anti-wrinkle, *12*
  bath, 19
  body massager with heat, 34
  head, *12*
  relaxing air, *12*
  (See also Cushions)
Place mat, non-slip lined, 92
Plates, Manoy, 89
Plates, scooper, 88
Playing cards (see Cards, playing)
Pliers, *151*
Pocket, bed, 7, *8*
  (See also Caddies; Wheelchairs, aids for)
Pool chair, *198*
Pot and pan rack, sliding, *81*
Potato peeler (see Peelers)
Potter's wheel, 198
Power failure light, 215
Power wheelchairs (see Wheelchairs)
Processor, food, 80
Purifier, air, *15*
  (See also Filter, water)
Push cuff, wheelchair, *104*

Racks:
  can, rolling, 71
  cup, revolving, 71
  dinnerware, *151*, *152*
  pot and pan, sliding, *81*
Radio(s):

  clock, miniature, 207
  headphone, 198
  with TV sound, 199
  wheelchair, *131*
  wrist, 198
Rail(s):
  bag for, *101*
  bath, *21*, 37, *38*
  bed, 6
  extender, side, 10
  stool with, *163*
  toilet guard, *47*
Ramp(s):
  access, *129*
  bowling, 192
  portable, 128
  van, *129*, *130*
Range buttons in front, 83
Range, self-cleaning, buttons front, 84
Razor, cordless electric, 53
Reachers, 161, *162*
Reaching tongs, 161
Readers' Digest, large-print, 168
Reading aids:
  for bathtub, *19*
  for bed, 4
  bookholders, 165–167
  eyeglass aids, 8, 9, 173, 174, 177
  magnifiers, 175–177
  page turners, 177–179
  reading machine, 181
  with scroll, *177*
  and writing aid, 188
  (See also Visually impaired)
Rear-view mirror, 209
Recliners (see Chairs, Wheelchairs)
Record adapter, 168
Recorded books and magazines, 168, 181
  (See also Time compression system; Visually impaired)
Recreational aids: 29–31, 191–203
  backgammon, computer, 197
  bicycle, hand-powered, *200*
  bicycle connector, 193
  bicycle power kit, 193
  bingo for visually impaired, 196
  blackjack, computer, 197
  bowling ball grip, *191*
  bowling holders, *192*
  bowling ramp, 192
  bowling stick, 193
  bridge, computer, 196
  camera, left-hand, 202
  car, children's row, *200*
  card holders, playing, 194
  card shufflers, 194
  cards, magnetic playing, 194
  cart, rolling, 200
  chair, buoyant, *198*
  chair, sportsman's, 193
  checkers, 196, 197
  chess, 196
  crawler, children's, *201*
  crochet holder, 195
  drawing kit, 195
  embroidery, left-hand, 202
  fishing belt, one-hand, 195
  game center, 197
  game table, revolving, 199
  gardening tools, 201
  guitar instruction, left-hand, 202
  handcycle, *200*
  hand controls, driving, 208
  hand controls, flying, 209
  knitting holder, 195
  Monopoly for visually impaired, 196
  motor home, *209*
  peg games, *195*, 196
  potter's wheel, 198
  radios, 130, 198, 199, 207
  scooter, 201

# INDEX

Recreational aids: (*continued*)
  scissors, left-hand sewing, 202
  shears, left-hand, 202
  shears, pinking, 203
  ski outrigger, flip, *199*
  sled, children's rolling, 202
  sportsman's four-in-one chair, 193
  swim sneakers, *39*
  television, 9, 170, 182, 199
  three-wheeler, electric, 201
  tricycles, 199, 200
  trimmers, 203
  vehicles, 132, 200, 209, 210, *212*
  video computer games, 197
Reminder box, pill, 36
Remote-control elevator, 159
Remote-control switches, 179, 180
Respirator alarm, *215*
Row car, children's, 200
Rubber glove, half, *75*
Rubber suction, for dishes, 82
Ruler, rolling, *181*

Safe, disguised, 222
Safety belts, 131
  (*See also* Accident prevention)
Scale, digital, 42
  talking, 50
Scissors:
  electric, 152
  folding pocket, 211
  left-hand barber, 41
  left-hand nail, 41
  left-hand sewing, 202
  (*See also* Papercutter, Shears, Trimmers)
Scooper-bowl, *87*
Scooper-plate, 88
Scooter board, round, 198
Scooter, children's, 201
Screwdriver, 151
Script guide for visually impaired, *189*
Seats:
  bathtub transfer, *23, 24*
  belts for, 131
  cane, *106*
  cushion, for wheelchairs, 112
  elevating, 130
  flip, 131
  lift, bath, *20*
  tip-up, 40
  toilet, 46–48
  shower, *40*
  (*See also* Chairs)
Security aids:
  alarm, door, *220*
  alarm, personal, 219, 220
  door viewer, wide-angle, *221*
  intercoms, 175
  locks, 159, 161, 216–218, 220–222
  safe, disguised, 222
  theft-prevention device, wheelchair, *135*
  timers, 222–223
  (*See also* Accident prevention; Alarms)
Shampoo in bed, 42, *43*
Shears, lightweight, left-hand, 202
Shears, pinking, left-hand, 203
Shock absorbers, wheelchair, 131
Shoe aids:
  for heel, *59*
  horns, *60, 61*
  lace fastener, one-hand, *59*
  laces, elastic, *59*
  lacing aid, *60*
  remover aid, 58
Shoes, wide or narrow, *61*
  (*See also* Swim sneaks)
Shower aids:
  caddies, 38, 40
  chairs, *41, 42*
  hand shower, *43*
  seat, fixed, 40

seat, retractable, 40
seat for wheelchair, *40*
sit-down shower, *26*
  and tub guard, *39*
  wheelchair, shower, *44*
  (*See also* Bathing aids)
Sifter, cordless, one-hand, 85
Signs (*see* Symbols)
Sink, wheelchair, *44*
Ski outrigger, flip, *199*
Sled, children's rolling, 202
Sleep sound, *13*
Sleeping aids (*see* Beds)
Slicer, food, 84
Slicing guide, *84*
Soap caddy, 38
Sock-aid, *62*
Socks, heated, *63*
Speech control, variable (hearing and visual aid), 181
Speech impaired, aids for:
  communicators, 169–173, 180
  larynx, artificial, *188*
  telephone, visual, 170
  voice amplifier, *187*
  (*See also* Telephone aids)
Spoon, angle-handle, *95*
Spoons, hanging, 82
Spoons, weighted, 94
  (*See also* Utensils)
Sporks, *96*
Sportsman's four-in-one chair, 193
Spotlight, portable, 211
Stabilizers for wheelchairs, *130, 134*
Stacker, cup, *72*
Stair climbing wheelchairs, *115*, 116
Stairway lifts, *123–126, 128*
Stand-up chairs, 113, 130
Stand-up wheelchair, *116*
Stapler, *152*
Stick, bowling, 193
Stick, dressing, *55–57*
Stick, typing, *183*
Stocking aid, *61, 62*
Stool, rail, *163*
Stool, safety, *163*
Storage bins, 152
Storage turntable, 144, *153*
  (*See also* Drawers; Racks)
Stove knobs, special, *83, 84*
Stove valve turner, *49, 82*
Stoves, special for disabled, *83, 84*
Strainer, colander, 84
Strainer, sink and cuttingboard, *83*
Straw holder, *93*
Straws, large, 93
Stroller, dual purpose, *211*
Stroller, therapy, *133*
Suction brush, manicure, 18
Suction, rubber, for dishes, 82
Swim sneaks, *39*
Switches, remote-control, 163, 179, *180*
Symbols:
  of access, *141*
  building, 141
  clearance sign, *141*
  medical alert, 34
  parking, *141*
  telephone, 141

Tables, multi-position, *14*
Talking aids (*see* Speech impaired)
Tape computer, 169
Teaspoon, self-leveling, *95*
Telephone aids:
  adapter, hearing aid, 186
  amplifying telephone, 185
  center, *153*
  communicator for speech impaired, 170
  cordless, 186
  cordless memory, 187

dialers, 185, *187*
for disabled, 180
extension arm, 184
headset, 185
for hearing impaired, 170
holding aid, *184*
indoor gong, 186
large raised numbers, 186
lo-vision pushbutton, 186
loud bell, 186
signalman, 185
silencer, 184
stand, clamp, and interrupter, 184
television phone, 170
toll-free guide for, 182
tone ringer, 185
voice amplifier, *187*
Television aids:
  channel selector, 182
  phone, 170
  sound, with radio, 199
  viewer for invalids, 9
Tellatouch, 170
Theft prevention device, wheelchair, *135*
  (*See also* Security)
Thermometers:
  easy-read, *64*
  electronic, 50
  indoor-outdoor, 64
  for shower, 39
  talking, 50
Three-wheeled vehicle, utility, 132
Three-wheeler, electric, 201
  (*See also* Tricycles; Vehicles)
Time-on-ceiling, 8
Time compression system, 181
Timers:
  automatic, 223
  big, 64
  light-sensitive, control, *223*
  master control, 222
  program, 222
Toaster tongs, 85
Toenail scissors, left-hand, 41
Toilet aids:
  chair, commode, 48
  hygiene aid, *33*
  lift, *45*
  paper holder, 44
  portable toilet, 210
  rails, 47
  seat, carrying case for, 46
  seat, cushioned, 46
  seat, raised, 46, 47
  urinal drainage bags, 48
  wash and dry toilet, 44, *45*
  wheelchair toilet, *16*
Toll-free guide, telephone, 182
Tongs, reaching, 161
Tongs, toaster, 85, 86
Tools:
  caddy, 146
  four-in-one, *151*
  gardening, 201
  pistol grip kit, 153
Toothbrush, angle, *17*
Toothbrush, cordless electric, 53
Toothbrush, large handle, 16
Toothpaste squeezer, 49
Topper, mattress, 10
Transfer aids, 24, *133, 134, 205*
Trapeze bars, *2*, 136
Travel aids:
  accelerator, left-foot, 206
  baggage toter, *206*
  car assist bar, 205
  car door opener, 207
  car transfer aid, 205
  chair, folding, two-inch, 207
  chair, travel, *114, 115*
  coffee maker, portable, 208

Travel aids: (continued)
  coin dispenser, 207
  cushion, supporting, 208
  electrical converter kit, 208
  flying controls, hand, 209
  hand controls, driving, 208
  luggage, rolling, 206
  luggage toter, *206*
  motor home, 209
  parking brake, hand, 207
  radio, miniature clock, 207
  scissors, pocket folding, 211
  spotlight, portable, 211
  strollers, 133, 211
  toilet, portable, 210
  transfer boards, 133, 134
  umbrella hat, 211
  vehicle, all-terrain, 212
  vehicle wheelchair lifts, 209, 210
  visually impaired, aid for, *132*
  wheelchair carriers, car, 212–214
  (*See also* Transfer aids)
Trays
  bed, *13*
  non-slip lined, *92*
  stacking, and frame, 93
  wheelchair caddy, 114
  (*See also* Caddies)
Tricycles, 199, 200
  (*See also* Bicycles; Vehicles)
Trimmers, 203
Tri-pan, 81
Tri-wheeled electric wheelchair, 119, 120
Trouser aid, *63*
Tube winder, *49*
Tubs (*see* Bathing aids; Bathtubs)
Turkey or roast lifter, *85*
Turner, food, *86*
Turner, page, 177–179
Turner, stove valve, *49*, 82
Turntable rack, *152*
Turntable, single storage, *153*
Tweezers, left-hand, 41
Two-cupper, 70
Typewriters:
  aids for disabled, 183
  Braille, 183
  large-size type, 183
  mask, 183
  one-hand, 183
  simplified keyboard, 182
Typing with one hand, instructions, 182
Typing stick, *183*

Ultrasonic cleaner, 146
Umbrella hat, 211
Urinal drainage bag, *48*
Urine sugar-ketone analyzer, talking, 50
Utensils, eating:
  built-up, *94*
  forks, *95*, 97
  horizontal grip, *96*
  knives, 77, *91*, *92*
  Manoy, *89*
  spoons, 82, *94*, *95*
  sporks, *96*
  three-function, *96*

Vacuum, portable, *154*
Van ramps, *129*, *130*
Vehicles:
  all-terrain, *212*
  cart, 200
  motor home, *209*

row car, children's, *200*
three-wheeled utility, *132*
wheelchair-carrying, *117*
wheelchair lifts for, *209*, 210
(*See also* Bicycles; Cars; Tricycles)
Versa Braille, 168
Vibrator, wake-up, 2
Video computer games, 197
Viewer, door, wide-angle, 221
Visually impaired, aids for:
  bed-ridden, eyeglass attachments for, *9*
  Bible, recorded, 168
  bingo, 196
  books, large print, *167*, 168
  books, recorded, 168
  Braille aids (*see* Braille aids)
  calculator, talking, 172
  checkers, 196
  chess, 196
  clocks, 8, 169
  communicator aid, 170, 171
  cookbooks, 69, 70
  copyholder, 169
  enlarger, illuminated, *174*
  eyeglass aids, 8, *9*, 173, 174, 177
  intercoms, 175
  labeler, large-letter, *150*
  large-print books, *167*, 168
  magazines, large-print, 168
  magazines, recorded, 181
  magnifiers, 175–177
  padlock, lever, 221
  pen, night, 178
  reading machine, 181
  record adapter, 168
  records, talking, 168
  scale, digital, 42
  scale, talking, 50
  script guide for, *189*
  speech control, variable, 181
  telephone aids, 170, 185, 186
  television viewer, *9*
  thermometer, easy-read, *64*
  thermometer, talking, 50
  time compression system, 181
  timer, big, *64*
  travel aid for, *132*
  typewriters, 183
  urine sugar-ketone test, talking, 50
  writing aid for, *189*
  (*See also* Braille aids; Reading aids)
Voice aids (*see* Speech impaired)

Walkane, adjustable, *107*
Walkers:
  adjustable seat, 139
  bags for, *99*, 100
  folding, 139
  folding seat, 137
  motorized, *132*
  one-hand, *138*
  rolling, *138*
  stair, *138*
  wheeled, *137*
  (*See also* Mobility Aid)
Warmer, bed, *3*
Warmer, body, 34
Wash cloth, *18*
Watches, left-hand, *189*
Water filter, *97*
Wheelchairs:
  electric, 116
  electric indoor, 120
  electric portable, 117–120

  glider, 121
  indoor-outdoor electric, *119*, 120
  lightweight, 140
  multi-purpose, 139
  power-drive, 118
  power-lift, *116*
  reclining back, retractable arm, *140*
  runabout, *139*
  self-propelling portable, *140*
  self-reclining, *118*
  stair-climbing, *115*, 116
  stand-up, *116*
  system, 119
  tri-wheeler, *119*, 120
Wheelchairs, aids for:
  ash trays, 91, 99, 114
  bags, *101*–103
  bathroom, *16*
  brake, attendant, *104*
  brake extension, 103
  caddy, *113*
  caddy tray, 114
  cane holder, 105
  car hoist, 212
  car racks, 213, *214*
  car tie down, 213
  car top loaders, *212*, 213
  car trunk loader, *213*
  carry-alls, 103
  carrying vehicle, *117*
  crutch holder, 105
  cup, 114
  cushions, *110*–112
  desk, 114
  heel strap, 121
  knee separator, *123*
  lapboards, *135*
  leg rest, *121*
  lift, stairway, 123, 124, *126*, *128*
  lift, vehicle, 209, 210
  loading chair, *115*
  narrower, 128
  power drive for, 119
  push cuff, *104*
  radio, *131*
  ramps, 128–130
  recliner for, 118
  seat, shower, 40
  shock absorber, 131
  shower, 44
  shower seat, 40
  sink, 44
  stabilizers, forward, *130*, 134
  theft-prevention device, *135*
  transfer aid, *205*
  transfer boards, *133*, 134
  travel chair, 114
  tray, 114
Whirlpools, 50–52
Winder, clock, *49*
Winder, tube, *49*
Wrap organizer, *144*
Wrench, *151*
Wrench, jar, 76
Writing aids:
  pen, lighted, 178
  pencil holder, 178
  and reading aid, 188
  script guide for visually impaired, *189*

Yardstick, left-hand, 154

Zipper pull, *65*